Opening Minds, Improving Lives

OPENING MINDS, IMPROVING LIVES

Education and

Women's Empowerment

in Honduras

Erin Murphy-Graham

Vanderbilt University Press

Nashville

© 2012 by Vanderbilt University Press
Nashville, Tennessee 37235
All rights reserved
First printing 2012

This book is printed on acid-free paper.
Manufactured in the United States of America

Library of Congress Cataloging-in-Publication Data on file

LC control number 2011023326
LC classification LC1811.M87 2012
Dewey class number 371.822

ISBN 978-0-8265-1828-6 (cloth)
ISBN 978-0-8265-1829-3 (paper)

In memory of

Eleanor Cavanaugh Murphy, 1923–2009
Virginia Hunter Ring, 1917–2010

With joy that you are free
from the fetters of this world

Contents

Acknowledgments

TWELVE YEARS AGO I volunteered to participate in a two-week evaluation of the SAT—Sistema de Aprendizaje Tutorial (Tutorial Learning System)—program in Honduras. My assignment during the evaluation was to explore the ways in which the SAT program empowered women. This took me much, much longer than two weeks, and many people helped along the way.

First, I am deeply indebted to the women and their families who agreed to participate in this research. They trusted me with their stories, and I hope I have faithfully shared their views and experiences. They welcomed me into their homes, and they believed enough in the importance of this project that they were willing to share sensitive personal information that highlights the complexity and contradictions of the empowerment process. Gracias por las tajadas, las siestas en sus hamacas, las risas que compartimos, y más que todo su confianza y amistad. I especially thank Leonidas Thomas and Lourdes Lino Mejia for letting us stay in their extra room and feeding us many delicious meals.

Thank you to the members of BASED-UK, particularly Michael Richards and Geeta Gandhi Kingdon, who supported my first visit to Honduras, and to Marcia Bernbaum, the team leader of the first SAT evaluation. The staff at Bayan, particularly Soheil Dooki, Alejandro Martínez, and Ricardo Edén, spent countless hours answering my questions to help me understand the history of SAT in Honduras. I am also grateful to the Dooki family for hosting me on multiple occasions during my stays in La Ceiba, and for welcoming and protecting me like a fourth daughter. I thank Azarnoosh Dooki for transcribing the interviews.

I would like to thank faculty members I worked with at the Harvard Graduate School of Education, including Fernando Reimers, Suzanne Grant Lewis, Pedro Noguera, and Carol Weiss. I am particularly thankful to Carol, whose mentorship and friendship were a sustaining feature of my final two years in graduate school. My dear friends from the Harvard Graduate School of Education, Sonya Anderson, Dorinda Carter, Allison

Gruner Gandhi, Heather Harding, and Michal Kurlaender, are the most amazing group of women, and I am blessed to have them in my life.

I have been surrounded by supportive colleagues at the University of California, Berkeley, and at New York University, many of whom encouraged me, read early drafts, and provided excellent advice. In particular, without the cheerleading of my department chair at UC Berkeley, Jabari Mahiri, I might have archived this project prematurely. Also at UC Berkeley, I thank Cynthia Coburn, Lisa García Bedolla, Sarah Freedman, Bruce Fuller, Glynda Hull, David Pearson, Janelle Scott, Na'ilah Suad Nasir, Laura Sterponi, and Tina Trujillo. At NYU I am especially appreciative of the support of my former department chair, Jonathan Zimmerman, and my colleagues Dana Burde, Floyd Hammock, Jennifer Hill, Phillip Hosay, Cynthia Miller-Idriss, Pedro Noguera, Lisa Stulberg, Marcelo Suarez-Orozco, Florencia Torche, and Niobe Way. The Center for Latin American Studies at UC Berkeley provided a generous travel grant that supported this work, as did the NYU Steinhardt Dean's Office. Thank you to Laura Feeney and Sarah Balistreri for their invaluable research assistance. Candace Morano, a gifted teacher, has nurtured my body and spirit while my mind has been occupied with the task of completing this book.

The William and Flora Hewlett Foundation provided funding for the data collection in Uganda. I would like to thank the research group I am currently working with for their patience while I finished up this book, particularly Patrick McEwan. The amazing team of graduate students we are working with, including Joseph Lample, Rebecca Tarlau, Kimberly Vinall, and David Torres, and the researchers at Universidad Pedagógica Francisco Morazán, including Renán Rápalo Castellanos and Claudia Aguilar, have allowed me to more comprehensively evaluate the impact of the SAT program. Thank you also to the staff at Kimanya-Ngeyo and the tutors and students in Uganda who shared their experiences with us.

A number of colleagues and friends have read and provided feedback on this work, or more generally helped shape my thinking and scholarship. They include Haleh Arbab, Monisha Bajaj, Joan DeJaeghere, Fran Deutsch, Gustavo Fischman, Holly Hanson, Nancy Kendall, Michael Karlberg, Kara Sammet, Nelly Stromquist, and Audrey Alforque Thomas. The shining star of this lot is Lesley Bartlett, who has provided support and encouragement at every stage of the process. Lesley, who introduced me to Michael Ames at Vanderbilt University Press, raved that Michael was a fantastic editor. I was not sure what she meant until I opened a chapter with his suggested changes and comments. His sharp eye and thoughtful feedback have improved my writing and made this book much better than the original manuscript. I would also like to thank the anonymous reviewers for their comprehensive suggestions, as well as the staff at the press, including the managing editor, Ed Huddleston, and freelance copyeditor Bobbe Needham. Any errors of course remain my own.

On a personal note, many family and friends have supported and inspired me. To my "BFFs"—Liane Baine, Mina Fazel, Sarah Illingworth, Marie-Claire Leman, Martha Marciel, Abby Norris Turner, and Jennifer Schuler—thank you for filling my life with the joy of enduring friendship. I would like to thank my parents for their ceaseless encouragement and my brother, Jeff, for everything he does to make my life better. Both my children were born during my work on this project, and the love I feel for them has given me a deeper understanding of what is truly powerful. To my shining light, Lucy Tahirih, thank you for joining our family and gracing me with your beautiful smile each day. To my peaceful warrior, Liam Thomas, thank you for asking me, "How many pages is your book now, Mama?" and for being impressed that I was working on a "really, really long" book. To the teachers, including Laureana Medrano-Otzoy, Jane Esposito, Chikako Yoda, Glennis Ramirez, Alison Kulman, Christine Grant, Odette Carthy, and Kamache Rajapa, who have cared for Liam and Lucy and taught me so much about parenting, I would not have been able to write a word of this text without seeing my children thrive in your care. Finally, to my better half, Bryan Graham, my deepest thanks for supporting my career and for being the best dad at the key park.

This work is dedicated to my grandmothers, both of whom passed away while I was writing the book. When I reflect on their lives, and the opportunities I have had that they were denied, I am inspired by how much change can take place in just two generations.

Opening Minds, Improving Lives

Introduction

THE BILLBOARD CATCHES MY eye as I dash to the departure gate at the Newark airport. Half of a woman's face—her dark brown skin, oval-shaped eye, and stoic expression—peeks out from under a bright yellow headscarf. The text scrawled across the black background reads, "I am powerful."

A blogger in Illinois reacts to the same image, which is part of the "I am powerful" campaign launched by the humanitarian organization CARE on International Women's Day, 2006. She writes: "Our daily routine is composed of countless visual assaults. . . . Every once in a while, and I have to hand it to Madison Avenue, they come up with something that jolts you. . . . Care.org has been creating some very powerful ads and on an issue close to my heart: focus on women's innate power in fighting global poverty."[1]

Women's empowerment is an issue that has gained increased attention in recent decades. According to representatives from CARE, the choice of women's empowerment as a marketing campaign was the result of research that suggested that the concept of "women's empowerment" resonated with women, echoing the comments of the blogger in Illinois. As CARE's vice president for communications and marketing explained: "We did some research and we were able to confirm that empowerment, even as a general concept, was more compelling to women." He continued: "Even if you weren't talking about women's empowerment specifically. If you take the old saying, 'Give a man a fish, he eats for a day,' men tended to say, 'Yes, give them a fish! If he's hungry, give him a fish!' Women tended to resonate more strongly to the concept of, 'No, no. Teach them to fish. Empower them and they can solve their own problems'" (Hicks et al. 2008).

The notion of women's empowerment, and empowerment more broadly, is now at the forefront of the international development agenda. In addition to CARE, other international organizations and declarations emphasize the importance of empowerment. For example, in September

1

2000, world leaders came together at the United Nations headquarters in New York to adopt the United Nations Millennium Declaration, a commitment to reducing extreme poverty around the world. The third of eight Millennium Development Goals is to "promote gender equality and empower women."[2]

The term is also overused. Tony Proscio, author of the book *In Other Words: A Plea for Plain Speaking in Foundations*, pokes fun at the term "empowerment": "To establish one's bona fides as a person concerned about the poor, the disenfranchised, or even ordinary people in general, it is essential in every setting to use empowerment, as early (and, in some circles, as often) as possible. The coiners of empowerment invested it with only the broadest meaning, perhaps to make it usable in nearly every context—or anyway, that has been the effect" (2000, 30).

Indeed, the word "empowerment" is used in a variety of contexts, and it appears in unlikely places. It is the slogan for Bank of America's campaign for recruiting new students, "Empower yourself!" An electric company claims to be "empowering New England." The act of brushing your teeth can also be empowering, if you use Colgate's "empowermint" toothpaste. Purchasing my morning bagel and coffee at Dean & DeLuca in New York City, I can add a "shot of power" to my bill to help empower women in Africa. In a *New Yorker* article about First Lady Michelle Obama's decision to wear sleeveless clothing that shows off her arms, we learn that even fashion is empowering: "Michelle Obama reminds women that they can make a place for vanity in their lives, and that, when they do, a little fashion can be supremely empowering" (Givhan 2009). Empowerment is a fuzzy concept, but the idea resonates—empowerment is a good thing.

But what, exactly, does empowerment entail? In what ways is the woman on the CARE billboard powerful? How can people be empowered to solve their own problems? The questions linger, and while "teach them to fish" is a catchy metaphor, the role of education in empowerment is unclear. What kind of education, if any, can empower individuals to take charge of their lives and work to improve their families, communities, and society at large? This is the central question this book addresses.

In this book, I draw on more than a decade of qualitative research to examine the relationship between women's education and their empowerment by providing an in-depth look at how and why education might spark the empowerment process. Through rich narratives, I explore the experiences of women who participated in an alternative secondary education program on the north coast of Honduras. The chapters that follow illustrate, through women's voices, how exposure to education changed the way women viewed themselves and the context where they lived. As women learned, they gained self-confidence. Their analytical capacities expanded, and they viewed their communities through a different lens. They began to recognize their inherent potential and the contribution they could make toward improving society. This altered outlook enabled some women to challenge dominant gender norms and renegotiate domestic responsibilities with their intimate partners.

Based on these findings, this book offers a fresh conception of women's empowerment through education as a process of recognition, capacity building, and action. I use the term "empowerment" to denote a process of change that includes many aspects of earlier definitions of the word, including an increase in gender consciousness, self-confidence, and participation in public life (Malhotra, Schuler, and Boender 2002). However, my understanding of empowerment stresses two concepts that are less prevalent in earlier discussions—recognition and action. I propose that empowered individuals come to recognize their inherent worth, the fundamental equality of all human beings, and their ability to contribute to personal and social betterment. They develop the capacity to critically examine their lives and broader society and to take action toward personal and social transformation.

The experiences of the women described in this book have much in common with those of women globally, and not just those in poor nations. Around the world, women spend more time than men on housework and child care (UNDP 2007).[3] While women's public roles have changed dramatically in recent decades, evidence suggests that fewer changes in gender relations have occurred in the private sphere (Hochschild 1990, 1996; Sullivan 2004). The women whose stories I tell here describe their struggle to work, take care of their children, and more equitably share domestic responsibilities with their partners. Their experiences are similar to those of women around the world.

Furthermore, these women viewed education as a way to move ahead in life, in their words, *"para seguir adelante."* Unfortunately, girls and women in many poor countries remain excluded from education because of their sex. Two-thirds of individuals who have no access to education are female, and more than sixty million girls are not in school (Lewis and Lockheed 2006). More than five hundred million women are illiterate (Herz and Sperling 2004). For more than two decades, international organizations and donor agencies have been working to increase girls' access to basic education. However, the majority of youths in poor countries have no access to secondary education, particularly in rural areas (UNESCO 2010a). The few rural students studying in secondary schools often do so in classrooms with abysmal conditions and a curriculum irrelevant to their daily lives. National governments and international institutions are now beginning to tackle the question of how to expand access to secondary education (particularly for girls, who are disproportionately underrepresented) and improve its quality.

The SAT Program: Empowering Education?

While *Opening Minds, Improving Lives* is centrally focused on empowerment, a crucial component of this research is to examine if, how, and why education sparks the empowerment process. I therefore provide an in-depth analysis of the educational program that students were exposed to, the Sistema de Aprendizaje Tutorial (Tutorial Learning System, or SAT). I examine the experiences of adolescents (who started the program when they were twelve to nineteen years old), as well as of older women with children who returned to school because, for the first time in their lives, they had the opportunity to study beyond primary school.

SAT's innovative approach and promising results have attracted international recognition and millions of dollars of funding from charitable foundations and international aid agencies.[4] The program has won two prestigious prizes, one at the German Educational Expo and one from the Club of Budapest, which designated SAT as a leading international educational program. Designed in Colombia in the early 1980s by the Bahá'í-inspired nongovernmental organization (NGO) Fundación para la Aplicación y Enseñanza de las Ciencias (FUNDAEC), the program is currently offered in Colombia, Honduras, Nicaragua, Guatemala, Kenya, Zambia, and Uganda.[5] Although it targets rural and marginalized populations to provide access to secondary education for youths and adults in developing countries, the theoretical underpinnings of the program are applicable to education in industrialized countries.

The SAT program's goal is to help students develop capabilities that enable them to take charge of their own intellectual and spiritual growth and at the same time to contribute to the building of better communities and the transformation of society (FUNDAEC 2007). There are five components of the SAT program: textbooks, tutors, the study group, the community, and the implementing institution. After finishing all the SAT textbooks and practical activities (in Honduras this takes approximately six years), students receive a secondary school diploma. Chapter 2 provides a comprehensive description of SAT and why it might empower students. Through an analysis of the SAT program, this book illuminates important questions and concerns about the purpose of secondary education and its potential to promote women's empowerment and gender equality.

Overview of the Book

Despite appeals from feminist scholars, our understanding of how schooling can challenge inequitable social norms and undo oppressive gender relations has advanced slowly. This book responds to recent feminist scholarship on undoing gender that calls for more research identifying the social processes that underlie resistance against conventional gender relations and how successful change in the power dynamics and inequities between men and women can be accomplished (Deutsch 2007). Throughout, I draw on the everyday experiences of women who participated in SAT to illustrate that change is a gradual and uneven process. Furthermore, unintended negative consequences can be associated with women's empowerment, including women's verbal and physical abuse by men who violently resist their taking on new roles. Education does not automatically result in women's empowerment, as the social and economic context in which women live can pose overwhelming constraints on their choices. Because of their poverty, poor health, geographic isolation, and lack of access to credit, the changes that SAT students experienced were often subtle. While their economic situation did not change drastically, some women spoke of having an altered worldview or "open mind," but this was not always accompanied by improved material conditions. However, over the course of six years (between 2004 and 2010), SAT graduates started small, income-generating activities or gained access to steady employment. They became more active in their communities, and several were elected to the village council. Some women left abusive spouses, and others began the process of negotiating a more equitable distribution of household labor. In short, the women who participated in SAT unanimously agreed that it was worthwhile and that it helped them improve their lives. Their experiences and perspectives shape the notions of what empowerment means, and the conditions under which it can be generated, that I articulate in this book.

In the first chapter, I briefly describe the research and policy context of this study. I summarize previous research on the role of education, particularly women's education, in development. I then chronicle the rise of educational policy and programs specifically targeting girls and women, and propose that empowerment is best understood as a process of recognition, capacity building, and action.

The second chapter provides an overview of the SAT program and my hypothesis of the ways in which it might empower students.

Chapter 3 sets the scene for the research, including a description of the challenges of implementing SAT and of the sites where the research was conducted, four Garifuna villages on the north coast of Honduras. Drawing from interviews with community members, I describe how individuals perceive the gender division of labor in Garifuna households, and how education is seen as a way to move ahead in life, or "*para seguir adelante.*"

In Chapters 4, 5, and 6, I develop the central arguments of the book. Chapter 4 describes how women experienced changed mindsets as a result of their participation in SAT and argues that empowerment is a process triggered by the acquisition of knowledge. As a result of their exposure to new knowledge, women describe changes in their self-perception, which, I argue, are deeply connected to the knowledge gains and attitudinal changes they experienced through their participation in SAT.

I discuss the consequences of the women's new outlook on themselves and the world in Chapter 5, where I describe the ways in which women who participated in SAT take action toward personal and community improvement. I also argue that education alone cannot change the social structures that place constraints on women's lives.

Chapter 6 examines a feature of women's lives that can block them or enable them to take on new roles: their relationships with their husbands or partners. I describe the intimate relationships of women who participated in the SAT program and those in the comparison group, drawing on interviews with women, their partners, and observations in their homes. My findings suggest that women who were able to successfully negotiate more equitable roles in their relationships used change-directed negotiating skills, were able to express their feelings clearly and control their anger, and demonstrated feelings of love and care.

In the final chapter I return to the guiding questions of the book, including: what is the relationship between education and women's empowerment? Under what conditions is education empowering? Drawing on my findings, I argue that for education to be empowering, it must accomplish several goals, the first of which is to allow individuals to recognize their inherent worth and the equality of all human beings.

My findings are significant for a number of reasons. They suggest that empowerment is not automatic. To return to the image that opened this chapter, the striking woman on the CARE billboard, my findings imply that education can be a key component of her empowerment. For her and millions of others around the world, access to education has the potential to spark positive change. However, empowerment is not synonymous with opening a bank account, wearing a sleeveless dress, receiving a microloan, or going to school, as some authors and marketing campaigns would lead us to believe. In the chapters that follow, I describe the lives of eighteen women and how participation in the SAT program sparked positive change in their lives. The findings from this study help us better understand how education can uncover talents and capabilities latent within individuals and can contribute to a more just and equitable society.

CHAPTER 1

On Gender, Education, and Empowerment

NAPOLEANA IS A SINGLE mother in her midforties. She lives in a simple concrete house with her adolescent son in one of the Honduran villages where this study was conducted. The house belongs to her sister and brother-in-law, who live in New York City. Napoleana separated from the father of her son after living with him for about a year. She explained that he was an alcoholic, and "he had his vices, and he deceived me, so I left him." She decided it was better for her to stay single. Napoleana was aware that many women in her situation do not have the option to live alone because they lack financial support. She received remittances, "from time to time," from her family in the United States. When I asked her why some women choose to remarry and others prefer to remain single, she explained that it is based on need: "There are some women with five or seven children, and for them it is obligatory that they get married again. There are some mothers that don't have any help from their family." She also believed that some women had bad luck: "This having children with various men, this is a woman's bad luck. Some women do it out of necessity because some men say that they are going to help economically . . . she has to accept it. Poor thing, because later this isn't a good home. There isn't understanding between them."

Napoleana, like many in her village, completed only primary school. When SAT opened up in her community, she eagerly enrolled. Previous research suggests that by participating in secondary education, she is more likely to earn higher wages, improve her health and that of her son, have fewer children, and become more involved in community affairs. These benefits of education are often associated with women's empowerment, and they explain why investing in girls' and women's education has become a top priority in international development. However, while research has consistently demonstrated a positive correlation between education and beneficial social and economic outcomes, we know relatively little about how and why education can trigger the empowerment process. Under what conditions can education alter a woman's circumstances in the community so that she does not have to partner with a man "out of necessity"?

Women's Education and Development

More than two hundred years ago, the father of modern economics, Adam Smith, wrote about the importance of education for national development in *Wealth of Nations*: "a man educated at the expense of much labor and time . . . may be compared to one expensive machine. . . . The work which he learns to perform . . . over and above the usual wages of common labor will replace the whole expense of his education" (cited in Psacharopolous 1988, 99)). Fast-forward two hundred years to the remarks of another economist, Lawrence Summers, who expressed a similar sentiment. This time the emphasis is not on "man" but on girls and women:

> If you think about the full social return on different investments in the developing world . . . there is a strong case that the highest return investment available is the investment in the primary and secondary education of young girls. . . . Part of the return to that investment is pecuniary in the form of the higher earnings those who are better educated have. Much of the return is social. Judged purely as a health program, education for girls looks pretty good. Judged purely as a family planning program, education for girls looks pretty good. Judged purely as a program for reduced maternal mortality, education for girls looks pretty good. Judged as all of the above, which it is, education for girls is an extraordinarily high return investment. (2004)

The notion of education as an investment has its roots in human capital theory. Although Smith introduced the idea as early as 1776, it was more fully articulated and backed by empirical evidence through the scholarship of Theodore Schultz (1971). His work emphasized the importance of studying the investment in formal education and quantifying the rate of return on this investment. The initial work on human capital theory made no distinction between men and women. However, in the late 1980s a Yale economist, T. Paul Schultz (Theodore's son), argued that there was an especially high rate of return from women's education (1987). By examining large-scale household surveys from a number of countries, he found that higher levels of female education were associated with a number of desirable outcomes, such as reduced rates of child mortality and reduced fertility. Unterhalter (2007) explains that while Schultz was careful not to assign causality, or to claim that women's education has a direct impact on other outcomes such as health or fertility, the policy recommendation that emerged from his work viewed women's education as a policy lever for poverty alleviation and development. She calls this the "instrumentalist argument" for the education of girls and women (2007, 43).

An influential book published in 1993 by the World Bank, *Women's Education in Developing Countries: Barriers, Benefits, and Policies*, summarized the research on the benefits of women's education, largely following this instrumentalist approach. The first chapter of the book argues that women's education is associated with increased earnings, lower infant mortality, lower maternal mortality, and lower total fertility rates (King and Hill 1993, 21–22). A number of publications and policy statements have expanded on these findings (e.g., Herz and Sperling 2004; Lewis and Lockheed 2006; Rihani 2006; UNESCO 2003). For example, Herz and Sperling (2004) present evidence suggesting that women's education is associated with:

- higher wages
- faster economic growth
- more productive farming
- smaller families
- lower infant mortality
- increased child immunization
- increased education for children
- lower rates of HIV contraction
- delayed sexual activity
- decreased risky sexual behavior
- reduced domestic violence
- decreased female genital cutting
- improved democracy and political participation

Policy appropriations of the instrumentalist argument are evident in a number of international declarations, publications, and policies, including the World Bank's 1995 education strategy (Unterhalter 2007). However, soon after the World Bank published King and Hill's book on women's education in developing countries, feminist scholars in the field of education began to critique the instrumentalist approach. In 1995, Nelly Stromquist delivered a presidential address at the Comparative and

International Education Conference, later published in a leading education journal, *Comparative Education Review*, where she argued that simply
expanding educational access for girls and women would not address the
underlying causes of their underrepresentation in education (Stromquist
1995a).

By the mid-1990s, an alternative to the instrumentalist justification
for female education was beginning to emerge. This was in part a result
of the growing influence of the publications of the scholar Amartya Sen,
who would go on to win the Nobel Prize in Economics in 1998. In a
number of lectures, articles, and books, Sen articulated what is now called
the "capabilities approach" to development. Rather than focusing on individuals as a means to economic growth, the capabilities approach frames
development as the expansion of what a person is able to do and be. A
capability is "a person's ability to do valuable acts or achieve valuable states
of being" (Sen 1993, 30). Development, in this framework, is essentially
about expanding people's opportunity to lead lives that they have reason to
value. Sen's capabilities approach influenced the way in which the United
Nations Development Program, and their annual publication, the *Human
Development Report*, conceptualized and measured development.

The philosopher Martha Nussbaum, a frequent collaborator with Sen,
has developed a list of ten specific capabilities that she sees as central to
human flourishing. Drawing on her work with women in India, Nussbaum explains this through the concrete example of a woman she calls
Vasanti:

> The central question asked by the capabilities approach is not, "How
> satisfied is Vasanti?" or even, "How much in the way of resources is she
> able to command?" It is instead, "What is Vasanti actually able to do and
> be?" Taking a stand for political purposes on a working list of functions
> that would appear to be of central importance in human life, we ask: Is
> the person capable of this, or not? We ask not only about the person's
> satisfaction with what she does, but about what she does, and what she is
> in a position to do (what her opportunities and liberties are). And we ask
> not just about the resources that are sitting around, but about how those
> do or do not go to work, enabling Vasanti to function in a fully human
> way. (2000, 71)

The ten capabilities that Nussbaum proposes are life; bodily health; bodily
integrity; senses, imagination, and thought; emotions; practical reason; affiliation; other species; play; and control over one's environment (ibid.,
78–80). Particularly relevant to education are three of these capabilities:

- *senses, imagination, and thought*, which, according to Nussbaum, include the ability to use the senses; to imagine, think, and reason in a way that is informed by an adequate education that includes but is not limited to literacy; numeracy; and basic scientific training
- *practical reason*, or being able to form a conception of what is good, and to engage in critical reflection
- *affiliation*, which means being able to live with and toward others, to recognize and show concern for other human beings, and to be able to engage in various forms of social interaction

Education plays a critical role in the capabilities approach to development because it can expand what people are able to be and do. More specifically, education can provide the opportunity for children and adults to develop their senses, imagination, and thought; their ability to reason; and their relationships with and concern for others (among other capabilities on Nussbaum's list).

The influence of the capabilities approach in development circles means that women's education is no longer emphasized solely because of its economic or social benefits. Rather, education is seen as a way to expand women's opportunities to live meaningful lives. Education is seen as a way to empower women.

Education and Women's Empowerment

In the decade that followed the publication of Sen's and Nussbaum's most influential work on the capabilities approach (2000–2010), women's empowerment as itself an important goal of development crept into the discourse of major development institutions. Even the World Bank, whose early emphasis on women's education stressed its "instrumental" role, came to embrace women's empowerment as a means to improving human welfare and social justice. In a paper commissioned by the World Bank, Malhotra, Schuler, and Boender explain:

> The World Bank has identified empowerment as one of the key constituent elements of poverty reduction, and as a primary development assistance goal. The Bank has also made gender mainstreaming a priority in development assistance, and is in the process of implementing an ambitious strategy to this effect. The promotion of women's empowerment as a development goal is based on a dual argument: *that social justice is an*

important aspect of human welfare and is intrinsically worth pursuing; and that women's empowerment is a means to other ends. (2002, 3; emphasis mine)

The World Bank was joined by a number of other international aid agencies, including the British Department for International Development and the Canadian International Development Agency in identifying women's empowerment as a strategic goal. "Empowerment" quickly became a buzzword in the international development community. Scores of development initiatives claimed "women's empowerment" as one of their aims (Mosedale 2005). Many of these linked women's empowerment directly or indirectly with women's education.

While women's empowerment emerged as a central goal of international development efforts, the mechanisms by which education sparks the empowerment process were not clearly specified. In the late 1990s, Malhotra and Mather argued that despite its theoretical appeal there was no concrete evidence that education leads to empowerment, and that to make this assumption was an "analytical leap of faith" (1997, 604). Scholars began to pose questions about how and what kind of education facilitates empowerment, and to make the point that not all forms of education are necessarily empowering.

Two 2007 books by Unterhalter—*Gender, Schooling, and Global Social Justice* and *Amartya Sen's Capability Approach and Social Justice in Education* (with lead editor Melanie Walker)—examine the connections between the capability approach, women's education, and social justice. This broader perspective on education moves away from equating years of schooling with empowerment. Furthermore, it acknowledges that schools can reinforce social norms or be of such low quality that little learning takes place. For example, Walker and Unterhalter convincingly argue that not everything "counts as education" if we wish to argue that education expands human freedoms, agency, and empowerment (2007, 14). Nussbaum, in a 2003 article entitled "Women's Education: A Global Challenge," makes a similar point. She argues that literacy and education in general are connected to women's ability to form social relationships and develop self-respect. By "education," she clarifies that she means not the mere rote use of skills but "an inquiring habit of mind and a cultivation of the inner space of the imagination" (2003, 336). "Real" education, according to Nussbaum, implies an "overall empowerment of the woman through literacy and numeracy but also the cultivation of the imagination and a mastery of her political and economic situation" (340). For Napoleana, the woman featured at the beginning of this chapter, or Nussbaum's

Vasanti to expand their possibilities, they must participate in empowering educational practices.

What Is Empowerment?

What does empowerment mean, and how is the concept different from agency or the expansion of human freedoms? I propose that empowerment is a process of recognition, capacity building, and action. Empowered individuals come to recognize their inherent worth, the fundamental equality of all human beings, and their ability to contribute to personal and social betterment. They develop the capacity to critically examine their lives and broader society and to take action toward personal and social transformation.

This notion of empowerment is somewhat consistent with how the term has been described in other studies. While there is no agreed-upon definition of empowerment, there is a great deal of overlap between how different scholars describe the concept. Researchers sometimes use terms such as "autonomy," "agency," "domestic economic power," and "participation" as synonyms for "empowerment" (Malhotra, Schuler, and Boender 2002). "Empowerment" has also been used as shorthand for the outcomes associated with the capabilities approach. For example, Raynor explains that she uses "empowerment" because there is "no easy shorthand term for the process of having a person's capabilities developed so that they are able to live a life that they have reason to value" (2007, 158). Despite the lack of overall agreement on the meaning of women's empowerment, Mosedale (2005) and Malhotra, Schuler, and Boender (2002) identify commonalities in how empowerment is conceptualized in the literature. These include:

1. To be empowered, one must have been disempowered. Women's empowerment is relevant because as a group women are disempowered relative to men.
2. Empowerment is a process rather than a product. People are empowered or disempowered relative to others and to themselves at an earlier time.
3. Empowerment cannot be bestowed by a third party. External agencies or programs cannot empower women but can facilitate the conditions for women to empower themselves.
4. Empowerment implies human agency and choice. A fundamental shift in perception or an inner transformation is essential to the for-

mulation of different choices. Empowerment includes people making decisions on matters that are important in their lives and being able to carry them out.

While conceptualizations of empowerment vary, a number of studies use some variation of Kabeer's definition: "the expansion in people's ability to make strategic life choices in a context where this ability was previously denied to them" (1999, 437; and see Malhotra, Schuler, and Boender 2002; Rowlands 1997; Unterhalter and Aikman 2005). In 2005, Mosedale proposed a framework of empowerment that is closely related to Kabeer's definition, but with two important differences. Mosedale defines empowerment as "the process by which women redefine and extend what is possible for them to be and do in situations where they have been restricted, compared to men, from being and doing . . . [and] the process by which women redefine their gender roles in ways which extend their possibilities for being and doing" (2005, 252). Mosedale explains that the key difference between her definition and Kabeer's is that hers stresses the gendered nature of women's disempowerment. Furthermore, Mosedale's definition focuses on individuals redefining and extending the limits of what is possible, rather than on individuals acquiring an ability to choose.

Empowerment and Power

The literal core of the word "empowerment" is power. The academic study of power has been approached in many ways, but there are two broad ways of thinking and talking about power: power over, or power as domination; and power to, or power as capacity. Karlberg (2005) describes the "power as domination" model as the traditional model of power in Western social theory, the implicit or explicit paradigmatic frame in the writings of Niccolò Machiavelli ([1513] 1961), Max Weber ([1910–1914] 1986), Thomas Hobbes ([1651] 1968), and Karl Marx and Friedrich Engels ([1846] 1967). Such power could be described as zero-sum—the more power one has, the less another has. It can also be thought of as the ability to convince someone to do something against his or her will. Lample (2009) proposes that this discourse on power that arises from tension or competition between individuals, between the individual and society, or between one group and another is a discourse of pathology, not health. As Lukes suggests, conceptions of power are themselves shaped by power relations, that is, "how we think about power may serve to reproduce and reinforce power structures and relations, or alternatively it may challenge or subvert them" (2005, 63). The idea that power relations shape conceptions of power informs the critique by feminist scholars that the power as domination model is itself a manifestation of male domination and patriarchy.

In contrast to the power as domination model, feminist writers have articulated alternative ways of thinking and talking about power (Allen 1999; Hartstock 1974; Miller 1982). Theorizations of power in the women's movement during the 1970s and early 1980s pointed to meanings of power that were associated with ability, capacity, care, and competence. Hartstock, commenting on the feminist theory of power, notes that "women's stress on power not as domination but as capacity, on power as a capacity of the community as a whole, suggests that women's experience of connection and relation have more consequences for understandings of power and may hold resources for a more liberatory understanding" (1983, 253). The view of power as the capacity or the "creative ability that individuals have *to do* something, rather than a dominance that is wielded over others," has also been called "power as empowerment" (Allen 1999, 21; emphasis in original).

This view of power as capacity places great emphasis on care, love, and the maintenance of relationships with others. Feminist scholars who align themselves with this model of power believe that redefining what constitutes "powerful" will form the basis for a feminist revisioning of society. A central goal of feminism is not for women to assume power over men, but for men and women to live in a world where "there is no domination, where females and males are not alike or even always equal, but where a vision of mutuality is the ethos shaping our interaction" (hooks 2000, x).

The idea of *power as empowerment*, or *power as capacity*, is at the core of the conceptualization of empowerment in this book. This way of viewing power calls into question one of the common themes in the literature on women's empowerment, namely that it is relevant to speak of women's empowerment because relative to men, women are disempowered. This notion echoes the power as domination model. A feminist understanding of power as capacity reframes the question of who is powerful and what constitutes empowerment. Women most certainly are unable to reach their full potential in a patriarchal society. However, the dominant form of masculinity, often called "hegemonic" masculinity (Connell 2005), also stigmatizes and ostracizes men who do not fit the vision of masculinity that sees men and boys as tough, aggressive, ambitious, unemotional, and self-reliant. As Kimmel explains, feminism offers a blueprint for a "new boyhood and masculinity based on a passion for justice, a love of equality, and expression of a fuller emotional palette" (2004, 258). In short, while men still outnumber women at the highest levels of a number of professions, in politics, and in what we might think of more generally as powerful positions in society, Gilligan reminds us that "the current system of gender relationships endangers both sexes" (2006, 53).

In conceptualizing the empowerment process, therefore, I argue that the very nature of power must be examined from a feminist perspective, and that from this vantage point men are also disempowered, because social norms limit their potential for being and doing.

Empowerment as Recognition, Capacity Development, and Action

With this notion of power as its core, I see empowerment as a process that involves recognition, capacity building, and action. These components are not necessarily sequential and are difficult to disentangle.

A key step in the empowerment process is that individuals come to recognize their inherent dignity and to gain self-respect.[1] This component of empowerment is similar to what Stromquist (1995b) and Rowlands (1997) call the "personal" dimension of empowerment, where one develops a sense of self- and individual confidence and capacity. I argue further that individuals must not only come to recognize their own dignity, but also learn to believe that their worth is equal to that of others. This entails the elimination of discrimination on the basis of race, sex, sexual orientation, ethnicity, caste, religion, disability, and national origin. Individuals must develop affiliation with others, or be able to live with and show goodwill toward others, and be treated as dignified beings whose worth is equal to that of others (Nussbaum 2003).

The empowerment process also demands that individuals expand what they are capable of thinking and doing. Although gaining concrete skills or abilities (e.g., learning how to sew, operate a small business, drive a car, or use a computer) might improve a person's life, these will matter in marginal ways compared with the capacity for critical thought. Empowered individuals build their capacity to critically examine their own lives and the broader society. Critical awareness, coupled with affiliation, serves as a powerful motivation for action that can improve one's life and the lives of others.

Indeed, action that leads to personal and social betterment is the third component of empowerment. Gaining self-confidence, recognizing the equality of all human beings, and developing the capacity for self- and social critique are in themselves insufficient. Thought alone will not lead to social change. The purpose of empowerment is to challenge oppressive relationships and structures and spark social transformation. It therefore demands action.

There are a number of ways in which the notion of empowerment as a process of recognition, capacity building, and action overlaps with earlier scholarship on empowerment and empowering education (Banks 1991; Kabeer 1999; McLaren 1999; Monkman, Miles, and Easton 2008; Mosedale 2005; Prins and Drayton 2010; Rowlands 1997; Stromquist 1995a). I see the convergence around these key ideas as a good thing, and I assume that frameworks of empowerment will continue to evolve as scholars conduct more empirical work on the topic. Indeed, I propose a new conception of empowerment somewhat reluctantly, as I do not think it is fruitful to endlessly debate semantics, particularly given the general convergence around key themes. At the same time, there are a few key features of this articulation that have not yet received prominent treatment. Furthermore, I have attempted to use clear, straightforward language that will be accessible to a broad range of actors interested in working toward social change through empowering educational practices.

Distinguishing Features of Empowerment as Recognition, Capacity Building, and Action

The feminist concept of power that informs my understanding of empowerment emphasizes the importance of relationships, of care, and of mutuality. The relational nature of empowerment, and gender more broadly, has been discussed in earlier research (e.g., Connell 1995; DaCosta 2008; Jackson 1999; Lorber 2000; Mason 2003; Rowlands 1997). However, few of these studies examine how or why men change their behavior in tandem with women who are undergoing the empowerment process. As Mason argues, "the *relational* nature of empowerment is critical. People are not empowered or disempowered in a vacuum. Rather, they are empowered relative to other people or groups whose lives intersect with theirs" (2003, 1; emphasis in original).

Among the people or groups whose lives intersect with women are, of course, men. So for women's empowerment to take place, they must become empowered relative to the men in their lives. This does not mean that women will have more power than men, or power over men. Rather, women's empowerment will lead to the improvement of women's relationships with the men in their lives. Many women find their marriage or domestic partnership the most difficult and challenging relationship in which they negotiate gender responsibilities (Adato and Mindek 2000; Bruce 1989; Rowlands 1997). For women to become empowered in the context of their intimate relationships, they must develop the ability to express their desires and concerns, communicate, and negotiate with their partners. In turn, the men must change their behaviors and attitudes so that the relationships are more equitable and satisfying for both parties. The centrality of relationships, and of men changing their behaviors so that these relationships are more equitable, is a key feature of my empowerment framework.

The emphasis on relationships also distinguishes my understanding of empowerment from the prevailing development discourse of individual empowerment. As Prins and Drayton (2010) explain, some development institutions (often influenced by neoliberal economic ideology) use empowerment as a synonym for greater financial independence. Likewise, these programs often view participation in the development process as synonymous with empowerment. Well-intended NGOs and fund-raising campaigns implicitly or explicitly equate empowerment with "capitalist individualism" (Feidrich and Jellema 2003). The "I am powerful" campaign described in the Introduction is a good example of this posture. From a feminist perspective, this slogan should be "We are powerful."

The capabilities approach is also referred to as an "empowerment" approach to development (Raynor 2007). Because of this, I want to briefly explain how my conception of empowerment overlaps with and differs from the capabilities approach. I would not use "empowerment" as shorthand for the capabilities approach, because empowerment is one of many processes that must take place in order to expand what individuals are able to do and to be. However, there is overlap between empowerment as I define it here and how Unterhalter describes the "capability approach line of travel in relation to empowerment." She explains that the capability approach perspective on empowerment "sets it as a feature of human-ness" (2011). In this way, the empowerment of women and the education that accompanies it carry significant normative dimensions. Education and women's empowerment aspire to make the world better through action and deliberative processes of reflection (ibid). Similar to Unterhalter, I see empowerment as a normative concept. I agree that empowering education should lead to actions that challenge inequitable social structures and improve individual and collective prosperity.

Because empowerment should lead to action, agency is inherent in the empowerment process. The term "agency," or the "culturally constrained

capacity to act" (Ahearn 2001, 54) is frequently discussed in empowerment research (Kabeer 1999; Maslak 2008). Sen, for example, uses empowerment interchangeably with well-being and agency, and defines an
"agent" as someone who acts to bring about changes that can be judged
in terms of the individual's values and objectives (Sen 1999,19, cited in
Unterhalter 2011). My understanding of empowerment as a process of
recognition, capacity building, and action that leads to personal and social
betterment therefore captures agency. However, I would not go as far as
to suggest that well-being is a requirement for empowerment (DeJaeghere
and Lee 2011; Sen 1999). Rather, empowerment is one of many processes
that lead toward improving self and social conditions.

When considering the relationship between education and empowerment, I think it is unrealistic to expect that education can directly change
oppressive social conditions and structures. I recognize that social relationships, conditions, and structures will facilitate or hinder the empowerment
process. However, I do not think it is feasible, at least not in the short
term, to expect that education can address many of the circumstances that
currently constrain the empowerment process. It is mainly for this reason
that I would not use the terms "empowerment approach" and "capabilities
approach" interchangeably. The capabilities approach is a comprehensive
framework for evaluating well-being. Part of the approach, as articulated
by Nussbaum (2011), is to identify the capabilities that a decent social
order must secure to all citizens, and education has been at the heart of
the capabilities approach since its inception. Therefore in attempting to
clarify the relationship between education and empowerment, in this book
I largely frame empowerment as a process that takes place at the individual
level. Over time, individuals may challenge oppressive social structures
and create new forms of social organization through their individual and
collective action. However, I see this as part of a longer-term outcome of
empowerment, not as a defining characteristic.

My understanding of empowerment draws from scholarship in the
fields of gender, development, and critical pedagogy. Literature on adult
education and literacy (e.g., Bartlett 2010; Prins 2011; Stromquist 1997)
has explored the links between critical education programs and empowerment. However, gender scholars who theorize women's empowerment
rarely draw on the work of critical pedagogy, including Ira Shor's book
Empowering Education (1992) and the work of Joe Kincheloe and Peter
McLaren. In this book, I merge two fields (critical pedagogy and gender and development) that have a common interest in understanding how
education can improve people's lives.

What We Know about Education and Women's Empowerment: Previous Research

While most previous research documents a correlation between an increase in women's education and outcomes such as lower fertility and improved child health, the cognitive and behavioral processes underlying these outcomes are unclear. As Malhotra and Mather (1997) argue, linking education to women's empowerment is rarely informed by empirical analyses. Some studies treat empowerment as a predictor variable, assuming that more years of schooling empower individuals, and that this will influence other social outcomes (such as health or fertility). Kishor's (2000) study provides an example of this type of research. She investigates the relationship between women's empowerment and contraceptive use. Women's education along with their role in household decision making, freedom of movement, and participation in waged work are used as predictors of whether a woman will choose to use contraception. In short, education appears as one variable in this empowerment equation, but we learn relatively little about the presumably empowering skills and dispositions that education imparts.

The second tendency in the literature is to investigate how a particular intervention or combination of social indicators (treated as predictors) fosters women's empowerment. In other words, empowerment is viewed as an outcome. For example, Adato and colleagues (2000) conducted a mixed-methods evaluation of Mexico's multifaceted federal welfare program, PROGRESA, which included an adult education component focusing on women's empowerment. They conclude that PROGRESA empowers women in that it increases their self-confidence and control over their movements and household resources. However, we learn little about the content of the educational program or how it fosters women's empowerment.

A study commissioned by the World Bank and published in 2002 provides an excellent overview of research on women's empowerment (Malhotra, Schuler, and Boender 2002). The two general trends the research review documents are that studies often focus on empowerment either as a predictor of other outcomes or as an outcome of a particular intervention. In cases where education is used as a proxy variable, an assumption is often made that more years of education lead to increased empowerment, neglecting the qualitative variations in schooling experiences and in the content of what individuals learn. In short, some research on women's empowerment tends to treat education as a magician's hat. The assumption is that schooling leads to somewhat magical transformations.

One of the goals of this book is to more thoroughly examine how and why (and even if) education works to empower women. In doing so, I add to a small but growing body of literature examining the empowerment process (Baily 2011; Bartlett 2010; Maslak 2011; Prins and Drayton 2010; Purcell-Gates and Waterman 2000; Stromquist 1997). In this book, because I examine the process of empowerment more explicitly and over a longer period of time, I identify the mechanisms through which empowerment came about for the women in this study. These findings generate insights about empowerment through education that could be transferred to and examined in other settings.

Empowering Education

While education is often described as a way to spark the empowerment process, or as a "resource" for empowerment, formal schooling can serve as a site of social reproduction, mirroring and reinforcing inequalities in society (Bourdieu 1977; Bowles and Gintis 1976). With regard to gender, for example, studies illustrate that schools reflect dominant notions of masculinity and femininity (Connell 1989; Pascoe 2007; Stromquist 1995a; Thorne 1993). Feminist scholars have called for "real" education (Nussbaum 2003, 340) that challenges the status quo and the ideological forces that operate against women (Stromquist 1995a). Because this kind of education is far more threatening to the status quo, it is more challenging to implement (Nussbaum 2003; Walker and Unterhalter 2007).

This more threatening conception and practice of education fits broadly into the domain of critical pedagogy, which links education with an analysis of politics and economics and takes as central the belief that schools are places where social analysis and the empowerment of students can take place (Weiler and Middleton 1992). Critical pedagogy is praxis, an exercise of action and reflection (Freire 1973).

Critical pedagogy is informed by critical social theory (CST), which has the implicit goal of advancing the emancipatory function of knowledge (Leonardo 2004). In CST, Leonardo explains, criticism functions to "cultivate students' ability to question, deconstruct, and then reconstruct knowledge in the interest of emancipation" (2004, 12). Such criticism is not a form of refutation or an exercise in rejection, faultfinding, or backbiting, nor is it valued in and of itself. Rather, the goal of criticism is to foster intellectual engagement and develop language that penetrates the core of relations of domination, such as race, class, and gender (Leonardo 2004). Critical pedagogy attempts to enable students to pose critical questions about the world, recognize social inequality, and work toward social justice.

The capacity to critically examine one's life and the broader society is essential to the empowerment process. Critical social theorists, drawing on the extremely influential work of the Brazilian educator Paulo Freire, refer to this as the development of critical consciousness, or *conscientização*. Education that is based on problem posing rather than a "banking" model of memorizing information is pivotal in the development of critical consciousness. Such education is active and grounds students' learning in their prior experiences and knowledge. Dialogue is the key instrument through which teachers and students learn.

As praxis, critical pedagogy requires both critical thought and action. As Monchinski explains: "Critical pedagogy as praxis *demands* we work to change the world. Critical pedagogy resonates with us because it affirms our suspicions that things aren't the way they should or could be. . . . Critical pedagogy offers us hope that things can change, but it is up to us to change them" (2008, 2–3; emphasis in original). Critical pedagogy requires both theory and action, and is oriented toward the betterment of society. Critical social theorists posit that education should enable students both to read the world more critically and to imagine a better world that allows the human essence to thrive (Leonardo 2004; Weiler 1988).

If empowerment is a process of recognition, capacity building, and action, "real" education, as Nussbaum concludes, requires much more than basic literacy and numeracy (2003). There are few examples of formal schooling (grades K–12) that draw on critical social theory or have a similar theoretical framework. More common are Freirean-inspired adult literacy programs (Bartlett 2010; Fiedrich 2004; Prins and Drayton 2010; Purcell-Gates and Waterman 2000; Stromquist 1997). These programs sometimes operate under the assumption that critical education automatically leads to certain ends, and this is not always the case (Bartlett 2008). Like linking education with empowerment, making the claim that critical education necessarily leads to certain outcomes is overly optimistic. However, a number of prominent scholars in the field of education and international development point to critical pedagogy as the most promising framework for tapping the transformative power of education (Bajaj 2009; Bartlett 2010; Walker and Unterhalter 2007). In fact, de los Reyes and Gozemba have coined the term "pockets of hope" to describe critical education projects (2002, 1). The SAT program, with over thirty years of history as a "pocket of hope" in Colombia, now reaches adolescents in Honduras, Costa Rica, Guatemala, Nicaragua, Zambia, Uganda, and Kenya. In both Honduras and Colombia, it is a formal, six-year secondary education program. Could SAT be more than a "pocket"—slowly and steadily growing to bring hope to thousands of youths, their families, and their communities around the world?

Research Design and Data Analysis

My research on the SAT program and the ways in which it empowers participants began in 1999, when I visited Honduras for the first time in my work as an external evaluator of the SAT program. With a grant from the British Department for International Development, a local Honduran NGO started implementing SAT in 1996, and between 1999 and 2002 I visited Honduras several times to help conduct external evaluations of the project. One of my tasks was to consider the extent to which the project was accomplishing the goals listed on its logical framework, including "to empower indigenous women" (Murphy-Graham et al. 2002). In connection with these evaluations I conducted interviews with female SAT students from several Garifuna villages along the country's north coast. Women in the program reported increased self-confidence and participation in community organizations, which they attributed to SAT. This experience sparked my interest in the general topic of women's empowerment through the SAT program and a more rigorous study that began data collection in 2004.

While I collected the bulk of data for this study over a six-month period in 2004, by the time I arrived in Honduras to conduct research I had visited the project each year for the previous five years. Some of the young women were just thirteen when I met them and were university students or graduates by 2010. Others who were newly married now have several children. My relationships with these women and my continued contact with them is one of the factors that helped them feel comfortable sharing their stories with me. This continued relationship has also helped me see how they have changed over time.

In 2004, I purposively selected four Garifuna villages along the north coast of Honduras for my study because of their economic and cultural similarities. Furthermore, their geographic proximity made fieldwork more feasible, as I could walk from one to another. Three of these villages had the SAT program for five years or more. In the fourth, comparison village, SAT was implemented for just three months before the site closed because of an unreliable tutor. Women selected from the fourth site served as an appropriate comparison group because they shared characteristics with those who participated in the program (all had finished primary school but not secondary, lived in poverty, and were of the same ethnic group) and they had elected to participate in the SAT program, although because of chance circumstances they were ultimately unable to do so. This feature of my sampling strategy—looking at women who were similarly motivated to study in SAT—helps address the important issue of selection bias.

To select participants, I created lists of all the women who were enrolled in SAT, based on registration information provided by SAT's administrative offices. I randomly selected twelve women from this list. I then randomly selected six names from the comparison group roster. I visited all the women to ask them if they would be willing to participate in the study. All those I selected in the SAT groups agreed; however, of the sample I initially selected from the comparison site, three of the women no longer lived there, so I selected three other names. In one case, a woman from the comparison site could not participate because her husband would not allow her to, so I selected another name.

In 2004, I conducted more than 120 interviews over a six-month period with this group of eighteen women and their relatives, spouses, tutors, and program coordinators. During these interviews we discussed a range of topics, including their family life, experience in the SAT program, thoughts and attitudes about the community, and plans for the future. I interviewed students' male partners (where applicable) and several male participants in the program (including students, tutors, and staff). I also interviewed community leaders and staff at community organizations. I conducted all the interviews in Spanish, which is not my first language, nor is it the first language of the women I interviewed. In this region of Honduras, Garifuna is the language most commonly used in the home, but Spanish is the language of instruction in school. All the women in the study were fluent Spanish speakers, and speaking with each other in our second language was a bond I shared with them. These (sometimes grammatically incorrect) interviews were recorded by me and transcribed by a Honduran university student. I translated all the interview excerpts that appear in the book, with the assistance of bilingual Hondurans who verified the accuracy of my translations.

In addition to interviews, I conducted more than two hundred hours of observation in women's homes and communities and took extensive field notes. I stayed with one of the SAT tutors and his family, in a small room adjacent to their home. He quickly became a key informant, providing historical and contextual information over our nightly meals together. I also spent time cooking meals with women, hanging out (and enjoying daily swims) with their children, and chatting informally with them in their homes.

In 2010 I returned to the four communities where this research was conducted to interview women again. I was eager to learn about the participants' experiences during the five years since my last visit. Had they executed their plans to continue their studies? Did they start the small businesses or projects they spoke about in 2004? Had their relationships become more or less equitable since our last conversations? Did those who participated in SAT think the experience was worthwhile, and how, if at all, had it altered the trajectory of their lives? I was able to interview seventeen of the eighteen women in the original study sample, as well as two former tutors in the program and three other SAT graduates.[2]

Limitations of the Study

Any analysis inevitably involves selection, translation, interpretation, and the influence of one's own beliefs. I believe that women and men should have equal opportunities and should determine how to share work equally through a consultative process. These beliefs likely influenced my attitude and posture when conducting interviews. For example, when women described how their spouses had additional wives or were abusive, it was difficult for me to react neutrally. As I describe in Chapter 6, one woman described how her husband threatened to kill her and said that subsequently she chose to leave him. After our interview I told her that I thought she made the right decision. In this instance I expressed my views blatantly. However, I may have also expressed my views in more subtle ways, including through my body language and facial expressions. On one hand, it is possible that because women picked up on these subtle cues, they told me what they thought I wanted to hear. On the other hand, it might have made them feel comfortable to express their own frustrations and confusion about their relationships and community.

I am also aware that I may have influenced the setting and the individuals studied. The villages where this research was conducted are quite remote and not on the tourist track. Much of the villagers' contact with North Americans and Europeans is through aid programs and charity groups. On numerous occasions individuals approached me to ask what "organization" I was from. Although I was very explicit about the fact that I was an independent researcher, it is conceivable that participants spoke highly of the SAT program because they hoped I might be able to obtain more aid for their community. Furthermore, my first point of contact with the individuals in these communities was as an external evaluator, and this may have also influenced people's responses. Additionally, my husband, Bryan, accompanied me during most of this research (becoming an avid bird watcher in the process as he occupied himself during my private interviews). People often assumed that he was my brother. The idea that a husband would follow on the heels of his wife to support her professional development seemed novel. Again, this view may have influenced how individuals interacted with us during the research process.

Finally, while I am an outsider to the communities where I conducted this research and so have a mostly "etic" position in relationship to the geographic and cultural contexts I studied, I am an insider (or have an "emic" position) in relation to the conceptual framework that underlies FUNDAEC and SAT. I became interested in the SAT program through contacts in the Bahá'í community. Raised Catholic, I investigated and came to accept the teachings of the Bahá'í faith as a teenager. I was initially intrigued by the faith largely because of its progressive social teachings, including the equality of men and women. The SAT program is implemented by institutions from a variety of backgrounds (including Catholic, Protestant, and secular). However, as I explain in the next chapter, many of the ideas that underpin FUNDAEC's approach to education and social change are informed by Bahá'í teachings, including the paramount importance of justice, the need for universal education, and the coherence of science and religion. One of my goals in this study is to better understand the challenges and accomplishments of SAT as praxis, or the process by which pivotal Bahá'í beliefs (particularly gender equality) are translated into action. As a member of the Bahá'í community, I share the same general underlying premises and concepts that inform the conceptual framework of FUNDAEC, and these beliefs may have shaped how I interpreted the data.

Like much research, this study raises more questions than it answers. While the interviews and observation in the household and homes with study participants offer insights into the empowerment process, the amount of time I spent observing students in the SAT classroom was limited to informal observations during my visits between 1999 and 2003. As I explain in Chapter 3, a number of individuals in these communities worked to convince educational authorities to open traditional secondary schools, triggering the closure of SAT sites because of low student enrollment. As Nussbaum predicted, "real" education is far more threatening and faces a tougher struggle (2003). In these four communities, a small but vocal number of individuals, largely to protect their own self-interests, worked to undermine the successful implementation of the SAT program. As a result the program was discontinued in these communities after six years. (It has since spread to other regions of the country, and a group of former students and tutors is lobbying to reopen these closed SAT sites.) I was not able to conduct any classroom observation with the study sample students because the sites had closed (I have, however, observed other SAT classrooms and students). I therefore rely on participants' testimonies of their experience in the program, and on the accounts of their tutors, their family members, and other community members, not on direct observation of classroom practice. Because this study is about how participants recognize and make sense of their experiences, direct observation of women in the SAT classroom would have been a nice way to triangulate my findings, but its absence does not detract from findings shared here.

I also chose to focus much of my research on better understanding how education could spark women's empowerment, as I was influenced by the scholarship and discourse in international development that identified women's empowerment as a paramount development goal. The findings from the study have influenced my thinking about empowerment and convinced me that any study of women's empowerment that does not give equal weight to male voices and experiences is flawed. While I did conduct interviews with and observations of several male SAT students, and some of this information is included in the chapters that follow, the majority of the research participants were female. In future research, I intend to explore how education can spark empowerment for both men and women.

CHAPTER 2

SAT as Empowering Education

MARTÍN, A LANKY TWELVE-YEAR-OLD boy with caramel-colored skin and close-cropped brown hair, stood next to me outside the classroom in the hot sun. "How is it going in SAT?" I asked. It was a question I had posed to many SAT students, but Martín's response, so concise yet so profound, lingers with me years later.

"It's going good. I like it."

"Why do you like it?" I asked.

"Well, there are some words in SAT, words that really affect me."

"What do you mean? Can you give me an example?"

Martín thought for a moment. I worried he wouldn't reply to the question and just shrug his shoulders. But he fired back: "Well, for example, the word 'latent.'"

"'Latent.' Hmm . . ." I said, my brow furrowed. "And why does this word affect you?"

"Well, I've learned that I have latent things, like capabilities, talent, inside of me."

He had been studying in SAT for only roughly half a year, but Martín already grasped one of the core goals of the program, to enable individuals to recognize that they are "mines rich in gems of inestimable value." Martín, his classmates, and thousands of SAT students in Latin America are engaged in a process of recognition that they are filled with latent talents and capacities.

I discuss in this chapter the core concepts that inform the work of the SAT program because, as noted earlier, "empowerment" has become a buzzword for companies, journalists, and international development agencies, an appealing word but often used in a way that is conceptually vague and empty, or as a synonym for feeling good. In SAT's case, a conceptually rich set of core values informs its curriculum. FUNDAEC—the Fundación para la Aplicación y Enseñanza de las Ciencias (Foundation for the Application and Teaching of the Sciences)—the NGO that created SAT, has a well-articulated vision of development, and my intention here is to describe the values that motivate its work.

When I describe SAT to other educators, they often ask if it is inspired by the work of Paulo Freire. Indeed, SAT has much in common with critical pedagogy, particularly in that both are hopeful that a better future is possible through the application of love, respect, and justice (Kincheloe 2005). However, while Freire's philosophy has deeply religious roots, this dimension of his work has not been the focus of contemporary critical education scholars. FUNDAEC emphasizes that individuals possess a spiritual nature. By and large, the field of development has overlooked religion and its potential role in fostering social change (Lunn 2009). FUNDAEC's vision of development places spiritual principles at the center of the process. As one of FUNDAEC's founders, Farzam Arbab, explains: "A vision [of development] is needed, and the proper vision will never take shape if the entire spiritual heritage of the human race continues to be neglected" (2000, 162).

FUNDAEC in Context: NGOs in Education and International Development

FUNDAEC is one of hundreds of NGOs that work to improve educational opportunities for adolescents around the world. The presence of NGOs in various sectors of social life has surged in recent years, particularly in education (Ginsburg 1998; Klees 1998; Stromquist 1998). Some scholars, such as Stromquist (1998), are optimistic about this trend and see NGOs as pursuing a progressive agenda that can help build bridges between donors, governments, and communities. NGOs often work with the most marginalized sectors of the population and act as the voice of the disadvantaged in many countries (Stromquist 1998). Indeed, major international organizations, including the United Nations, the World Bank, and bilateral aid agencies, partner with NGOs in their work.

However, as Klees (1998) describes, while the work of NGOs is potentially transformative, NGOs have also been seen as co-opted by neoliberal policies that emphasize a reduction in the provision of social services by the state. Carter and O'Neill (1995) describe a "new orthodoxy" in the relationship between politics, government, and education that, among other elements, is characterized by a reduction in the costs of education to the government. Indeed, NGOs often provide educational services in instances where the state is unable or unwilling to do so. Despite this, many

NGOs have serious commitments to social justice and grassroots activism, which make them an important force in the struggle for sustainable development (Klees 1998).

While FUNDAEC works both directly and indirectly with the Colombian government and those in countries that have SAT, its mission goes beyond providing basic educational services. FUNDAEC believes that religion and faith have a role to play in the future of development, particularly in ensuring that it is appropriate and sustainable. A global resurgence in religion is under way (Lunn 2009; Thomas 2004; Tyndale 2003). In developing countries this trend may be the result of the failure of the secular state to produce democracy or development, as well as an outcome of the widespread inequalities of wealth brought by the neoliberal prescription of free markets and open economies (Thomas 2004).

Evidence of this renewed interest in religion and development is the World Faiths Development Dialogue (WFDD), started in 1998 by James Wolfensohn, then president of the World Bank, and Lord George Carey, then archbishop of Canterbury. WFDD brings together a network of roughly thirty faith-inspired partner organizations from around the world to bridge the gap between faith and secular development. At around the same time (fall of 1997), the Canadian International Development Research Center (IDRC) launched an inquiry that aimed to investigate how its efforts relate "to the spiritual and religious dimension of human well-being" (Harper 2000, vii). This inquiry brought together scientists from diverse religious backgrounds to explore the theme of science, religion, and development (Harper 2000).[1] In 2007 UNESCO held a conference titled "Faith-Based Organizations and Education for Sustainability." Mary Evelyn Tucker, a keynote speaker from the Forum on Religion and Ecology at Harvard University, opened that meeting by suggesting that "sustainability needs to be placed within a larger, spiritually inspired context" (Pigem 2007, 8). Since the early 1970s, FUNDAEC has argued that development efforts need to recognize the spiritual heritage of humanity. This notion is now more prevalent among and accepted by prominent scholars and major development organizations.

A Brief History of FUNDAEC

In October 1974, a group of like-minded scientists and professionals at the Universidad del Valle in Cali, Colombia, founded FUNDAEC, which would become the parent organization of the SAT program. However, the group did not form around a desire to create an alternative secondary education program. They were interested much more broadly in "seeking strategies for developing, within specific populations, the capacity to generate knowledge and to put that knowledge at the service of their own social and economic development" (FUNDAEC 2001, 1).

The group was convened by Farzam Arbab, a physicist from Iran who migrated to the United States for his doctorate. After completing his PhD in physics at the University of California, Berkeley, he moved to Colombia and took a position as a visiting scholar at the Universidad del Valle. He worked, as part of a broader university reform effort sponsored by the Rockefeller Foundation, to help reorganize the physics department to meet the standards of universities in North America and Western Europe.

Arbab and the group of colleagues with whom he founded FUNDAEC saw a gap between the work they were doing at the university and the needs of individuals in the rural areas in the Colombian departments (administrative units similar to states in the United States) of Valle and Cauca, the regions outside the city of Cali where the university was located.[2] They were motivated by a desire to find a more appropriate role for science, technology, and education in the development of rural areas. Arbab explains: "I was uncomfortable with the distance that separated our formal academic endeavor from the lives of the millions of people whose needs and aspirations demanded immediate attention. . . . What was most striking about my new community was not material poverty per se but the wealth of talent that went uncultivated, together with the dreams of noble futures that went unfulfilled, as injustice systematically blocked the development of potentialities" (Arbab 2000, 153–154). The group critiqued development processes set in motion after World War II that had done little to improve the lives of the majority of the inhabitants of Colombia who lived in rural areas. Arbab and his colleagues thought that development efforts had created separate social groups or sectors: a small modern sector, living the lifestyle of the industrialized nations, and "popular" sectors, mostly rural or in the process of migration to urban slums, that struggled to meet their basic needs for food, clothing, and shelter (Arbab, Correa, and de Valcálcel 1988).

FUNDAEC's founders believed that the majority of development programs and projects known to them "treated development as a package to be delivered to the 'underdeveloped by the developed countries'" (ibid., 2). They wanted to come up with a strategy that instead allowed rural populations to be on an equal footing with those delivering the "development package." In other words, they wanted rural populations to cease being the objects of the plans of other individuals and institutions (ibid.). They believed that for this to happen, individuals must genuinely participate in the development process. Unlike many development projects of the era that viewed "participation" as including villagers in the implementation of a project they had no say in, FUNDAEC's founders believed that significant participation required that individuals work together in existing institutions (e.g., cooperatives, clubs, businesses, other community organizations) and create new structures. These might include new local decision-making bodies or new structures for marketing the goods of small farmers.

Arbab describes the process of recognizing the importance of "interconnected structures" for social and economic development: "The creation of institutions of a global society, a web of interconnected structures that hold society together at all levels, from local to international—institutions that gradually become the patrimony of the inhabitants of the planet—is for me one of the major challenges of development planning and strategy. Without it, I fear, globalization will be synonymous with the marginalization of the masses" (2000, 161). Along with appropriate structures, the group believed that rural populations needed access to a "systematic learning process with access to global knowledge" (Arbab, Correa, and de Valcálcel 1988, 3). They believed that rural populations could only participate in meaningful ways in the development process if they had access to knowledge. The group decided they needed a series of "learning processes" and looked for volunteers to participate in their development. These they found in a group of eager youths from villages and towns in the north of Cauca, whom they invited to participate in a variety of educational activities—learning processes that would lead to positive change at the individual and community level—which eventually would lay the groundwork for the SAT program.

These initial educational activities are also referred to as "action research" in some of FUNDAEC's documents (e.g., FUNDAEC 2001), echoing the participatory action research tradition that emerged in the late 1980s and early 1990s (Fals-Borda and Rahman 1991; Greenwood and Levin 1998; Selener 1997). FUNDAEC was trying to identify the kinds of practical projects and educational materials that could set in motion a "systematic learning process" and enable individuals to become active participants in the development process. Their process for learning, whose components often take place simultaneously, included: (1) taking action, trying out new ideas; (2) reflection—individually and collectively thinking about and critically examining the action that has taken place; and (3) learning, which stems from reflection and informs future action.

Between 1974 and 1980, FUNDAEC's action research projects focused on alternative, more environmentally friendly agricultural production and effective forms of community organization, including the development of more than twenty microenterprises for small farms. The knowledge generated during these first action research projects formed the content of FUNDAEC's first educational materials (the eventual SAT textbooks).

Between 1980 and 1990, FUNDAEC expanded as an organization and consolidated its work. Additional educational materials were written, and FUNDAEC increased its collaboration with other development organizations in the region. The Colombian Ministry of Education approved its materials as "effective and valid" for secondary education, spanning grades 7–12 (FUNDAEC 2001), and the SAT program was born. Although "FUNDAEC had never looked at SAT simply as a program to fill the vacuum in secondary education, but rather as a strategy for advancing social and economic development" (FUNDAEC 2001, 3), approval by the Ministry of Education was a great attraction to institutions whose main concern was to extend access to secondary education in rural areas of Colombia. The SAT program began to expand rapidly when two other NGOs, Comunidad por los Niños (Community for the Children) and the Federación de Juntas de Acción Comunal (Federation of Community Action Boards) began offering the SAT program in two additional Colombian departments, Antioquia and Risaralda. Later in the decade, institutions in two more departments, Valle and Santander, began offering the program.

FUNDAEC and SAT Today

FUNDAEC's role has evolved since it began the SAT program. During the 1990s, the SAT program expanded rapidly in Colombia and in other Latin American countries (including Ecuador, Costa Rica, Guatemala, and Honduras), and forty-two institutions signed collaborative agreements with FUNDAEC. These institutions implement and manage the day-to-day activities of the SAT program. FUNDAEC no longer directly supervises SAT groups or students, but rather works in partnership with the institutions that do so. In Colombia, SAT now operates in eighteen of the thirty-two departments, and roughly twenty-five thousand students are currently enrolled in the program.

The increased demand for the program was seen as both an opportunity and a challenge for FUNDAEC, which needed a mechanism to ensure that the quality of the program did not decline as it expanded. In 1990, FUNDAEC founded the CUBR, the Centro Universitario de Bienestar Rural (University Center for Rural Well-Being, often called the Rural University), which offers a five-year bachelor's degree in rural education. Many of its graduates go on to be tutors in the SAT program. FUNDAEC also is responsible for maintaining and updating the SAT textbooks, which is another mechanism used to ensure the quality of the program.

While the role of FUNDAEC has evolved over time, its assessment of development has remained relatively stable. Although FUNDAEC no longer has its own SAT students, one of its main activities is offering a graduate program in specialization in education for development.[3] The program targets those who are involved in the implementation of the SAT program in and outside Colombia. According to the group's website, participants study a set of materials that FUNDAEC has developed to "share the learning generated in the University for Integral Development through more than 25 years of work in investigation and action, revolving around the search for possible and necessary ways to use education as a motor to promote the integral development of rural communities."[4] One of the core components of the specialization is a module entitled "Constructing a Conceptual Framework for Social Action."[5] In this module, FUNDAEC presents some of the core elements of SAT's conceptual framework, the system of concepts, assumptions, expectations, beliefs, and theories that inform its critique of mainstream development thought and its work with SAT.

SAT's Conceptual Framework

Curriculum is never value neutral, yet in many instances the ideological nature of education is "hidden."[6] FUNDAEC is explicit about the set of beliefs that inform SAT textbooks and pedagogy, and also frank that "translating our principles into action and making our ideals a reality is something we have to learn." Those engaged in the process of social action must have a "learning attitude; . . . we exert our utmost to study, to act, and to reflect on our action within a framework which, itself, is gradually constructed" (Arbab and Arbab 2003, 5).

In a talk delivered at a colloquium on science, religion, and development in New Delhi, India, Haleh Arbab, a longtime collaborator at FUNDAEC and the sister of Farzam Arbab, explained that the conceptual framework links the lines of action and research that FUNDAEC undertakes: "Social action needs to be consistent and coherent. The way we have tried to achieve such coherence is to ensure that our action and research occur within an evolving conceptual framework, which we examine often, taking the necessary time and energy to make it explicit" (cited in Lample 2009, 138).

Many of the ideas that underpin FUNDAEC's approach are inspired by Bahá'í teachings, as mentioned earlier. However, as one of its publications states:

> FUNDAEC is not administered by Bahá'í institutions and not dedicated to the propagation of the Bahá'í Faith per se. Its purpose is not to convert people. Many of our fundamental beliefs are, nonetheless, shaped by Bahá'í teachings, and you should be aware of this fact from the outset. In a spirit of oneness, we will refer to the Bahá'í writings as the source of certain ideas. It is natural that the adherence to these ideas by the students will vary depending on whether they are members of the Bahá'í community or not. Yet this is entirely immaterial, for the unit does not address the specific issue of religious belief. As you will see, however, we do take a strong stand against rampant materialism, but this is a position shared by the vast majority of the inhabitants of the planet who are spiritually inclined, independent of the particular religion to which they adhere. (Arbab and Arbab 2003, 3)

SAT's conceptual framework is inspired by Bahá'í principles explicitly mentioned in the SAT textbooks, including conceptions regarding the oneness of humanity, the role of justice, human nature, gender equality, the role of knowledge, and the process of social change. Many of these ideas are echoed in the teachings of major world religions, including Buddhism, Hinduism, Judaism, Christianity, and Islam. For example, the Golden Rule appears in some form in all religions and spiritual traditions of the world. This rule—"In everything, do to others as you would have them do to you" (Matt. 7:12), or "Not one of you truly believes until you wish for others what you wish for yourself" (Prophet Muhammad, Hadith), according to Tyndale, "points us towards an understanding of 'development' which requires nothing short of a new world order in which generosity and caring are essential values, the community becomes more important than the individual, and people relate to each other on the basis of cooperation rather than competition" (2003, 22–23).

I focus in this book on the ways in which participation in SAT can spark women's empowerment; I did not examine in my fieldwork the fidelity with which the program is implemented, or the extent to which participants in the program are aware of how these principles permeate the curriculum.[7] However, these ideas inform the curriculum that SAT students study and therefore are important to take into consideration when investigating the relationship between SAT and empowerment.

Oneness of Humanity: End Goal and Strategy

The purpose of religion, and of working individually and collectively for social transformation, is the unification of the human race (Arbab 2000). At the same time, developing consciousness of the oneness of humanity is also the strategy or means by which FUNDAEC believes this end will be realized: "The bedrock of a strategy that can engage the world's population in assuming responsibility for its collective destiny must be the consciousness of the oneness of humankind. Deceptively simple in popular discourse, the concept that humanity constitutes a single people presents fundamental challenges to the way that most of the institutions of contemporary society carry out their functions" (Arbab and Arbab 2003, 9, citing Bahá'í International Community 1995). The analogy that best demonstrates the principle of the oneness of humanity, as FUNDAEC understands it, is the human body. The principle that governs the functioning of the body is cooperation. Human society is composed not of a mass of differentiated cells but of networks and associations of individuals. No cell lives apart from the body, whether in contributing to its functioning or deriving its share from the overall well-being of the whole. Consciousness of the oneness of humanity is therefore crucial in building world peace. "Only through the dawning consciousness that they constitute a single people will the inhabitants of the planet be enabled to turn away from the patterns of conflict that have dominated social organization in the past and begin to learn the ways of collaboration and conciliation" (Arbab and Arbab 2003, 10, citing Bahá'í International Community 1995). FUNDAEC is careful to point out that this belief "in the oneness of humankind does not represent a mere plea for tolerance or a romantic dream of brotherhood." Rather, this concept is at the "center of a conception of existence within which we define the nature and fundamental processes and structures of our collective life" (FUNDAEC 2004, 23).

Justice

Tightly linked with the concept of oneness is justice. The purpose of justice is the establishment of unity. Justice is the one power that can "translate the dawning consciousness of humanity's oneness into a collective will through which the necessary structures of global community life can be confidently erected" (Arbab and Arbab 2003, 37, citing Bahá'í International Community 1995). Justice can be thought of as the practical expression of awareness that to achieve human progress, the interests of the individual and those of society are inseparable.

FUNDAEC believes that justice is not a mere construct of society but has its roots in the qualities of the human soul, that is, "the principles of justice represent spiritual truths that already exist and must be discovered and understood; they are not something invented to ensure the survival of society" (2004, 37). When justice is viewed as a spiritual attribute, commitment to justice is a tangible expression of faith. Further, one meaning of justice is "to have no regard for one's own personal benefits and selfish advantages [but] . . . to consider the welfare of the community as one's own" (Arbab and Arbab 2003, 60).

Thus, FUNDAEC conceptualizes justice as an evolving capacity that individuals, communities, and institutions must continually seek to develop in order to establish unity (Arbab and Arbab 2003).

Gender Equality

The principle of gender equality is a "core element" of FUNDAEC's conceptual framework, and the theme is discussed in a number of units in the organization's graduate study materials. Without gender equality, "development simply will not occur" (Arbab 2000, 202). Guiding the goal of gender equality is a vision of men and women working together in all fields—scientific, political, economic, social, and cultural—with the same rewards in equal conditions. According to FUNDAEC, the application of this principle will "revolutionize every aspect of society, from the family to government, from the smallest productive unit to large financial organizations, from structures that support individual creativity to the most complex channels for the collective expression of culture" (Arbab 2000, 202). This conception of gender equality envisions not just opening opportunities for women to do what men do, but replacing prevalent attitudes of domination with those of cooperation (Arbab and Arbab 2003, 63).

Knowledge

FUNDAEC believes that "the power that can ultimately raise humanity from its present condition is the power of knowledge" (Arbab 2000, 163). However, the knowledge system currently propelling the development of the world is fragmented. Citing the physicist and philosopher David Bohm, Haleh Arbab explains that the way most intellectual disciplines treat theory today is intimately connected with the fragmentation of thought prevalent in society. Furthermore, she holds, fragmented knowledge cannot address the highly complex and interrelated problems of contemporary society (Arbab 2007).

FUNDAEC believes that two main sources of knowledge are religion and science: "With their aid we discover in ourselves the powers of nobility, freedom, and oneness and learn to apply these powers in building an ever-advancing civilization" (Arbab 2000, 157). Religion, as a source of knowledge, has been largely overlooked by the field of development. According to a document prepared by the Institute for the Study of Global Prosperity (ISGP), an institution affiliated with the Bahá'í International Community and FUNDAEC, religion must be taken into consideration as a body of knowledge: "The international development agenda has for the most part ignored the fact that the great majority of the world's peoples do not view themselves simply as material beings responding to material exigencies and circumstances, but rather as moral beings concerned with spiritual awareness and purpose. It has thus become evident that the mainly economic and material criteria now guiding development activity must be broadened to include those spiritual aspirations that animate human nature" (ISGP 2005).

In addition to neglecting religion as a source of knowledge, FUNDAEC problematizes the increasing superficiality of the education received by the majority of the children and youths in the world today: "In most cases the result of such education is the fragmentation of the student's mind and its final outcome is compliance with the social and spiritual vacuum that characterizes present-day society," says Haleh Arbab (2007, 9). She points out that many education systems organize knowledge into distinct disciplines, and so children aggregate bits of information year after year but gain inadequate understanding of the concepts covered. Moreover, even if students are able to gain a reasonable level of understanding in one subject, they rarely get a glimpse of knowledge as a connected whole. In SAT, traditional subjects are set aside and the curriculum integrates knowledge from various disciplines in a way that attempts to promote such deeper understanding (Arbab 2007).

FUNDAEC also believes that the field of development needs to focus on expanding knowledge and does not want to replicate current arrangements where certain sectors of society have access to modern science and an increasing number of poor people do not. Rather, "a fundamental concern of any program of social and economic development has to be the right of the masses of humanity not only to have access to information, but to participate fully in the generation and application of knowledge" (Arbab 2000, 206). The flow of knowledge in the world must be rearranged so that new knowledge can be generated by an increasingly diverse population. Focusing on locally generated knowledge can promote the institutional capacity that the population needs to tackle specific problems.

To summarize, at the core of the development process is knowledge. The major challenge facing the field of development, according to FUNDAEC, is how to engage populations in the process of knowledge generation. Examples of this perspective on knowledge from the SAT texts, included in the Appendix, illustrate how the curriculum attempts to allow students to participate in this process.

Social Change

FUNDAEC sees the process of social change, or the transformation of human society, as a result of a complex set of interactions that have to occur within the individual and in the structures of society (Arbab 2000). Social change will not take place unless individuals and social structures evolve to reflect the foregoing principles. Enduring change depends on simultaneous efforts to transform both the individual and society (ISGP 2005).

One social structure that FUNDAEC focuses on in its training materials is the family; to establish gender equality, the family as a social structure requires profound transformation, FUNDAEC believes. In training sessions, SAT tutors and coordinators ponder the following question, for example: "The structure most affected by the relationship between men and women is the family. . . . Discuss in your group the profound changes that the unit of the family as a basic structure of society must undergo in order to reflect the principle of the equality of women and men" (Arbab and Arbab 2003). Change in existing social structures and the emergence of new ones are key to the social change process. But according to FUNDAEC, these changes must be accompanied by changes in the human heart, which cannot be separated from its environment.

How SAT Operates

This conceptual framework informs not only the SAT curriculum but also the overall pedagogical approach of the program, which includes five key components: textbooks, tutors, study groups, communities, and accompanying institutions.

Textbooks and Practice

While the curriculum is not organized around traditional academic subjects, it is divided into roughly eighty textbooks written by FUNDAEC over the past thirty years. Organized by concepts and capabilities that FUNDAEC believes are necessary for students to develop, the texts attempt to build students' skills and abilities, attitudes, and habits, and to provide concise bits of information.

After several years of deliberation, the professionals at FUNDAEC agreed that the concepts and capabilities they saw as necessary in the SAT curriculum fell into five basic categories: mathematics, sciences, language, technology, and service to the community (Arbab, Correa, and de Valcálcel 1988). Each textbook has a general theme, with concepts drawn from several disciplines. For instance, "a unit in the area of mathematics may include the analysis of health conditions in a village. [The] main thrust is the application of fractions and percentages as health indices and rates, and its main purpose is the development of needed mathematical abilities in the context of a real and significant social problem" (ibid., 21). The textbooks' units of instruction are designed to help students acquire a small set of related "capabilities," defined in this context as "an instrument for the integration of knowledge in the development of curricula" (FUNDAEC 2008, 187). Students study several textbooks simultaneously.[8] In the preface of a language textbook called *Systems and Processes*, for example, the authors explain that the lessons aim to enable students to perceive the reality around them and describe it at higher and higher levels of sophistication (Arbab 2005). The capabilities that the textbook emphasizes include the ability to "describe the world they see and experience with increased clarity" through greater understanding of systems and processes (ibid., vii).

Lesson 13 of this book presents a brief overview of the process of digestion, along with a diagram of the digestive tract. The text begins: "Imagine you are eating an apple. What would have to happen to the apple so that, ultimately, the cells of the body can use its nutrients to carry out their functions? (See Appendix.) The text proceeds to describe the components of the digestive track, including the mouth, the esophagus, the pyloric sphincter, the stomach, and the small and large intestine. A series of "extension" exercises follow, asking students to look more carefully at a set of more detailed diagrams and answer a few questions. This is followed by "Reflection on internalizing ideas," which reads:

> Our digestive system is in charge of taking in food and converting it to a form that can be absorbed by the cells of our body. This is an entirely physical process over which we have little control once we have swallowed the food. In the world of thought, our mind does something similar to digestion. It receives ideas and works with them. Some it keeps and makes its own. Others it rejects and tries to forget. Think of one of your convictions, for example, your belief in the equality of men and women. Do you remember when you first encountered this idea? Were you convinced of its truth immediately? Can you describe what you thought and did until it became part of your systems of beliefs?

This lesson demonstrates that SAT's curriculum is interdisciplinary. Here a language textbook includes information that would normally appear in a science lesson, and integrates one of the core principles of the conceptual framework, the equality of men and women. Students are expected to discuss this reflection question, and even if gender equality is not part of their belief system, they have the opportunity to talk about the concept. Written in an informal and active style ("Imagine you are eating an apple"), the textbooks attempt to engage the student in a dialogue. A FUNDAEC grant proposal explains: "The main instrument of our pedagogy is an ongoing dialogue pursued by the student—with us, with the tutor, with other students, and increasingly with the community and the institutions of society. Our textbooks are records of this dialogue; they are revised from time to time to reflect the way our discourse is advancing" (FUNDAEC 2001, 8).

The emphasis on dialogue reflects how FUNDAEC views the student: "The student is not considered an empty container to be filled drop by drop but a mine of hidden talents and potential that need to be discovered, perfected, and directed toward the service of others" (Arbab, Correa, and de Valcálcel 1988, 22). Critical pedagogy similarly stresses the importance of dialogue for learning (Shor 1992).

In addition to their study of SAT textbooks, SAT students are required to complete a number of practical or applied learning activities. The program places strong emphasis on technology as it applies in rural areas, mainly on farming and small-scale agro-industrial development, since the vast majority of students are from farming communities. Through a participatory agricultural research process, SAT students and their tutors develop subsystems—more diversified farming systems that reduce the risks of crop failure, minimize the use of expensive chemical inputs, make a profit, and improve and diversify family nutrition (Richards 2005). Each group of students has a "learning plot," where they grow a number of crops often not traditionally grown together. Although students do not usually develop full-scale farms, their exposure to agricultural technology allows them to connect relevant academic, traditional, and practical knowledge.

Tutors

A tutor works with groups of students, as a teacher would in a traditional classroom. The use of the word "tutor" instead of teacher, and the overall program title, Tutorial Learning System, emphasize the idea of guiding a student in a learning process, rather than teaching a student information. "The purpose is to increase participation without denying the special position of the teacher who has access to much more knowledge in a specific field than the students" (Arbab, Correa, and de Valcálcel 1988, 22). The tutor is viewed as a leader in the classroom who guides the students through the textbooks and educational activities. Tutors "do not lecture or dictate, but nor are they mere facilitators of group discussion" (Arbab and Lample 2005, 187). Tutors are supposed to learn alongside students from the SAT textbooks and practical exercises, and not adopt a know-it-all attitude.

The program attempts to hire and train tutors with the same social and cultural background as the students. The tutors receive training in the textbooks' content from FUNDAEC or the local implementing institution. In Honduras, for example, training sessions are designed to mimic how tutors will conduct their classes, and tutors study the same set of textbooks that they will eventually teach. During one tutor-training session I observed, the coordinator facilitating the class asked me to suggest a *dinámica*, an interactive activity for the tutors in training. They were studying a science textbook on insects, so I had them make lists of all of the insects they could think of in two minutes. Then the tutors shouted out an insect and had to cross it off the list if any other tutor had the same one. Not only did this exercise help me learn the Spanish names for a number of critters I had never heard of, but also it was an example of how the tutors could make learning more interactive for their students when they returned to their classrooms.

Ideally, the training also prepares tutors to participate in community development activities. The goal of the preparation is to help tutors develop a teaching style that inspires "service to others and to work towards becoming a responsible, creative, and moral leader" (Arbab and Lample 2005, 190). Additionally, tutors should have an authentic interest in rural life and a sincere love for the community where they work.

More concretely, what does the tutor do in the classroom? Often, to start the day, the tutor briefly reviews what the group has been working on. The tutor may call on a student to read aloud from a text. When the text asks a question, or asks students to do something, the tutor interrupts and allows students to answer. The text that begins, "Imagine you are eating an apple" is not rhetorical; here the tutor might ask students to respond and to talk about the steps of chewing, swallowing, digestion, and elimination. The reading is thus an interactive process that the tutor leads. In sum, the view that learning is "educed" or drawn out of students rather than induced or given to students is reflected in how FUNDAEC describes the role of the tutor and the overall method of teaching the curricular content.

Of course, this describes an ideal tutor, and not all the SAT tutors are equally qualified. During my classroom observations I have seen tutors chatting outside the classroom during class time or interrupting the class to take a cell phone call. Tutors sometimes cannot teach because of family emergencies or personal illness, and since there is no one to replace them, students can go long stretches between classes. When the program started in Honduras, it was difficult to find tutors able to understand and then facilitate student learning of the academic content of SAT texts, particularly in the last two years of the program. As is the case in any educational program, SAT tutors vary in the extent to which they fulfill their job responsibilities.

Study Groups

Ideally, a SAT group/class has fifteen to twenty-five members. The program targets adolescents who have finished primary school, but often adults study in the program as well, as was the case in the Honduran villages where I conducted this study. The group meets during the week for twenty to twenty-five hours according to a schedule designed with their tutor. The schedule ideally allows them to complete all their study requirements as well as meet their family and economic responsibilities. Once set, the schedule is implemented with formality but flexibly enough to accommodate the needs of students. During periods of intense agricultural production (e.g., coffee harvesting), the group can postpone class and make up for missed hours. Some groups meet only on weekends, some have afternoon schedules, and some have a combination of morning and afternoon meeting times.

Communities

The community plays a role in the SAT experience at several levels. Because one of the goals of SAT is to help students perceive the reality around them and describe it, the curriculum focuses on the community as part of this reality that students must engage in, learn about, and learn from. SAT attempts to link what students learn during their official hours in SAT and their experiences in the community. Several exercises in the text ask students to investigate specific phenomena in their communities, to reflect on their communities, and to carry out service activities in their communities.

Service to the community, an essential component of the SAT program, motivates students to interact and share what they are learning with their friends, family, and other community members. Along with their tutor, students participate in a wide variety of community educational, productive, and organizational activities. For example, the first unit of the first service to the community textbook introduces students to a variety of diseases that might affect individuals in their village. After reading about these and answering a series of questions, they are asked to visit households in the village to complete a short survey about household health and to share with community members what they have learned about various illnesses. Other examples include organizing vaccination campaigns, participating in environmental education through reforestation or sanitation projects, growing new varieties of crops, and offering literacy classes for adults. During my research, the SAT students had started a palm tree nursery because the trees in their communities were infected with a blight and were dying. Palm trees, coconuts, and coconut milk are an important food source and cultural product, so the students planted palm seedlings resistant to the blight, which they distributed to community members for a nominal fee. SAT service projects attempt to connect what students are learning in the classroom with action; specifically, "the tutor and the group live an educational experience that integrates rigorous intellectual activity with action" (Arbab and Lample 2005, 190).

The relationship between SAT and community members is reciprocal. While the community benefits from the involvement of SAT students, community members also help students in a variety of ways. For example, community members have supported SAT by donating land, providing technical assistance in agriculture, and assisting with classroom construction.

Partner Institutions

FUNDAEC works with institutions that implement the SAT program, in most cases registered nongovernmental organizations that oversee the day-to-day operation of the program. FUNDAEC and the majority of these institutions cover their operating costs with grants from private foundations and bilateral and multilateral donors. However, in Honduras and Colombia, the Ministry of Education covers the tutor salaries, which is the largest recurring cost of program implementation.

The collaborating institutions conduct the training of tutors, the evaluation of students, and social promotion of the program in new communities that are unfamiliar with SAT. In Colombia and Honduras, where SAT has the official recognition of the Ministry of Education, they also serve as a liaison between SAT groups and the ministry. Often, the staff members at these institutions have completed their undergraduate degree at FUNDAEC's Rural University, and a number of individuals at these institutions study in FUNDAEC's specialization course to deepen their understanding of the concepts that guide FUNDAEC's work. The program coordinators at these institutions should therefore fully understand that SAT is not a mere system of secondary education, but an educational endeavor that develops the human resources necessary for progress in the region where students live and coordinators work (Arbab, Correa, and de

Valcálcel 1988). FUNDAEC trains individuals at its partner institutions (it acts as a trainer of trainers, so to speak) and continues to produce and revise the SAT textbooks.

In Honduras and Colombia, SAT has received recognition from the Ministry of Education; when students complete levels of study corresponding to lower secondary and upper secondary school, they receive diplomas. In these countries, SAT is therefore part of the formal education system, available to thousands of youths who finish primary school. FUNDAEC, in one of the texts of the specialization program, describes the advantages and disadvantages of working under the auspices of the Ministry of Education:

> The recognition SAT has received from the official system in Colombia has been a necessity and a blessing, but at the same time an obstacle to the natural unfolding of our pedagogy. Obtaining the resources needed to maintain the system and to continually enlarge it, requires the support of the government. . . . Yet, such close collaboration with the ministry implies that there must be many points of contact between SAT and the official programs of the country. FUNDAEC simply has to accept certain educational contents and methods with which it is not in agreement. But this is far better than hiding in a small experimental school and developing the "ideal education" which no one can ever implement. And, the results of the application of the pedagogy, even with these constraints, are so impressive that there is no reason for us to complain. This immersion in society and involvement with real social processes is an essential characteristic of all the efforts of FUNDAEC to generate and apply knowledge, and formal education is not an exception. (Arbab and Lample 2005, 189)

As noted here, there have been instances where FUNDAEC's ideas about education were compromised because of its close collaboration with the Ministry of Education. In fact, the executive director of Asociación Bayan, the institution that sponsors SAT in Honduras, uses the term *escolarizado*, which roughly translates to "schooled," to describe how SAT has taken on many characteristics of formal schooling to facilitate its implementation throughout the country. Nevertheless, FUNDAEC viewed the benefits of reaching thousands of youths as greater than the costs of adapting to meet government requirements. Whether these compromises have had a detrimental effect on program quality requires additional research.

Research on SAT

Despite SAT's operation in Colombia for more than twenty years, only a small body of research and evaluation is available. Nevertheless, the program has gained recognition by a number of different donors, policy makers, and scholars. While empirical evidence is scant, those who visit the program (myself included) are often impressed by the students, tutors, pedagogy, and textbooks. For example, during her visit to a SAT community, a senior education specialist at the Inter-American Development Bank (IDB), Claudia Uribe, started chatting with a group of students and asked, "What do you like about SAT?" One replied, "I like the methodology." Thinking this was a term the student was parroting or had been prodded to say by the SAT tutor, she pressed further. "What do you mean by methodology?" The student immediately went into a lengthy description of how she enjoyed reading the texts, discussing ideas and questions with her classmates and tutor, learning through the practical activities, and having the opportunity to reflect on her ideas, all of which elicited a nod and wide grin from Uribe. In addition to their articulate responses to her questions, Uribe was impressed by the students' level of leadership and roles of responsibility in their communities.[9] This anecdote is not hard evidence of the program's effectiveness, but it does convey the impression that many individuals who have visited the program share: it is a promising model, perhaps of higher quality than traditional rural secondary schools.

According to FUNDAEC (2001), during the years of its operation, various consultants and students have visited and written reports and evaluations about its programs, including SAT. Several midterm and final evaluations on SAT in Honduras have been conducted as part of multiyear projects funded by the Department for International Development of the United Kingdom and the Canadian International Development Agency. The nature of these evaluations (short time period, limited resources) precluded them from gathering sufficient data to make any claims about SAT's impact. They are descriptive in nature, summarizing the main activities of the project over the time period (e.g., Murphy-Graham et al. 2002). The Inter-American Development Bank and the World Bank have also commissioned descriptive reports on SAT (Perfetti, Leal, and Arango 2001; Ramirez 2003; Roldan 2000), but they have not funded or conducted any research or comprehensive evaluations.[10]

Is SAT Empowering?

While the quality of the SAT program appears strong, determining the extent to which SAT accomplishes the more ambitious goal of empowering individuals to become protagonists of social change is not a straightforward enterprise. I began this study with several hypotheses about why SAT might trigger the empowerment process, which I developed using research and theory in the field of critical pedagogy, particularly drawing on Ira Shor's *Empowering Education: Critical Teaching for Social Change*. The pedagogy of SAT shares much in common with critical pedagogy as articulated by Shor (1992) and Kincheloe (2005), including motivating principles, understanding of the relationship between individuals and the larger society, and beliefs about the roles of knowledge, teachers, and students.

Both SAT's pedagogy and critical pedagogy emphasize that the purpose of education is self- and social transformation. However, an important distinguishing feature is that FUNDAEC is explicit about, and labels as "spiritual," the values that need to be cultivated at the individual level in order to promote social transformation. Among these are love, mercy, kindness, generosity, selfless service to others, and justice (Arbab and Arbab 2003). While scholarship in the field of critical pedagogy also emphasizes many of these characteristics, it does not consider them spiritual, per se. SAT and critical pedagogy view the role of the individual and society as interconnected: "society cannot be made unless people create it together" (Shor 1992, 15). In short, in both SAT and critical pedagogy, education is seen as a tool that can transform individuals. Through their collaboration and sustained efforts, individuals can work together to change society. In this process of social change, knowledge plays a key role. Both approaches also link knowledge with action, claiming that students learn best when they can directly apply their knowledge to the context where they live. Finally, critical pedagogy and SAT have similar beliefs about the roles of students and teachers. The teacher is not an expert but rather an individual who can guide students in their studies and learn alongside them. The teacher should encourage questioning and should hold high expectations of the student. Participation of students in the learning process is essential for this interactive learning to occur.

In the chapters that follow, I turn to the narratives of SAT students and explore the ways in which their participation in SAT triggered the empowerment process, and I draw on FUNDAEC's conceptual framework and critical pedagogy to uncover the attributes of education that are potentially empowering.

CHAPTER 3

"SAT Came to My Feet, It Came to My Doorstep"

Understanding the Context of SAT Implementation in Honduras

In May 2008, I spoke at a workshop exploring SAT as a strategy for poverty alleviation during the UN Commission on Sustainable Development. Participants in the workshop, including representatives from several countries in Africa, wanted to know how they could start SAT in their home countries. FUNDAEC currently supports the work of local organizations that sponsor SAT in Honduras, Nicaragua, Guatemala, Kenya, Uganda, and Zambia. However, outside of Colombia, Honduras has the most extensive SAT program. But this did not happen overnight. It took roughly a decade for SAT to gain momentum and spread nationally.

The National Context

Until a military-backed coup ousted President Manuel Zelaya early one morning in June 2009 while he was still in his pajamas, the Central American nation of Honduras scarcely made the headlines. Located in Central America between Guatemala to the north, El Salvador to the west, and Nicaragua to the south, Honduras is the original banana republic—a primary exporter of bananas to the United States, with much of its early infrastructure developed by fruit companies. It is a country roughly the size and shape of the state of Kentucky and has a population of 6.5 million (INE 2001).

It is also one of the poorest countries in the Western hemisphere. On average, Hondurans earn close to US$1,000 per year less than their neighbors in Guatemala, the third poorest country in the region. Table 3.1 presents key development and educational indicators for Honduras relative to other Central American countries.

Education in Honduras

Part of the national strategy to reduce poverty is to expand access to education, particularly at the secondary level (grades seven through twelve, roughly corresponding to ages thirteen to seventeen). While primary school net enrollment rates are approximately 80 percent, few students, particularly those in rural areas, have the opportunity to continue their studies beyond the sixth grade (see Table 3.2). In fact, a recent study comparing educational opportunities in Central America found that secondary-school-aged Hondurans suffer the greatest disparities in access to education (Porta Pallais and Laguna 2007). A glance at the data presented in Table 3.3 suggests that Honduras lags behind only Guatemala in terms of secondary education coverage, with net enrollment rates of just 36.8 percent in grades seven through nine and 18.9 percent in grades ten through twelve (see Table 3.4), according to a report by the Inter-American Development Bank (IDB).

A report commissioned by the U.S. Agency for International Development finds that secondary education in Honduras faces multiple challenges: "First, access to secondary schools must be improved. While more than 11,000 public primary schools operate nationally in Honduras, there

Table 3.1. Key development indicators for Central American countries

	2004 GDP per capita (purchasing power parity, US$)*	2006 Human Development Index rank†*
Nicaragua	2,570	124
Guatemala	4,562	122
Honduras	3,796	112
El Salvador	5,804	106
Belize	6,734	93
Panama	11,391	60
Costa Rica	10,842	54

Source: Data compiled from UNDP 2009.
*GDP = gross domestic product
†The Human Development Index is a composite index measuring average achievement in three basic dimensions of human development—a long and healthy life, knowledge, and a decent standard of living.

Table 3.2. Honduran net enrollment rates in primary and secondary education by gender, 2007 (in percentage)

	Primary	Secondary
Urban female	78.5	57.5
Urban male	80.0	54.5
Rural female	78.6	31.0
Rural male	77.3	24.8

Source: Honduran household surveys (EPHPM 2007). Retrieved 26 July 2011 from www.trabajo.gob.hn/oml/bases-de-datos.-encuesta-permanente-de-hogares-de-propositos-multiples.
Note: Net enrollment is defined as the number of students enrolled in a level of education who fall within the official school range for that level, as a percentage of the population of the official age range for that education level. The official age range for primary school is seven to thirteen, for secondary school, thirteen to seventeen.

Table 3.3. Secondary education gross and net enrollment rates in Central American countries, 2005

	Gross enrollment rate*	Net enrollment rate**
Belize	86	71
Costa Rica	66	53
El Salvador	59	49
Guatemala	43	30
Honduras	50	35
Nicaragua	61	39
Panama	71	63

Source: DiGropella (2006).
*The number of pupils enrolled in a secondary education regardless of age expressed as a percentage of the population in the theoretical age group for that level of education.
**The number of pupils of secondary school age enrolled in secondary school as a percentage of the total population of children of secondary school age.

Table 3.4. Honduran net enrollment rate by area and education level, 2003

	Grades 7–9 (ages 12–14)	Grades 10–12 (ages 15–18)
Urban	54.8	33.7
Rural	22.7	6.3
Total	36.8	18.9

Source: Inter-American Development Bank (2004).
Note: See definition of net enrollment rate in Table 3.3.

are only about 900 upper secondary schools" (Umansky et al. 2008). The report also describes the need for more sufficient learning resources, better infrastructure, and better-prepared human resources, explaining that schools lack telephones, science laboratory space, libraries, desks, and qualified teachers.

In addition to the challenges of access, education in Honduras is typically of low quality. According to the IDB, this presents a number of problems, including the obsolescence of the curriculum and its lack of relevance to labor market needs (IDB 2004). The IDB disbursed a $34 million loan to the Honduran government to help address the lack of available secondary education options, as well as to improve their overall quality. Part of this loan went directly to support the expansion of three alternative secondary education programs, one of which was the SAT program.

The communities where I conducted my research had no secondary education programs before the implementation of SAT in 1996. Scores on a standardized test given to a nationally representative sample of Honduran communities suggest that the quality of primary education in the study villages is slightly lower than the national average (UMCE 2003). In the only village I studied for which data were available, students scored 30 percent in Spanish, compared to a national average of 43 percent. In mathematics, students in the village scored 25 percent, compared with a national average of 35 percent. SAT fills a need in Honduras by expanding secondary education opportunities, potentially improving educational quality for rural youths.

History of SAT in Honduras

Implementing SAT in Honduras was a process that spanned more than a decade, beginning in the mid 1980s when the Center for the Development of Human Resources in Honduras (CADERH) collaborated with USAID to investigate the possibility of introducing SAT in Santa Lucia, an agricultural community located outside the Honduran capital, Tegucigalpa. This effort gained the attention of numerous local educators, including individuals from the Ministry of Education and international organizations, who saw SAT as a means to improve Honduran education. Unfortunately, the program never became fully functional because organizational priorities shifted at CADERH.

In the early 1990s, Asociación Bayan (Bayan Association, hereinafter referred to as Bayan), became interested in starting SAT in Honduras. Bayan was a small NGO that operated a health clinic in Palacios, a community in La Mosquitia—the Mosquito Coast, an area with about 100,000 to 200,000 inhabitants.[1] Four ethnic minority groups live in La Mosquitia: the Garifuna, Miskito, Pech, and Tawahka. Arguably the region most neglected by the Honduran government, the area is often referred to as the eighteenth department, that is, at the bottom of a list of the country's eighteen departments (Landsdale 2002). Along with this neglect come some of the highest illiteracy rates, poorest health conditions, and overall lowest standard of living in Honduras. Bayan concentrated its efforts in La Mosquitia largely because of the area's need for health services. Over time, staff at the organization became convinced that, in addition to the provision of basic health services, a more comprehensive development strategy was required. In 1993, Bayan sponsored two individuals to enroll in the undergraduate program at FUNDAEC's university—Ricardo Eden, a Miskito from the community of Belen, and Alejandro Martinez, a Garifuna from the community of Batalla. Bayan hoped that Ricardo and Alejandro, upon completing their studies, would return to help implement SAT in La Mosquitia.

In 1994, Bayan invited two FUNDAEC representatives to visit La Mosquitia and conduct an exploratory study that would assess the feasibility of Bayan's plans to introduce SAT in that region. The study included interviews with schoolteachers, district educational authorities, and community leaders and parents. The results suggested a strong desire among interviewees for access to secondary education.

In 1995, FUNDAEC invited a representative of Bayan to participate in a SAT seminar financed by the Kellogg Foundation. With the information obtained there, Bayan created a proposal for the initiation of the SAT program in La Mosquitia. Later in the same year, Ricardo and Alejandro returned to Honduras during a short vacation from their studies in Colombia and began assisting with the preliminary identification of communities where SAT could function, meeting with parents of prospective students in order to share the goals and vision of the SAT program.

Shortly thereafter the proposal to start SAT in La Mosquitia was presented to the Canadian International Development Agency and the Kellogg Foundation; both organizations provided funding. During this same period, Bayan sent forward a request to have the Ministry of Education legally recognize SAT. In March 1996, with funding from USAID, representatives from the Honduran Ministry of Education and Bayan staff visited FUNDAEC in Colombia to develop a deeper understanding of the experience of SAT in that country, and ultimately to identify appropriate mechanisms for its implementation in Honduras. The ministry officials found the program quite promising and encouraged Bayan to move forward with its plans.

Establishing the First SAT Groups

In June 1996, with Ricardo and Alejandro having returned from their studies at FUNDAEC, Bayan selected eighteen communities in La Mosquitia to pilot the SAT program. In choosing these communities, three main criteria were established as indicators of ideal environments: (1) the community should have a functioning primary school; (2) the community should have a considerable number of youths that have not had access to secondary schools; and (3) members of the community, particularly parents and community leaders, should express the desire to collaborate with SAT.

Even though SAT did not yet have official recognition from the Ministry of Education, approximately 380 students enrolled in the program. The first groups were 70 percent female, and 36 percent of these were mothers. Participants ranged in age from thirteen to forty-eight.

In addition to recruiting students, Bayan recruited young professionals from the region to work as tutors and field coordinators, advertising through word of mouth and community meetings. Finding qualified tutors was a serious challenge. Although a number of communities had experienced and trained teachers at the primary school level, few of these individuals chose to collaborate with SAT as tutors. Only twenty-five people applied for the nineteen available positions, and Bayan was forced to hire individuals who did not match its criteria. The newly hired tutors participated in training sessions initially intended to last about forty-six hours; however, because of perceived difficulties in participants' mastery of the academic content, it was decided that more time would be needed to adequately cover the curriculum. Even after the intensive training, several of the tutors in this first cohort struggled with the academically demanding nature of the SAT texts.

These first groups of students used SAT textbooks from Colombia. Between 1997 and 2000, a curriculum specialist hired by Bayan began adapting the SAT texts to the Honduran context by removing references to Colombia and infusing the texts with locally relevant examples. Furthermore, to receive official recognition from the ministry, Bayan had to adapt the curriculum to meet national requirements. For example, it had to add English language textbooks, as English is a required subject in Honduras.

During these early years, Bayan staff received ongoing training by a team from FUNDAEC that visited Honduras approximately every three months. Training sessions focused on the pedagogy of instruction, on providing technical assistance in agriculture, and on covering the academic content of the textbooks. In consultation with FUNDAEC, Bayan decided to alter the organization of the curriculum to correspond with the two three-year cycles of Honduran secondary schools, rather than with Columbia's three two-year phases.

Official Recognition of SAT by the Ministry of Education

From the beginning of its work with SAT, Bayan worked to establish strong relationships with educational authorities at the regional and national levels. This process is challenging, given the frequent turnover in these positions—with each election cycle, and often even more frequently, these positions are restaffed. Soheil Dooki, the executive director of Bayan, explained that efforts to build a close understanding with the government played an essential role in the establishment of SAT in La Mosquitia. Such efforts included, for example, inviting ministry officials to participate in training sessions that presented information about the program and activities taking place in SAT communities.

After sustained efforts to build recognition with the Ministry of Education, Bayan signed a preliminary agreement with the government in December 1997 that granted SAT temporary ministry authorization for the first two years of its six-year curriculum. This important achievement helped strengthen the confidence of the program's students. In 2002, after much effort on the part of Bayan, a law was enacted that recognized SAT as a permanent six-year secondary school program, stipulating that graduates of SAT were entitled to enroll in any Honduran university. This step was crucial for the reputation of the program and its eventual expansion to other regions of Honduras. Along with this agreement, the ministry began absorbing the majority of SAT's operational costs; it now pays the salaries of tutors and some supervisors.

Key Challenges of SAT Implementation in Honduras

Official recognition by the Ministry of Education was a major milestone for SAT in Honduras. Between 1996 and 2002, numerous obstacles forced the program to close in a number of villages where student enrollment dropped substantially.

Lack of Community Trust and Acceptance

Because the program received only temporary recognition from the Ministry of Education, parents, students, and community members had reservations about SAT. They feared that a SAT diploma would not be recognized if students wanted to enroll in university or seek outside employment. A handful of primary school teachers were skeptical about the quality of the program and thus unsupportive of it because (1) SAT requires only one tutor, whereas official state-sponsored secondary schools require subject-area specialists; (2) unlike teachers in the formal system, SAT tutors do not have specialized training in education at the secondary or tertiary level (the only requirement is that they have completed secondary schooling); (3) SAT tutors work with temporary annual contracts and were paid less than the starting salary of a teacher in the formal system. Additionally, some primary school teachers hoped that if the government started an official secondary school, they would be able to work a double shift as primary school teachers in the morning and secondary school teachers in the afternoon; Bayan did not hire primary school teachers to work as SAT tutors.

These teachers raised doubts about the SAT program among parents and students. One went from house to house encouraging parents to withdraw their children from the SAT program. The teachers argued that SAT was a waste of time, an informal education program that would get students nowhere. They pointed to its lack of uniforms as evidence of its informality and poor quality. Subsequently, many students dropped out of the program, producing a ripple effect among their classmates. After the official ministry recognition in 2002, this problem diminished somewhat, but teachers continued to be the most vocal opponents of SAT because it eliminated the possibility of a double shift

Increase in Traditional Secondary Schools

Because the SAT program initially received only temporary recognition by the Ministry of Education, during its early years district offices, often in response to pressure from teachers, requested that the ministry start middle schools (*centros básicos*) in several villages where SAT already operated. The state did open secondary schools in some villages, which exacerbated the dropout rate in SAT because students switched over to these schools.

Low Academic Levels of Students

According to SAT coordinators and tutors, the SAT curriculum was too academically challenging for most students. Although they had completed the sixth grade, some students had been out of school for decades, and others entered the program barely able to read and write. This resulted in frustration and very slow academic progress (which also contributed to the drop-out rate). SAT required four hours of work a day, and many adult students had household responsibilities that prevented them from maintaining this schedule.

Student Dissatisfaction with Slow Progress

SAT requires students to progress from one unit of textbooks to the next, and the group determines the pace. The pace was very slow because of the poor academic preparation of the students. However, students were used to state-sponsored schooling, where whatever a class covered in a year was enough to move to the next level. In SAT, students must complete all the textbooks in one level before they can progress to the next. It took approximately three years to cover what Colombian students normally cover in two years. This frustrated students who wanted to advance more rapidly.

Unqualified Tutors

Bayan had difficulty hiring qualified tutors since so few individuals from the region have attended secondary school. Those who met the minimum requirements (completion of secondary school and being native to the region) had low academic levels. They had difficulty mastering and teaching the SAT curriculum, which further frustrated students and impeded progress. In three communities, groups were closed because the tutor was unreliable (this was the case with the comparison group in this study) or simply could not teach the academic content.

Geographic and Infrastructure Challenges

La Mosquitia is possibly the most difficult and expensive Honduran region in which to begin a program—there are no roads but only inland waterways, and no electricity or telephone service (cellular phone towers began operating in 2008). Its remote location and lack of infrastructure essentially ruled out regular communication with experts at FUNDAEC. SAT coordinators at Bayan had to make decisions on their own, rather than consult with individuals with many years of experience with the SAT program. Furthermore, the lack of transportation infrastructure made monitoring the SAT groups very difficult. At certain times of year the only way to travel from one village to the next was to walk along the beach, a journey sometimes of up to twelve hours.

Bayan's Response to the Challenges

Bayan responded to these challenges in a variety of ways. To formalize the image of the program, for example, it distributed student uniforms (a cotton T-shirt with the SAT logo on it and a pair of dark trousers) and asked students to wear them. Additionally, it began to cast a wider net to recruit tutors. The requirement that tutors be from the community where they work was adjusted to focus on tutors with satisfactory academic backgrounds. Furthermore, while adults still participate in the program (particularly young mothers), the target group for SAT became more clearly defined as adolescents because they had more time to commit to the program. Bayan also decided to establish a few criteria, incorporated into the 2002 agreement with the Ministry of Education, regarding what was necessary for a SAT group to operate in a community:

- The community must have a primary school with at least three teachers, preferably with at least thirty-five sixth-grade graduates.
- Parents and other community members must petition the local authorities, requesting SAT in their village.
- The community must provide at least 1.5 *manzanas* of land (roughly 2.5 acres) for students to use for agricultural experiments.
- No other secondary school should exist within seven kilometers of the location where SAT functions.

Despite the challenges, early evaluations of the program were positive, emphasizing its high academic quality, relevance, and potential to expand to other areas of Honduras (Bernbaum et al. 1999). Ministry of Education officials who visited the program were consistently impressed with what they observed (ibid.; Murphy-Graham et al. 2002). In 2003, the program expanded to two additional Honduran departments. Between 2003 and 2004, Bayan received funding to expand and augment SAT from several international organizations, including the Canadian International Development Agency, the Pestalozzi Foundation, and the Ford Foundation. The IDB funded the expansion of the SAT program through a major loan to the government of Honduras (a $34 million loan to improve Honduran secondary education quality and coverage). By the end of the 2009 school year, approximately thirteen years after SAT began in the country, there were 6,800 students in 142 communities in twelve departments in Honduras.

The Honduran experience illustrates that SAT can be successfully implemented in other countries—the viability of the program is not unique to Colombia. At the same time, Bayan's ability to adapt the program to the Honduran context (e.g., establishing criteria for SAT to operate in a community, adapting the curriculum to meet Honduran national standards) was essential in the implementation process. This suggests that for SAT to take root in other environments, the local sponsoring institution will play a pivotal role. Competent and committed personnel able to simultaneously make connections with educational authorities at the local and national levels and to oversee the day-to-day operations of the program are indispensable to SAT's successful implementation.

In summary, the implementation of SAT in Honduras and the scaling up of the program spanned more than a decade. The first years of SAT operation were particularly challenging because of the high costs and geographic isolation of La Mosquitia, the region where the first groups were located (and where my research was conducted). The spread of SAT took off when Bayan decided to open groups in Atlántida and other departments. While still rural, these communities were more accessible and had better infrastructure, which facilitated program monitoring.

Research Site: Garifuna Communities on the Honduran North Coast

The four villages where this research was conducted were among the first eighteen communities in Honduras in which SAT was implemented. They are inhabited by Garifunas, who originally settled in La Mosquitia in the early 1800s. They trace their origins to the Caribbean island of St. Vincent, where intermarriage between African slaves and Carib Indians produced a black Carib culture of Garifuna speakers (Herlihy 1997; Sunshine 1996).[2] After a long conflict between the British (who claimed hegemony over St. Vincent and its inhabitants) and the Garifuna (who claimed autonomy), the British launched an armed conflict in 1795.

This conflict ended in the decisive defeat of the Garifuna in 1796 (Kerns 1983). In 1797 the British deported more than five thousand Garifuna to Roatan, one of the Bay Islands off the coast of Honduras. Shortly thereafter the Spanish visited from mainland Honduras and persuaded most of the Garifuna to abandon the island for the mainland. Those who remained on the island formed the first permanent Garifuna settlement, Punta Gorda. Those who left Roatan established settlements along the Caribbean coast from Belize to Nicaragua.

Today, there are an estimated fifty-one to fifty-four Garifuna settlements along this long strip of coastline (Herlihy 1997; Yuscaran 1991). The vast majority of these, roughly forty-four villages, are in Honduras (Herlihy 1997; Yuscaran 1991). Estimates of the total Garifuna population in Honduras range from 45,000 (INE 2001) to 300,000 (Herlihy 1997).

The Garifuna culture retains visible Afro-Caribbean influences (Herlihy 1997). Most individuals in the villages speak Garifuna, a language with roots in Native American, West African, and European languages, but learn Spanish in school (Cayetano and Cayetano 1997). The predominant religion is Catholicism, although traditional religious practices are also observed (Yuscaran 1991).

Economic Context

These communities depend on the sea and subsistence farming for their livelihoods (Dodds 2001). Garifuna men fish by casting nets from dugout canoes; the women are subsistence farmers, primarily growing yuca, a root vegetable. Men are often at sea for long periods of time, employed on the deep-sea vessels that ply the Gulf of Mexico fisheries. Women typically head their households for a significant part of the year. Very few job opportunities exist in these villages—a handful of individuals work as teachers in the local elementary schools, nurses in the health clinics, or office workers in the municipal offices. Most income comes through in the informal economy, the fishing industry, and remittances from family members living abroad.

Although no data are available on employment opportunities at the municipal or departmental level, the Honduran Survey of Household Income and Expenditures provides a national estimate of the economic sector in rural areas. Nationally, 66 percent of individuals in rural areas work in the agricultural sector; 14 percent in commerce, hotels, and restaurants, and 9 percent in manufacturing. However, in the study villages there are no hotels or restaurants, nor are there shops or manufacturing. Therefore, the percent of the population employed in these sectors is likely much lower than the national average. Finally, roughly 9 percent of the population works in social services, construction, and public administration. Again, I suspect this number may be lower than the average in the study villages.

Infrastructure and Geographic Remoteness

Until 2003—about two years after I started this study—the four villages included in my research were accessible only by sea or light aircraft. A dirt road recently opened up access to the region for vehicles with four-wheel drive during the dry season when rivers do not flood the road. Three or four buses (usually old school buses from the United States) make the trip from these villages to Tocoa, a regional town roughly four hours away. There are no telephones or electricity. The closest major city is La Ceiba, which is the third-largest city in Honduras. The trip to La Ceiba takes approximately seven hours during the dry season.

Gender in Garifuna Communities

Few studies exist on women and gender relations in Honduran Garifuna communities. One of the most cited ethnographies on Garifuna women, *Women and the Ancestors: Black Carib Kinship and Ritual*, by Virginia Kerns, is based on fieldwork in Belize. Kerns's work offers preliminary insights on Garifuna culture and gender relations. Other studies on the Garifuna tend to focus on Garifuna folklore, history, dance, and religious practices and include only sparse references to gender relations (Gonzalez 1988; Yuscaran 1991).

Courtship and Cohabitation

Roughly 75 percent of the women in the sample were living with a man. Courtship looks slightly differently for each couple, but according to an NGO worker from San Pedro Sula, Andres Thomas, who had worked in the study villages for a number of years, courtship was not like what he was used to in the cities. "It's no fairy tale. . . . Here people leave their [parents'] houses and start their lives." What surprised Andres was that many couples began living together after a very brief courtship, often because their parents suspected they might have had intercourse. For example, Andres explained, if one day he and I went to the town fair together and were seen chatting or hanging around with each other, and my parents became aware of this, the next day "they might take your things out of the house, and tell you to go to my house." He said that as soon as a girl's parents suspect that she may have had intercourse with a boy, they send her to the boy's house. "It is not like in the city where you might go to the movies or out to get a milkshake," he exclaimed.

Andres also said that he never sees couples holding hands, hugging, or kissing: "Here a kiss is on the verge of sex." He thought that couples often don't know each other very well before they begin to cohabitate but that after they get accustomed to living together, they may develop affection for each other:

> Many girls are looking for an opportunity to get out of their houses. If a man comes by, they like each other, or maybe they don't even like each other, but they get used to living together, you see? After time there is understanding, communication, you get used to living together, which I guess you could call affection, but I wouldn't call it love like you or I from the city have. I think that you're not going to find that here.

When couples do begin to live together, it is most often in common-law marriages.[3] Only one of the women in my sample was legally married.

Three of the eighteen women in the study were involved with men who had more than one common-law wife. The traditional Garifuna practice of polygamy, while less common than at the turn of the nineteenth century, still exists in the communities I studied. This practice has historical roots among the Island Carib that extend back at least to the seventeenth century, when European observers described it (Helms 1981). Today, some Garifuna men associate with several common-law wives, sometimes concurrently (Bateman 1998).

Having more than one wife is, however, less common than men leaving their wives to cohabitate with another woman. According to women I interviewed, if the abandoned woman has several children, she must find another man to provide financial support, as women depend largely on men for their meager income. As a result, it is not uncommon for women to have children with multiple partners. As one interviewee, Soraida, explained: "It is because of poverty that women have children with different men, because there are men who only give children and then they take off. And as I have told you, there is no source of work, so she has to look for another person who will give her bread, soap, things like that, for her and her children. That's why they look for another man, to survive."

Angela, another study participant, shared Soraida's view that women are obliged to look for another partner because they can't survive on their own: "Sometimes a woman does this [has children with multiple partners] because the one she is with will get her pregnant and then leave her, so because of this she has to look for another man. Then another might deceive her, and well, the same thing happens. . . . Poverty obliges women to do this." There seems to be little social stigma attached to having multiple partners. Soraida and Angela do not look negatively upon women in this situation. Rather, they see it as a result of poverty and financial dependence on men. Bateman explains that residents of Garifuna communities are bound by complex ties of kinship, "owing in no small measure to the fact that so many women and men had children by more than one mate" (1998, 214).

Division of Labor

All the women I interviewed agreed that women work more hours per day than men do. As Alejandra explained: "Men don't like to work. Women work more." One of the reasons women work more is because of their responsibilities in agriculture. Men help clear the fields for planting, but after that their role is minimal. Women plant, tend, and harvest the crops. They then turn the crops into a finished product. On top of this they bear the burden of the household responsibilities, including cooking, cleaning, and child rearing. Sonia explained that "women do almost everything in the home. All men do is work in fishing. She is the one who washes, cleans, takes the children to the doctor, goes to meetings. . . . Men do maybe one-quarter of what women do."

The words of a Garifuna woman in Yuscaran's study are similar to Sonia's comment: "You have to realize that Garifuna women have little freedom. In a way, they are like slaves. All they do is work. They have the major responsibility for raising children, providing food, and often, making an income. I believe this should change" (1991, 68). There is no dispute in the literature that women are primarily responsible for raising children in Garifuna communities (Kerns 1983; McCauley 1981; Yuscaran 1991). As Kerns writes: "Women bear ultimate responsibility for their children. . . . On a daily basis, women must see that their children are adequately fed and clothed. They are also responsible for care when their children fall ill"

(1983, 108). Kerns describes a father's responsibility toward his children primarily in terms of the financial support he provides (116).

McCauley's study is also consistent with what the women I interviewed said; the chapter "Women Working" begins: "While the men dream, women have to continue with their daily labors" (1981, 53). Kerns describes the daily life of the Garifuna in the following way: Men normally wake in predawn darkness and paddle their dugout canoes out to sea or into a lagoon. A few men will return early (around the time of the morning meal); most will not return until midday, and then they will relax and socialize with friends. Women wake between 5:00 and 6:00 a.m., spending the next hour on a variety of tasks that include chopping firewood, sweeping the yard and the inside of their houses, and procuring food for the noon meal. During the early hours of the morning, women cut firewood or work in the fields, returning with upwards of fifty pounds of wood or crops balanced on their heads. Women then cook and serve lunch. In the afternoon they draw water from the well and bathe. By 4:00 p.m. they begin the evening meal. Between 5:00 and 6:00 women serve the evening meal. By 8:00 p.m. most women have retired for the night, with their husbands joining them shortly thereafter (Kerns 1983, 53–55).

Women's main source of cash income comes from their work in subsis-

Women working together to grate yuca for cassave bread

tence agriculture. Thirteen of the eighteen women I interviewed work in subsistence agriculture, growing yuca, plantains, corn, and several tropical root vegetables (yams, malanga, and taro). Yuca, the most commonly tended crop, is processed into a flat bread, cassave. Women often work collectively with their neighbors or relatives in making cassave, a laborious task that takes at least two days. The yuca must be peeled, pressed, grated, dried, and then finally cooked on a large woodstove. They eat part of the cassave they produce and sell the rest, mainly to Garifuna communities in peri-urban areas. These communities, such as Sambo Creek, Corozal, and Trujillo, consume cassave but no longer produce it, creating a market demand. With the construction of the road, women now have better access to this market and can ship cassave on the bus to these purchasing com-

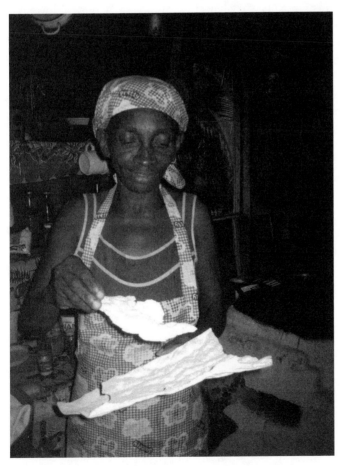

A SAT student's mother holding the finished product, cassave

munities. While women do earn some income from cassave, they largely depend on the financial assistance of their spouses to meet the needs of their households.

Financial Dependence on Men: "Who Will Help Me?"

Men commonly work in the fishing industry, often leaving the community for months at a time to work on commercial vessels from the Bay Islands, as I have noted (Herlihy 1997; Kerns 1983). Out migration has been common for decades, as men seek opportunities in the larger cities of Honduras and in the United States (Herlihy 1997; Kerns 1983). As one woman in Yuscaran's study explained: "The men work outside the village or go to sea, returning when they have made money. My husband worked for a long time as a net fisherman. He is now at sea, working on a boat which sails to the United States. I am waiting for him. Here, women are always waiting for the return of their men" (1991, 62). Between 1991 and 2006, 6 percent of the population of Honduras left rural areas in search of a better life in the cities (Hoyos, Bussolo, and Núñez 2008).

One of the reasons why women wait for their men to return is that they depend on the earnings of their partners to maintain their household and pay for their children's schooling. Seven of the women I interviewed used the word *ayuda* (help) in connection with men's roles. Help, in this context, refers to financial support. Alejandra and Esmeralda both asked, "Who will help me" (*Quien me va a ayudar*) with my children? They depend on their partners' financial support to raise their children. How else would they get by? For example, although Esmeralda was not satisfied with her relationship, she asked: "With three children, who is going to help me more than him [her partner]?" Alejandra believes that the primary reason people get married is so that a man will help a woman financially. I asked her why a woman decides to get married and she replied: "Well, so that a man will financially support [help] her."

Women must often ask their partners for money, even though they eventually decide how this money is spent. Dulcinea and Teodora both described how they must ask their partner for money to purchase basic goods for the household. When I asked Teodora, "Who decides to make small purchases such as rice, sugar, flour?" she explained that she must ask her partner for the money: "I decide to buy it, only he gives me the money." Likewise, Dulcinea explained that when her husband gets back from fishing, "I have to follow him around so that right away he will give me a little bit of money to buy goods for the house."

Male Alcohol Consumption

Women were also critical of how men spent their money. Several women described men as financially irresponsible because they spend their money on alcohol instead of on basic household necessities. In my interviews with women, alcohol abuse was the most frequently mentioned problem facing men in the community. Women were also frustrated because men spent their money on alcohol. For example, Sonia, Teodora, and Renata said that men spend what little money they earn on drinking when they should put the needs of their children and household first. Renata: "There is hardly any money, and if there are five *lempiras* [US$0.30] they use it to drink." Teodora: "When men have money, they look for a drink, but a woman uses it for the household."

Empirical studies confirm Teodora's observation that women are more likely to spend their money on the household than are men (World Bank 2001).[4] In a qualitative study in four Honduran Garifuna communities commissioned by the Inter-American Development Bank, respondents describe the connection between unemployment and drug and alcohol abuse in Garifuna communities. Lack of employment coupled with the "easy money" from remittances is viewed as exacerbating irresponsible conduct, including alcohol abuse (Tercero 2002, 43).

Education as Hope for the Future

Education is frequently touted as a way to improve the lives of the millions who live in poverty around the globe (Sachs 2005; Stiglitz 2006). According to *New York Times* columnists Nicholas Kristof and Sheryl WuDunn in their best-selling book *Half the Sky: Turning Oppression into Opportunity for Women Worldwide*, education is essential. In fact, the slogan that runs as a banner across the home page of their Half the Sky website (*www.halftheskymovement.org*) reads: "The best way to fight poverty and extremism is to educate and empower women and girls." In poor countries such as Honduras, implementing innovative educational programs that can change the life circumstances of marginalized populations is a challenge. There were a number of obstacles for the SAT program, particularly during the early years of operation, as we have seen. For women, poverty, poor health, natural disasters, cultural norms, and the demands of household labor made it difficult to participate in SAT, even if they were highly motivated.

Yet despite the numerous structural challenges facing the women, many believed firmly that education would help them move ahead in life, or "*para seguir adelante.*" The phrase encapsulates why the women in the study (both in the SAT group and the comparison group) value education. It allowed them take steps forward, or at least to have hope for doing so. Through education, they believed, they could become protagonists in improving their living conditions.

CHAPTER 4

"My Mind Is Different"

*Developing Confidence
and Critical Perspectives through SAT*

"WHATEVER I LEARNED I'VE already forgotten," Margarita explained sheepishly when I asked about her participation in SAT. She was in the program for only about three months, and so she did not have much to tell me about her experience. Margarita dropped out of SAT for a good reason: an offer to work in San Pedro Sula. She was excited about this opportunity, as it was her ticket out of the village and into waged labor. For two years, Margarita worked as an assistant cook at Que Chicken!, a buffet restaurant attached to a gas station outside San Pedro Sula, Honduras's second-largest city. She prepared salads, meat, and other dishes to serve at the buffet. She enjoyed this work and was promoted to supervise other assistants.

Although she liked her job, Margarita found city life dangerous. "I had to take more than one bus to work," she explained, as she lived in a marginal neighborhood some distance from the restaurant. One night, she did not leave work until eight o'clock. As she waited to catch the second of three buses that brought her home, she was mugged at knifepoint. "He pulled off my bracelet and threatened me with a knife!" Margarita spoke disparagingly of all of the "thieves and delinquents" in the city, and explained that their presence was one reason why she decided to return to her village, although her boss at Que Chicken! wanted her to stay. He sent her off with a letter of recommendation for future jobs, which Margarita proudly retrieved from her house to show me. She read aloud: "To whom it may concern, Margarita Dolmo has worked here for several years, all with excellent conduct, honesty, and above all a desire to excel. For these reasons I recommend her for any future services you may need."

For a short time after Margarita returned to her village, she ran a shop in a small thatched-roof hut adjacent to her home. She showed me its remnants: beer bottles were arranged in a haphazard semicircle on the floor, and a pile of glass Coca-Cola empties mixed with some plastic *guaro* bottles sat in crates near the side wall. She explained: "I used to sell flour, sugar, candies, but now I only sell beer and *guaro*." Her customers would seat themselves either inside or outside her home to drink and hang out.

Margarita mentioned that she would like to continue her studies someday so that she could get a job, but she did not want to return to San Pedro Sula. Several of her classmates in SAT were enrolled in universities, and I wondered if Margarita would have enrolled had she turned down the job in San Pedro Sula and finished her studies in SAT. One SAT *bachiller* graduate, Juanita, had material circumstances similar to Margarita's. During the course of her studies in SAT, she and her partner began operating a *comedor* that sold cold drinks, beer, and hot meals. While her business sold more than alcohol, she and Margarita earned their livelihoods through the operation of small businesses. Though Margarita seemed remorseful regarding her decision to discontinue her studies, it was difficult to pinpoint the tangible ways in which Juanita and Margarita's circumstances differed because of their participation (or lack thereof) in SAT, at least from a material perspective.

Does SAT Make a Difference?

In questioning the impact of SAT on women's empowerment, I often returned to Margarita and Juanita. The concrete ways in which women's lives had changed as a result of their studies were difficult to define, particularly for the women who remained in the villages. After all, only a handful of SAT graduates were enrolled in universities. Exactly how, then, were women's lives different as a result of their studies? The answer to this question emerged in subtle ways through my conversations with women. They spoke of "seeing the world differently." Juanita said that SAT "opened [her] mind." Teodora explained that her "mind opened more" through her studies. Like a potter molds clay, she explained, SAT had "formed" her into a different person.

Participation in SAT sparked a process of recognition. It altered the way women viewed themselves and their communities. Learning, or acquiring knowledge, triggered self-reflection and discovery. Often linked to learning was an improvement in self-confidence, as women began to recognize their inherent worth and to see themselves on an equal footing with others for the first time. Some women who participated in SAT developed the capacity to critically examine their lives and their communities, particularly manifestations of gender inequality. These findings demonstrate key components of the empowerment process, namely, individuals come to recognize their inherent worth and their equality with others, and are able to critically examine their lives and the broader society.

Becoming a Professional:
Views on the Importance of Schooling

Several SAT participants believed that education was important because it allowed a person to press on, or move ahead (*"para seguir adelante"*) and become a "professional." They used the term *profesional* in Spanish, and I have translated it literally here. However, the term seemed to mean stable, paid employment. For example, a paid construction worker, clerical worker, teacher, nurse, or social worker is a professional. In fact, any formal employment is considered "professional." Several women specifically mentioned the professions of nursing and teaching as fields of work an educated person would have access to. If an individual is able to get a job as a nurse or a teacher, she will get paid monthly. This job security will allow her to improve her living conditions and send her children to school. This is the basic trajectory (school → more school or professional training → steady job → improved living conditions) that encompasses the notion of getting ahead.

Margarita, for example, explained that "when you get a degree, you work, because when a person has a degree, she gets a job." Renata, Lola, Esmeralda, and Isadora all mentioned that education helps a person become a "professional" and have an occupation. For example, according to Soraida, education prepares a person to enter the labor market, and this allows them to take better care of their household: "An [educated] person is prepared—wherever they go they get a job and earn money, and this money helps them in a lot of ways; it helps them to maintain their household, help their children, give their children support so that they can keep studying." Here Soraida describes the trajectory of schooling, stable work, and improved living conditions. Juanita also stated that education is the key to earning a living: "Whoever isn't a professional now has few opportunities to earn money." Alejandra said that education is important because it can help alleviate poverty and offer "economic help." Even though she is not earning any additional money because of her studies in the SAT program, she still believed her experience was important because it prepared her for the future. She had only finished the ninth grade but wanted to continue studying so that she could become a professional, particularly a teacher or a nurse. She explained: "Studying is important because a person can get out of poverty. Here in this village there is a lot of poverty, but if a person is a professional or is a teacher your check doesn't arrive every month, but when it does arrive it is a large sum of money. A person can pay off their debts and save some money for the future."

Renata summarized her views, and the views of many women I interviewed, in one comment: "We need to study. Now we have access to education. The only thing we have to do is to finish our studies so we can work."

Unfortunately, the nature of the economy in the remote villages where these women live will make it very difficult for them to get jobs. Life there follows a predominantly subsistence pattern. The modest assets that families do have come mainly from earnings in the fishing industry (which only men have access to) and remittances from family members who live in urban areas of Honduras or in the United States. There is virtually no formal economy in these villages, so earning opportunities for women are confined to the informal economy, such as selling basic foodstuffs out of their homes, or selling cassave. The only salaried employment amounts to a few government jobs in health clinics, schools, the municipal offices, or with an NGO or aid organization. In total, these salaried jobs might amount to thirty to forty jobs across the four villages, hardly enough for the six thousand people who live in these communities.

The constraints of the context create a somewhat paradoxical situation. The women who studied in the SAT program were not likely to reap the financial benefits that they associate with education, at least not in the short term. Nevertheless, there was some evidence in 2004 and more evidence in 2010 that women who participated in SAT had taken small, albeit significant, steps toward improving their lives. Even if they did not have stable employment, they viewed themselves as *profesional* (see Box 4.1).

Unlike those in the SAT group, women in the comparison group had not started any new activities between 2004 and 2010, with the exception of one woman who moved to the city to work in a *maquila* (factory) (see Box 4.2).

In summary, the differences between women in the comparison group and those who studied in SAT, subtle in 2004, grew over time. There was no noteworthy difference between the two groups in terms of their access to paid employment in 2004, but by 2010 a number of SAT participants had steady incomes (see Chapter 5). Furthermore, those in SAT described a process of coming to recognize their inherent worth and an altered perception of their communities.

Box 4.1. Are women getting ahead through SAT?

Renata, age twenty-seven, with three years in SAT, did not earn a higher income but valued her experience in the program. She claimed that it helped improve her attitude with others and that she was more involved in community activities. She wanted to continue her studies so she could become a professional.

Napoleana, age forty-four, with three years in SAT, believed her studies helped her "advance." She manages and does the accounting for a village store, a *bodega.*

Alejandra, age twenty-three, with four years in SAT, valued her studies because she wanted to provide a better example for her children. In 2009, Alejandra moved to La Ceiba to enroll in a nursing program.

Sonia, age twenty-nine, with four years in SAT, started a small business out of her home. She was elected to the village council (*patronato*) and was active in community life. Sonia confronted her husband about his infidelity and wished for a more equitable relationship.

Isadora, age forty-eight, with five years in SAT, grew more yuca as a result of the agricultural techniques she learned in SAT. Isadora's husband verbally abused her because he did not want her to study. Isadora went to the municipal authorities to report his abuse and she moved to a different house in their village.

Teodora, age thirty-eight, with five years in SAT, grew more yuca because of the agricultural techniques she learned in SAT. She started a cooperative beekeeping business with her cousin.

Soraida, age thirty-four, with five years in SAT, worked as a teacher in a number of alternative education programs.

Juanita, age twenty-six, with six years in SAT, opened a small *comedor,* or eatery, in her village. She and her husband gradually expanded the business, applying some of the accounting and business skills she gained through her studies.

Kenia, age twenty-two, with six years in SAT, enrolled in a university in La Ceiba to study nursing. She planned to return to her community to work in one of the health clinics when she finishes her studies.

Leticia, age twenty-eight, with six years of SAT, was enrolled in the National University in Tegucigalpa, studying social work. She wanted to return to her community to work for a community development organization.

*Box 4.2. Summary of women in the comparison
group and those with minimal exposure to SAT*

Angela, age forty-five, was the only woman who had a steady job in 2003. She
worked at the municipal registry. Her husband owned several businesses. Her
family was one of the more economically prosperous in the village.

Carolina, age thirty-one, grew yuca and sold cassave. She had no other source of
income.

Esmeralda, age thirty-three, did not have access to income. She depended on
the earnings of her partner, who lived with his first wife in another village. In
2010 Esmeralda described her situation as "desperate" because her husband
had not sent any money for more than three years.

Maria Josefina, age forty-three, did not participate in any productive activities
aside from agriculture.

Susy, age thirty-two, lived with her mother and ten-year-old daughter in 2004.
She sold home-brewed alcohol (*guaro*). In 2007, she moved to San Pedro
Sula to work in a *maquila.*

Dulcinea, age thirty, grew yuca and other crops to feed her family. She depended
on the income of her spouse, who had a second wife in the village.

Margarita, age twenty-two, was in SAT for approximately two months. She
returned to her village after working in San Pedro Sula for three years. In
2004 she sold alcohol out of her home to make a living. In 2008 she and her
husband opened a bar.

Lola, age twenty-seven, attended SAT sporadically for one year. She was a
subsistence farmer.

What Did They Learn? SAT,
Social Mobility, and Agricultural Skills

The most concrete way in which SAT made a difference in women's lives
was that they attained more years of schooling. Their diplomas alone made
new opportunities available to them, including formal employment and
further study. But educational attainment, or years of schooling, should
not be equated with women's empowerment. In terms of empowerment,
a woman's years of schooling fail to capture the knowledge, attitudes, and
beliefs she possesses.

Nevertheless, completing a secondary degree allows individuals to enroll in higher education, an option that a handful of the first cohort of SAT *bachiller* graduates exercised. In 2010, Kenia, Alan, and Leticia, were all in their final year of university studies. Alan was finishing his degree at Earth University (I was unable to interview him because he was in Costa Rica). Leticia was completing her degree in social work. Kenia was on track to complete her nursing degree in July 2010. Juana completed her studies in agronomy at Earth University in Costa Rica. These four former SAT students are the only young adults from their village in the past five years to study at the university level. The SAT program no longer operates in their community because a traditional secondary school opened; it takes students only through grade nine, so graduates have to complete their upper secondary degrees elsewhere. Few students do so, and none in the past five years have made it to university.

Reflecting on their experiences in the program, Leticia and Kenia described how they had to resist the criticism of community members, who told them they were wasting their time in SAT, that their studies in SAT would amount to nothing, and so on. "We knew we were learning," explained Leticia. Now, she said, those who dropped out of the program regret their decision. "Now they are seeing the fruit. They could have stayed in SAT but they didn't. And look where we [SAT graduates] are now!" She went on to say that "without SAT, my only option would have been to start a family and work in agriculture." She continued: "I never imagined I'd be in the university. Never. SAT has helped me so much. It has given me a set of expectations for my life." Leticia was the only one of her seven siblings to study in the university.

Kenia said that at first it was difficult for her to adapt to the teaching style in her nursing program. "It was a lot of memorization, and I wasn't used to that in SAT. Also, they don't care about your opinion. They just want regurgitated information." Because of these differences, Kenia explained, she failed one of her tests and had a "little problem" with one of her teachers. She had to repeat a course, and then she would be finished with her degree. Both Leticia and Kenia emphasized that SAT had given them a solid academic foundation. Juana stressed that few university students complete their studies within five years, as she had, because the courses are too challenging. Kenia, Leticia, and Juana agreed that SAT had adequately prepared them for higher education. Juana's studies have already led to a stable job, and Leticia and Kenia expect to find jobs when they finish.

Students who finished their studies in SAT but did not go on to higher education also unanimously agreed that SAT was a worthwhile and valuable program of study. Lola said: "There are things that I didn't know when I was in school but when I entered there [SAT] I learned." Soraida commented: "I have acquired a lot of knowledge—things that I didn't know. You know, it has helped me in a lot of ways."

Some women were more specific. One woman explained that her vocabulary had increased as a result of SAT. Because SAT texts are in Spanish and their first language is Garifuna, SAT provided women with a means to improve both their written and spoken Spanish. For example, Alejandra explained that before she participated in SAT, she would overhear conversations and not know some of the words people used, such as the word "theory":

> Sometimes when I was on the bus people would say some words, but these words I barely understood . . . but in SAT there it said it in our book . . . when I started in SAT I said, "Ah! That is what those people were saying." . . . I didn't know this word. For example, "theory." They were talking about theory and I said, "What is theory, what is this?" I didn't know anything because I hadn't studied, but now, yeah, I know.

Several women described the agricultural skills and knowledge they gained in the program. This is significant given the role that agriculture plays in individual and community life. Most women grow yuca and other root vegetables, as I have noted. Two varieties of yuca are grown—"sweet" yuca and "bitter" yuca. Bitter yuca is used to make cassave bread, prized for its long shelf life. It requires no refrigeration, and if stored properly is good for many months.

As part of the SAT curriculum, women experimented with various planting techniques. They planted yuca seedlings in vertical, horizontal, and diagonal positions and observed which planting techniques seemed to work the best. They also learned how to mix other crops with their yuca, a technique referred to as *policultivo* or polycrops, which encourages thinking systemically because different crops draw from and replenish certain nutrients in the soil. The SAT groups also experimented with crops not typically grown in this setting, such as radishes, tomatoes, and cucumbers. Because of the central role that agriculture plays in women's lives, it is not surprising that they spoke of the practical skills they learned in this domain.

Isadora described how she learned how to plant in beds in a row. She explained that before SAT she planted yuca haphazardly. After our interview Isadora proudly showed me her straight beds of yuca plants. Teodora made a similar comment. "I plant a little different from the traditional

A SAT tutor feeding the chickens that students raised during their studies

way," she explained. "I still plant traditionally, but I also use the techniques that I learned in SAT." She said that she now has a higher yield because of these new techniques.

Another common skill that women mentioned they learned in SAT was chicken raising. The SAT textbooks describe production systems, and the practical activity that goes along with this theoretical material is raising chickens. SAT students are required to build a chicken coop, acquire young chicks, immunize and feed them, and complete all other tasks necessary for raising chickens. At the end, they write a report documenting what they did and learned. For most students, this was the first time they had raised chickens in a systematic way. It is somewhat common for households to have a few chickens, but medium- and large-scale production attempts are rare. In some instances this project was the first thing women mentioned when I asked them what they had learned in the program.

For example, I asked Sonia what she learned in the program and what her experience was like and she replied: "Well, in SAT I had many experiences, like raising chickens." Unfortunately, a variety of factors contributed to the failure of the chicken-raising projects. One was the weather. They started the project during the rainy season, and floods killed most of the small chicks. Nevertheless, many spoke optimistically of their experience. Sonia and some of her classmates have a plan to restart the chicken-raising project when they can raise the funds to purchase chicks.

The clearest beneficiaries from SAT were the students who went on to study in universities, as they will most likely obtain stable employment when they graduate. However, women who stayed in the villages described learning experiences in SAT that provided them with concrete skills that improve their daily lives. These skills often translated, according to participants, into increased self-confidence. Women described feeling better about themselves because they had completed more years of schooling and because they could communicate more clearly and effectively. This improved confidence was also a component of their self-perception as "professionals."

"Before I Felt Like Less": Self-Confidence and Self-Perception

All the women in SAT were the first in their families to study beyond the sixth grade. They were proud of this accomplishment, and many felt happy that they could serve as a role model for their children. In addition to feeling proud about their increased educational attainment, women also described an altered self-perception. Several used the term "professional" to refer to themselves, a sharp distinction between those in the SAT and comparison groups.

Women in the comparison groups struggled to think of and say things they felt proud of. For example, when I asked Dulcinea, she paused for quite some time. I then asked her if she understood the question. She said yes but did not mention anything that she was proud of. Instead, she said: "There are times when I worry about myself, and I ask God not to give me so many worries. Because I am still young . . . I ask God not to give me troubles." I was taken aback by her response, because rather than mention something that she felt proud of, she commented on the worries she had in her life. Her lack of education is a source of shame for her, and Dulcinea said she wanted her children to study "so that they don't turn out like me."

In contrast, women in the SAT group frequently mentioned being proud that they had studied. For example, Juanita replied that she was proud of "having studied, serving my community, and being a mother."

Sonia's answer was similar: "Having studied through the ninth grade be-cause I can defend myself [*defenderme*] better, because I know something from there [SAT]. I know how to analyze my problems. When they give talks or workshops, I have seen it. My mind is not closed. I can read and analyze things." Here Sonia links her knowledge with her confidence—she was proud because she "knows something." She could analyze her prob-lems because of her knowledge, and she felt confident when she attended talks or workshop because often the material presented was familiar to her. Isadora mentioned that she felt proud when "we are at Mass and I read from the Bible and then explain what I have read." It is possible that before her participation in SAT, Isadora did not have literacy skills required for this task. Now she is able to read in public (which requires self-confidence) and can explain what she has read to others (which requires reading com-prehension). This is particularly significant in the context where she lives, where most adults have very low levels of literacy, as they did not have access to quality education. Her ability to read and interpret for others provides a concrete example of how literacy skills enrich Isadora's life, even where there are few opportunities for their application. Both Isadora and Sonia felt more confident because of their increased knowledge.

Like her classmates, Leticia was proud of having studied. Her pride stems from being able to accomplish something she had always wanted to do. From the time Leticia was a young girl, she had wanted to study. How-ever, there were no educational opportunities available to her beyond the sixth grade. She never lost hope and eagerly joined the SAT program when she was in her early twenties. She explained that she was proud of having studied because "I would say that I forced myself to get my *bachillerato*, my parents didn't encourage me, nobody forced me. I called on myself [*me invoco*] to study, this desire was latent within me. And I feel proud and I am moving ahead [*sigo adelante*]." In fact, Leticia explained that unlike most girls, she decided not to get married when she was in her late teens/early twenties because getting married "would cause difficulties because I wouldn't be able to study." She was proud that she was turning this dream into action and believed that she was moving forward.

Juanita similarly explained that before studying she felt inferior to "professionals" in her community, that is, individuals with at least a sec-ondary education and stable employment (e.g., teachers, nurses, doctors, NGO workers). "Before I felt like less when I was around professional people. But now I think we are equal." Here Juanita hints at one of the key components of the empowerment process, the recognition of her inherent worth.

Similar to Juanita, Alejandra believed that she was on the road to becoming a professional. "Having studied makes me feel good. . . . When I complete my studies I am going to be a professional." The ability to organize and express their thoughts, even in public settings, was another concrete benefit that women in SAT described. Several explained that before their studies, they seldom if ever spoke out in public. For example, Soraida explained that now she is trained and so she is not afraid of sharing her thoughts with others: "I mean, I didn't do it [speak in public] because I was afraid and ashamed because I—because I hadn't studied. So now that I am a professional and trained [*professional y capacitada*]—now I am not afraid of confronting any situation and expressing myself."

Leticia made a similar remark. She explained that through her participation in the SAT program she has gained public speaking skills. "I have seen a great change in myself, because before I couldn't speak in public. Now I can give a presentation at the university. I couldn't do this before, no way!" One of the women's explanations for why they are not afraid to speak in public is their improved communication skills. For example, Juana said: "SAT has helped me in a variety of ways. The way I like the most is to be able to speak in public, to not be afraid of anyone, to say whatever I feel. To not be shy and to speak in a way that does not go against any individual person." Juana's mention of not speaking in a way that goes "against" any individual person hints at a more nuanced communication style. SAT encourages students to share their ideas and participate in class discussion, as we have seen. In the SAT classroom, women practiced expressing themselves in front of others, and now they can speak in other public settings in a sophisticated way.

In contrast with the SAT group, four of the six women in the comparison group mentioned that they do not like to speak in public. Their response on this topic also illustrates their low level of self-confidence in comparison with the SAT group. For example, Dulcinea, who is not a member of any formal community organization but likes to go to meetings, explained that when she attends, she just listens. She does not like to speak in public because she is "ashamed." Esmeralda, who also attends meetings but is not a member of any community organizations, also goes only "to listen." She does not like to speak in public. Another woman in the comparison group, Susy, neither attends meetings nor speaks in public. When I asked her why, she replied: "I don't like those things."

The ability to speak in public reflects both self-confidence and communication skills. The differences between those in the SAT and comparison groups suggest that this is one way that women's outlooks have changed. Women who studied in SAT reported an increased ability to express themselves in front of others, at least in part because they believe in themselves and know that they can say what they feel.

Education "Opens Your Mind"

Two women in the SAT sample spoke about seeing the world differently. Juanita described how the knowledge she gained in SAT had given her a new level of awareness about her surroundings. Her knowledge has made her view the world differently: "The SAT program has helped me with everything, you know, because it has opened my mind. Because before I didn't think about anything. I looked at the world as if [it was] nothing. But now after SAT my mind is different."

Sonia made a comment similar to Juanita's. She explained that as a result of SAT she is aware of things for the first time. Her statement also implies an expanded awareness or level of consciousness; she said: "My mind is not closed." These remarks of Sonia and Juanita might reflect the emphasis of SAT on the discovery of knowledge. Because the program did not simply require them to memorize information but encouraged them to investigate their own context, they now see their environment through a different lens. Alan, one of the two male students to finish the *bachiller* degree, explained that "SAT students are quite different; say, for example, you come across a student that has studied in a *centro basico*, even in their last year, they won't have the same thinking, the same capabilities as a SAT student. SAT students see things in a more general, broader way, analyzing each problem."

While only three female and one male student specifically made reference to a new mindset, one of the tutors in the program, Leonidas, mentioned this change as the most notable impact of SAT that he observed in his students: "In general, SAT has made them [students] see the world differently." He reiterated this statement, explaining that they see the world differently because they recognize their own capacities and potential. "SAT has made them see the world differently because they have studied that they have potential, that they can continue to grow, and they can continue to learn."

In addition to women's own claims, as well as those of key program staff, there are other indicators that SAT has sharpened women's abilities to critically examine their communities—the differences in the ways in which women in the SAT and comparison groups describe community life and their beliefs about gender.

Views on Community Life

I asked Alejandro, one of the SAT coordinators, if he could identify any benefits of the SAT program. He replied that when the SAT program began, students were unable to critique their context:

> I remember when we started out with SAT. We asked the students what problems they saw or identified in their communities. Honestly, we didn't get answers, or there wasn't the possibility of problems. It was all, "everything was fine," there weren't any problems in the community in the students' eyes. After a period of working, of studying in SAT, after having done some community service activities . . . it was then that people could see things, you know? Before, it wasn't so easy to see them. So even though they still don't take decisive actions in an organized way to confront them, an important first step is to identify them.

Alejandro provided a specific example of how SAT allows students to see their community through a new lens. Being able to critique one's context requires the ability to think analytically and critically. Before their study in SAT, women lacked this capacity.

Coincidentally, in my interviews I asked women in both the SAT and comparison groups to identify and propose solutions to challenges facing their communities. My intention was to see if they brought up any themes related to gender and women's empowerment. However, their responses to these questions confirm Alejandro's statement about women's ability to see their environment differently as a result of their studies.

The responses to my questions about community life highlight a consistent difference between those who had studied in SAT and the comparison group in terms of their abilities to identify and propose solutions to challenges facing the community. All those who had studied in SAT were able to name specific issues requiring attention, whereas only two women in the comparison group were able to do so. Women in SAT identified the following issues:

- lack of men's involvement, male abandonment, and male domination
- alcohol abuse by men
- lack of jobs, and of the opportunity to learn a trade
- community disintegration, lack of unity, and lack of educational opportunities

- lack of a stable market to sell their products
- threats to their land rights

For example, Juanita explained: "There are many single mothers, no jobs, community disintegration and lack of unity, low education levels. Many women want to study but there are few opportunities." When I asked her to think of ways to confront these challenges, she focused on poverty alleviation: "Institutions could come into the villages and we can lend them land if they provide jobs, or they can give small loans so each person can realize their potential." Like Juanita, Soraida focused on poverty: "There's no work, no jobs. We don't sell or export agriculture. It stays here and we lose the surplus. That's why the Garifuna don't get ahead, because there is no employment." When I asked her how she thought this could be resolved, she replied: "First we have to find help from other places, where they will give us some projects constructing buildings and creating jobs for people so that they can earn money and earn a living. Without work there is no saving; we'll always be poor."

Other strategies to confront challenges facing the community included:

- counseling and talking with men about their attitudes and alcohol use
- studying so that one can get a job in the future
- raising the consciousness of youths and educating them so that they can start a healthy family
- encouraging men to join the church so they won't drink (several churches discourage or prohibit alcohol consumption)
- limiting the amount of alcohol a man can buy, and not selling alcohol to those already intoxicated

Only one of the women in the comparison group, Carolina, was able to articulate a challenge facing the community and propose a solution. She explained that one of the main problems in the community was the lack of "outside help." Her solution was for more institutions to provide "help" to address poverty. The inability of women in the comparison group to identify and propose solutions to community problems suggests that SAT may enable women to think in new ways and to see their community through a different lens. The contrast between the groups may also reflect increased communication skills, because women who had studied in SAT are able to explain their opinions. This increased awareness and communication skills may be clearly linked to their desire for and actions toward self- and community improvement. If individuals do not see or are unable to articulate lacks in their community or in their own lives, there is little likelihood that they will work for betterment. SAT seems to foster the necessary critical thinking skills and equip women with knowledge that helps them identify areas that need improvement. This is a key component of their altered outlook.

"We Both Have Two Hands, Two Feet": Beliefs about Gender

The mindsets of women in the two groups were also different in terms of their beliefs about gender. The analysis of their answers to interview questions about gender again suggests that women in SAT view their surroundings through a different, more critical lens.

In the course of my interviews with women, I asked ten questions intended to investigate their level of awareness of gender issues, that is, matters of public concern that arise from questioning gender roles and recognizing instances of gender inequality as unjust. This exercise allowed me to directly compare the responses of women in the comparison group and SAT students. While open-ended interviews yielded more nuanced data, the direct comparison of these two groups is noteworthy. I asked women if they agreed or disagreed with a series of statements about the roles and capacities of women and men from a list of questions I compiled based on earlier interviews:

1. Women can offer better care for children than men.
2. Cooking is a woman's job.
3. Men shouldn't cook because it is a woman's job.
4. Men shouldn't clean clothes because it is a woman's job.
5. Men are more intelligent than women.
6. Men are physically stronger than women
7. Men are spiritually stronger than women.
8. It is okay if from time to time men hit women.
9. Women should be part of the village council and other community activities.
10. Earning money for the family is a man's responsibility, not a woman's.

I posed these questions to thirteen women who had participated in SAT and the six women in the comparison group. Women in both groups unanimously agreed that women offer better care for children than men, that women should be part of the village council and participate in other activities, and that it was not okay if from time to time a man hits a woman. Their answers to the remaining questions showed interesting variation. I compiled their answers and calculated the percentage of gender-sensitive responses by group. Women in the comparison group scored 38 percent; those in the SAT group scored 71 percent. The raw difference in scores, 33 percentage points, suggests that women in the comparison group have less equitable views about the roles and capabilities of men and women.

In in-depth interviews I also probed women about their attitudes about gender issues, particularly the gendered division of labor. I asked women what the responsibilities and daily tasks of men and women were, and what they thought of this. As mentioned earlier, traditionally in these villages women are responsible for the household and men work in fishing. The great majority of women I interviewed thought that women worked more than men.

Three women from the comparison group and two women from the SAT group thought that the traditional division of labor was fine. From the comparison group, Dulcinea's answers were consistent with what I heard from most women. Women typically do more work, taking care of the household and children and growing yuca and other crops. Men, in contrast, work in fishing for part of the year but have next to no household duties. Dulcinea explained that she saw this scenario as fine: "Women behind men." She viewed the man as the authority figure and believed that women were inferior. At another moment in our interview she said that "the man comes first in the home."

Other women in the comparison group also saw the current division of labor as natural and even divinely ordained. When I first asked Angela, for instance, about her views on the division of labor in her household and in the community, she replied: "That is how it should be." However, only a few moments later she explained that she thought that men and women should work together, but that in Garifuna communities women work more than men. One of the coping mechanisms Angela used to justify inequality was her religious belief: "Since the beginning, man has been the head of the household. God made man . . . he is the head of the household, and the woman follows him."

While two women in the SAT group saw no problem with the current division of labor, most were more critical. They thought that men should take on more responsibility in the household and share work equally with women because it is unfair that women work more than men. For example, Sonia said: "It shouldn't be like it is. Work should be shared equally among the two [men and women]." Juanita too believed that the current division of labor "is bad because we all have to earn our daily bread. Sometimes a woman works for four people in her house and she gets tired and kills herself from this, from so much work, she is spent." Leticia shared Juanita's views. Of the division of labor, she explained: "I think it is machismo, because the two have to do the same, both men and women. They have a commitment, and both have to fulfill it."

The notion of fulfilling a commitment also came up in my interview with Napoleana, who expressed the opinion that men are irresponsible: "There are men who like to have kids and then take off. The one who sacrifices is the mother. This isn't right, but that is how it is. The mother has to be responsible, because who would throw away their child? That's why I say that a mother suffers more for her child than a child suffers for his mother." In a conversation a few weeks later, Napoleana repeated these sentiments. She argued that women are more responsible than men, using a creative term to explain the role of the mother—"mapa"—joining the first two letters of the Spanish words for mother (*madre*) and father (*padre*): "A mother is more responsible than a man. She signs the name *mapa*, *madre* and *padre*"—that is, mothers play both roles. Men do not assume the parental role that they should, and so a woman must assume her role as mother and his role as father.   When I asked respondents about problems facing women in the community, three women in the SAT group mentioned machismo. *Macho* is the Spanish word for male. The term "machismo," which has seeped into the English language, refers to a strong or exaggerated sense of masculinity that stresses attributes such as virility, domination of women, and aggressiveness. Although the term is contested and its meaning varies (see Gutmann 2007), these women's use of the term suggested that they were frustrated by, and aware of, gender inequality in their communities.

While SAT students, on average, seemed to have higher levels of gender awareness than those in the comparison group, not all the women in the SAT group had more equitable ideas about gender. For example, Alejandra mentioned in our first interview that her husband was in charge (*él manda*). I asked her in a follow-up interview what she meant by this, and she explained that "I have to go along with everything that he says . . . that I am under his responsibility." However, Alejandra was an exception among SAT participants in this regard; most were quite adamant that men and women were equal and that they deserved equal rights.

When Teodora spoke about gender roles, she did so in an ironic and

Teodora holding her granddaughter

questioning tone. She asked: "Why does a man have to feel so macho? He doesn't have to be the one who has the final say at home. We both have a say, and we both have two hands." Teodora also explained that a man didn't have to be so manly, because a woman could also be very womanly. She did not think that either of these situations was desirable. Her views on gender roles were more fluid. She stated that "we are all human beings . . . we all have two feet, two hands. I mean, we are all equal." She joked: "Why does a man have to act so macho in front of a woman? A woman can be aggressive if she wants, too!"

Leticia also spoke about gender equality in our interviews. She told me about her experiences growing up; in her household her male siblings were allowed to do certain things that the girls couldn't do. She believed that parents should give equal rights to their male and female children: "men and women have equal rights." Isadora echoed Leticia's remarks about equal rights for both women and men. She used a very practical situation to express this opinion: "When both a man and a woman go up to the fields, and if the woman gets home first she should clean the house, and if the man gets home first he has the right [*tiene el derecho*] to clean the house and see what else needs to be done." Most people might not think that sweeping or cleaning the house is a "right." However, Isadora raised an important point. Gender equality does not mean that only women engage in activities previously denied to them. Men, also, should have the opportunity to partake of the full range of activities, even mundane ones like sweeping the patio. If there are cultural norms that dictate that sweeping the floor is a woman's job, men may feel that they don't have the "right" to sweep. They might be ostracized by others (both men and women) for doing so. In Isadora's scenario of gender equality, both men and women would have opportunities to participate in aspects of daily life that fall outside the traditional realm.

Comparing the beliefs about gender of women in the SAT group with the comparison group highlights another example of how those who participated in SAT had different outlooks. There are at least two plausible explanations for this difference. First, women in SAT have been exposed to specific content in the curriculum that questions traditional gender roles. Second, women's increased analytic or critical thinking capabilities as a result of SAT study prompt them to consider gender from a different perspective. It is likely that both these mechanisms help explain the differences in the groups' beliefs about gender. However, egalitarian beliefs do not necessarily translate into choices or actions; it is also important to examine the concrete steps women took toward self- and social betterment.

Implications and Conclusion

In attempting to define and conceptualize women's empowerment, several authors focus on the notion of expanded choice (Kabeer 1999; Rowlands 1997). Increased educational attainment expands women's choices, as they will be able to enroll in further education or apply for certain jobs. A case in point is Margarita, whose situation I described at the beginning of this chapter. Margarita, having only a sixth-grade education, cannot apply for many jobs nor can she enroll in higher education. For the near future, she will likely continue to sell liquor out of her home.

However, Juanita is in a similar situation, earning her livelihood through the sale of liquor and other goods. The key differences between Margarita and Juanita include Juanita's "open mind" and her self-identification as a professional. Rather than concrete material differences, a positive self-perception emerges as a crucial first step in the process of empowerment. My conversations with women suggested that part of the process of redefining and extending what was possible for them was developing a new way of seeing the world. At the same time, an altered perception needs to be coupled with concrete opportunities for action. (In the next chapter, I explore the actions that women took to improve their circumstances.)

The analysis of the differences between those in the SAT and comparison groups provides robust evidence of a different or altered worldview among SAT participants. Three students in SAT and two staff members mentioned "open minds" and "seeing the world differently." This different world outlook is evident in how women describe the challenges facing their community, as well as in their ideas about gender.

Self-confidence is a key dimension of this new outlook, which is well established in earlier research and theoretical work on empowerment (Kabeer 1999; Mosedale 2005; Rowlands 1997; Stromquist 1995b). Education that challenges gender norms and promotes critical thinking can play a particularly important role in boosting women's self-confidence. This kind of education can allow individuals to recognize their inherent potential and their equal worth with others, and helps them learn skills that they can put into practice. Women's increased ability to speak in public demonstrates that many factors work together to allow women to see themselves differently. It is not just women's self-perception that enables them to speak in front of others, but the combination of this self-image and their communication skills. The ability to participate in community life (in everyday interactions, community organizations, and small businesses) is closely related to women's increased self-confidence and public speaking capabilities.

The comment of the tutor Leonidas included earlier in this chapter sums up the findings presented here: "SAT has made them see the world differently because they have studied that they have potential, that they can continue to grow, and they can continue to learn." SAT's conception of human beings as "mines rich in gems of inestimable value" places great confidence in education: "education can, alone, cause it [the mine] to reveal its treasures and enable mankind to benefit therefrom." The international development community, at least in its articulation of Millennium Development Goals, also touts the role of education as a powerful force for change. But, as Vavrus (2003) points out, education too often prepares youths for futures that are unattainable. Discourses of development that champion education as universally empowering and transformative are potentially debilitating.

Education and knowledge are not synonymous, nor are schooling and education. Formal schooling can provide individuals with access to knowledge, but not all education will allow individuals to see themselves as "mines rich in gems of inestimable value." While the findings presented here do suggest that education can act as a resource for empowerment, education programs vary widely in their content and effectiveness. The question, "What kind of education?" should always accompany any claims made for a relationship between education and women's empowerment.

CHAPTER 5

Taking Life by the Reins

Steps toward Self- and Social Betterment

They [SAT students] seem more self-confident and are
taking the reins; . . . they aren't just waiting.
—Alejandro, SAT coordinator

LETICIA WALKED ACROSS THE lobby of the hotel in Tegucigalpa
where we had agreed to meet. I was delighted to finally see her in person
after multiple rounds of telephone tag. Leticia had been living in Tegucigalpa for the last year, and I traveled to the city for our interview. She was
enrolled as a student at one of the top national universities. Her goal is to
become a social worker, because "it is a career oriented towards service,
and that's why I like it." She explained that the SAT program played an
instrumental role in her life: "Here I am now in the university because of
SAT."

Leticia's case illustrates that while one of the main effects of SAT is a
"different mind," women have benefited from their studies in more visible
ways. Leticia was older than many of her classmates when she entered the
university, for she finished high school at twenty-seven. As a young girl,
she said, "I wanted to study, but, well, since there wasn't a *centro basico* in
the community and my family couldn't afford to send me to the city, there
wasn't a possibility for me to continue studying." In 1996 when the SAT
program started, she was one of the first to enroll.

Neither of Leticia's parents studied beyond the third grade. Her father
worked as a fisherman, and her mother worked in subsistence agriculture.
Both Leticia and her mother told me that one of the challenges Leticia
faced growing up was that her father drank heavily. Leticia explained in
2004: "My father hasn't been a good father. He is not responsible at home.
When a man dedicates himself to drinking, well, sometimes he fails at
home." During our 2010 interview, Leticia revealed that her father had
stopped drinking to help support her university studies.

Leticia was in no rush to marry or have children, for whom she wanted to set a different example. She intentionally put off getting involved with anyone because she did not want it to interfere with her plans to enroll in further study. "I didn't want to [marry] because this would have caused problems because I wouldn't have studied." When she does marry, Leticia wants the relationship to be one where "we share the housework and share ideas—to me this is important for a couple."

Before moving to Tegucigalpa, Leticia was one of the most active women in her community. For many years she was the president of a youth group in her village, sponsored by the Episcopalian group Pastoral Social. She also served as treasurer. In 1999, she was elected by her peers to go to Rome as part of the Jubilee 2000 celebration. She explained that she was selected because "I was active in groups and they elected me as coordinator."

In this chapter I describe how, closely linked with their increased self-confidence and critical perspective, women who participated in SAT (including Leticia) were taking steps toward personal and community improvement. Their perspectives and actions, when viewed through the lens of social capital (Bourdieu 1993), may in the long run contribute to community development because they strengthen the social fabric of the community. Furthermore, in some instances women were creating new structures in the form of income-generating enterprises. These initiatives improve women's lives through increasing their access to income and allowing them financial independence from their male partners. These small businesses may also improve the community by providing needed services and goods. Nevertheless, the context in which these women live places serious constraints on their ability to contribute to self- and social change. They are geographically isolated, and there is little access to a market for their agricultural products. While education has begun to expand their outlooks and actions, education alone cannot change the social structures and physical conditions that constrain their lives. However, in the context of where these women live, the small changes that do take place should not be overlooked.

Sociability and Relationships with Others

SAT participants frequently mentioned improved relationships with others as a direct consequence of their participation in the program. For example, before her participation in SAT, Sonia rarely left her home. She described how through SAT she formed friendships that made her realize the importance of working with others. She was now involved in several community organizations, including a women's group that formed as a spin-off of her SAT group. I asked her if she has always been involved in the community, and she explained that before SAT she "didn't even get together with other people. I only went to my mother's." I asked her if she thought her participation in SAT had anything to do with this, and she replied: "Yes, because in SAT I learned that one should have friends when they are in a group wherever they are. I learned this because in SAT we accomplished this, and after this I liked it [having friends]."

According to Sonia, in SAT she formed friendships, and this experience encouraged her to socialize and seek out relationships with others. This pattern is also described in research conducted by sociologists Anthony Bryk and Barbara Schneider examining the role of trust in schools. They explain that when an individual sustains a relationship with some person or organization (as Sonia did with her SAT group), these social connections can take on value in themselves. "Feelings of friendship evolve and alter subsequent exchanges; . . . social participation entails not only material benefits to individuals, but also important social-psychological rewards" (2002, 15). Sonia described how she came to enjoy her social relationships and said that she "learned" a group social norm of being friendly and in relationships with others. She also described her participation and her friendships with others as something she felt proud of, which supports the hypothesis that fostering relationships with others has social-psychological rewards.

Perhaps as a prerequisite of forming friendships, several SAT students described a more social posture toward others. They described this as part of acting like a "professional," which means treating others with dignity and respect and getting along with other people. For example, Teodora explained that SAT helped her "not to have problems with other people." Another student, Isadora, explained: "I am respectful. I am not like I was before, when nothing mattered to me. After I started studying, I changed my attitude with people. I like to talk with them because I like it when others understand me and answer me with kindness."

I asked Isadora to elaborate on this comment, because I wanted to know what she meant by "respectful." She explained that before she started the program, she would get into public arguments with her friends, especially if they criticized her. She explained that they would make "fools" of themselves, yelling and shouting foul words at one another. She doesn't do this anymore because "it would make me ashamed. A person who has studied can change their attitude, because now this [behavior] on the street, now I don't do it." Isadora is no longer ashamed of her behavior, and this stems from and reinforces her improved self-confidence.

Isadora's description of these encounters speaks to one of the characteristics of living in a small Garifuna community, at least according to Andres Thomas, the community social worker mentioned earlier, who said that "since there is no TV, there is nothing to do." Spreading gossip about others and finding out other people's business was a major pastime for community members. Andres explained that men and women alike spread rumors and gossip with gusto: "In this, yes, there is gender equality!" Spreading rumors about others, or saying bad things about someone, often resulted in arguments and tension, which Isadora hints at in her description of acting inappropriately. Several other women noted that participation in SAT diminished their participation in the rumor mill.

Alejandra, for example, explained that individuals had spread rumors about her in the past, that someone had told her husband that she was doing "this, that, and the other." "It was all a lie! This person just wanted to blackmail my husband." She explained that gossip spreaders often approach men seeking payment for "information" about their wives' misdeeds: "This is just a way for them to get money." This practice used to anger Alejandra, who would get very worked up and "would violently ask them to take it back!" Alejandra said that after participating in SAT, she tried to remain calm and ignore these comments. "Everything is calm; . . . I don't get angry. When they say something to me, I don't get mad, I am always good with them."

Ana described her own role in spreading rumors in the community before she studied in SAT: "I used to behave in a controversial way." I wasn't sure what she meant by "controversial," so I asked her to elaborate. "I used to fight with people or go look for gossip with my friends." She traced this behavior to the violent nature of her stepfather, who used to beat her and was "a little violent." She explained that she no longer does this: "Now I don't, I've changed my ways . . . what I did wasn't good" She attributed the changes in her behavior to "studies and also to God." Ana is an active member of a local Pentecostal church.

Women who participated in SAT often mentioned being kind or "good" to others and being social. One specific example two women spoke about was the importance of greeting other community members. When they cross paths with another individual, regardless of their age, they look at them and say, "Good morning," or "Good afternoon." This is a way that they can demonstrate their respect for other community members. As Juanita explained: "I learned that one should greet older people, respect them and everything, even young people. Some older people say that you don't have to greet someone younger than you . . . but you have to greet the younger person just like you greet the older person." Renata echoed

Juanita's comment. She described one example of good conduct: "In the morning you have to greet people and speak with grace to all of the people you encounter." The simple act of greeting fellow community members, according to Juanita and Renata, demonstrates respect for others, and this is an important component of conducting themselves in a way that makes them proud.

Related to greeting others, two students mentioned that before participating in the program they were moody or unfriendly. As Juanita explained: "I was moody, someone would walk by me on the street and I wouldn't talk to them—they didn't do anything to me but I wouldn't talk to them. Today I don't do this because I learned those things [to respect others]." Juanita said she still gets in a bad mood from time to time, but she tries to treat others with respect. Renata's experience was similar. Her sister, Kenia, said that before Renata studied in SAT, "a whole day would go by when she wouldn't say a word in the house!" Kenia thinks that Renata is now more talkative and less moody. Leticia explained that she was friendlier after completing SAT: "I am not as nasty as I used to be. I like to listen to others."

In addition to listening to and greeting others, women mentioned "respecting," "helping," and "being generous." In sum, one of the most frequently mentioned self-reported changes attributed to SAT was more "professional" behavior. Just as individuals came to recognize their own worth, they also recognize the importance of treating others with respect, and they change their actions to demonstrate these beliefs. Here, SAT participants describe shared social norms, perhaps developed through their experience as SAT students. In putting these norms into action through everyday activities such as saying hello to their neighbors, being nice to others, and listening with respect, they are taking steps toward personal and community improvement. All the women who mentioned these changes spoke of them in a positive light. They felt "good" about their participation in SAT because it helped them become more social. Their increased sociability also allows them to become more engaged in community affairs and to start new enterprises.

Participation in Community Improvement: Orientations and Actions

Two important distinctions between SAT participants and the comparison group relate to SAT students' actions toward community improvement. First, that SAT students emphasized the importance of serving their communities may be a result of the emphasis on service as an integral component of the SAT curriculum. Second, SAT students did not mention a reliance on help from charitable organizations or other outside groups in order to work toward community improvement.

Kenia, Alejandra, Juanita, Inita, and Leticia particularly emphasized the importance of community service and hope their eventual careers will serve their communities. As Leticia explained, she chose to study social work in Tegucigalpa because it is a service-oriented career, and she wants one day to return to her community to put what she is learning into practice. Kenia also mentioned that she wanted to return to her community when she finished her studies, "to serve my community." Juanita explained that service to the community was important to her because "that is how our community will improve." She said that "there are some people, they just want to live, they don't want to give anything back, they just want to be left alone."

These women's orientation toward service and working toward community improvement contrasted with that of women in the comparison group, who frequently mentioned that outside agencies were responsible for community welfare. All the women in the comparison group talked explicitly about poverty and how it affects their lives. In contrast with women who participated in SAT, these women tended to mention financial assistance from outside groups as a solution to this problem, another indicator of their lack of financial independence. They not only relied on the income of their partners, but also they viewed outside financial assistance from donor organizations as a way to increase their income.

For example, financial help, *ayuda*, was a recurring theme in my interviews with Carolina, who seemed to feel strongly that outside help was necessary for her to change her situation. When I asked her what challenges women face in the community, she replied: "In the first place, the lack of help." Later in the interview I asked if she has any ideas for how to resolve community problems, and she replied: "Getting financial help from people that support the community." She wanted to study but said she could not without outside financial support or "*ayuda*." My interpretation is that she was specifically referring to financial help, although she could have also been referring to other forms of support.

Instead of relying on outside financial help, women in SAT seemed to be "taking the reins" and generating their own opportunities to increase their income. As the tutor Leonidas said: "SAT has created a more productive mentality, particularly in terms of creating and managing businesses." By 2010, a number of women had started their own businesses and several were formally employed. In short, several women who participated in SAT seemed to conceptualize their role in the community differently. They emphasized service and downplayed the role of external organizations. Several described becoming involved in community organizations as a result of their participation in SAT.

Civic Engagement: "I Am Awake!"

Before leaving her village to study in Tegucigalpa, Leticia was one of the most active women in the community, according to a representative from a local NGO, Martha Ordonez. Leticia explained that she had been active in the community since her childhood, but SAT had helped her be more vocal: "I like to participate, but sometimes I would get nervous [about speaking]." She admitted that she still felt nervous before speaking but said that she was much more confident and could give a presentation at the university with ease.

The majority of women in the SAT and comparison groups said that they went to meetings in the community. Alan, one of the two male SAT graduates, explained that "if there is a meeting in the community, there are always more women than men, but men participate more than women. For example, when a community is forming a village council and is electing its directors, there are normally three times as many men as women. More women attend the meetings, but they don't participate because they are afraid or think that they will be made fun of." In this context, speaking out in meetings or being elected to the village council is quite significant. Many women described being able to speak in public in ways they could not before their participation in SAT. Others described participating in community events or forming small collectives.

Renata, Alejandra, Sonia, Soraida, Teodora, and Kenia all mentioned that they feel proud of having participated in community events or organizations. Some of them had not done so before to their participation in SAT. Although two women in the SAT group, Leticia and Juanita, have always been active in community organizations, others, like Teodora, are involved in the community for the first time. Teodora told me she was on the village council (*patronato*) in 1998, 2000, and 2002. When I asked why she had not belonged to the council before, she explained:

> It was when I started with SAT. I can say that it helped familiarize me with other people and participate. To not be ashamed to be in meetings. . . . I can say that SAT shaped me (*me formó*). Before, I was always ashamed. People would say to me, "Let's go to meetings." I would say,

"No way." After being in the program, we used to go to meet with other students in [neighboring villages], so I got better at this.

In SAT students are forced to speak in front of others, even others from different communities. Teodora explained that before SAT she was "ashamed, or better said, afraid [to speak in public], but not now." She said that whenever something is happening in the community, she is there, when before, "I was so shy to participate in things. If someone asked me something I wouldn't know how to respond. But after, my mind opened more. I am awake."

Sonia too was elected to the village council and in 2010 was serving as the treasurer. She was also elected to the board of Organización Fraternal Negra Hondureña, an alliance of Garifuna and Caribbean people in Honduras. She participated in a yearlong women's empowerment program sponsored by a Canadian Christian NGO, CAUSE, that taught women how to interact with their children and husband, as well as practical agricultural skills. As mentioned earlier, before her studies in SAT Sonia left her house only to visit her mother or sister, or to work in the fields. She explained that SAT helped her "integrate into the community."

While some SAT participants were less involved in community life than Teodora and Sonia, they showed signs of improved participation in public spaces. Renata, a student who finished ninth grade, did not belong to any community organizations and said she was still somewhat afraid to speak in public. In SAT, however, she attended a meeting in another village where she was asked to present herself and say a few words: "When they called on me to speak, I got up and went to speak. I had never done this before. I thought that I wouldn't be able to speak, that I would be afraid, but I was fine."

Women's self-confidence and participation in public events were strongly connected and seem to reinforce each other. Women gained confidence through their studies and were able to participate in new spaces. In turn, having participated in new spaces made them, like Renata, feel proud. Teodora said: "I feel better for the simple reason that I participate in more things"; for example, "a little while ago they came from another department, and I went with some friends, always learning new things."

There was not a striking difference between women in the comparison group and those in the SAT group in terms of participation in community organizations. Four of the six women in the comparison group belonged to some form of community organization. The two women who did not participate both explained that they "don't like" being a member of these groups. One woman in the comparison group, Maria Josefina, was on the village council. However, when I asked her if she is a good communicator, she replied: "No, me, no." Carolina also did not have confidence in her communication skills and does not like to speak in public: "No, I couldn't say that I am a good communicator, but I could learn."

Just as three women in SAT explained that even before their participation in the program they were active in community organizations, some women in the comparison group are active in the community despite having completed only the sixth grade. These findings suggest that for some women, participation in public spaces may not be related to their educational experience. For others, however, furthering their education increases their self-confidence, which allowed them to speak and participate in public settings in a way they had not done previously. Education provided women with an opportunity to enrich their lives, and enabled them to contribute to the improvement of their communities.

Income Generation and Financial Independence

In addition to higher levels of participation in community groups, some women started small businesses or obtained "professional" employment. Although the stated goals of the SAT program do not include an increased income, there is some indication that women had access to cash earnings for the first time after SAT study. Independent access to income is important in these villages, because women largely depend on the earnings of their spouses to cover the majority of household expenses.

The women in the SAT sample had access to cash earnings to varying degrees. Fifteen of the eighteen continued to grow yuca and, together with other women, processed this raw product into cassave. Sonia, Isadora, Alejandra, Renata, Teodora, and Napoleana all mentioned that they harvest more yuca now than they did prior to SAT. This increase has not necessarily translated into higher earnings, however. Teodora and Napoleana explained that while the market has improved in recent years, it is still not stable. They are not always able to sell their product for a fair price. As Andres Thomas commented: "Unfortunately, they don't have a stable market, there are many difficulties to sell it [cassave]. People don't sell it at the right price, it is undervalued and because of this they hardly earn a profit. It is practically free labor, because they need some income to satisfy their minimum, immediate needs." Nevertheless, the women's new agricultural skills may bring financial benefits in the future if the market stabilizes.

Some women did earn more money than they had before their participation in SAT. One reason why this might be the case is that they learned practical skills through the program, such as working together to raise money, which they put into practice. Alejandra explained that from the beginning, her SAT group tried to be self-sufficient. With the guidance of their SAT tutor, the students started a small *chiclera*, a little shop where they sold gum and candies (the Spanish word for gum, *chicle*, is the root word for this term). With the earnings from this shop and by selling cassave made from yuca they had grown, the students bought their SAT textbooks.

> So, we said it was important to start a *chiclera* because there are times when we can't even find five *lempiras* [about twenty-five U.S. cents]. So we started the *chiclera* and with the earnings from the *chiclera* we paid for the books. We also planted yuca, because in the first practical lesson you do this, and this yuca, wow! We had so much! The first day when we baked it we had a hundred loaves and we sold this cassave and paid for the books. And this is how we got started in SAT.

One of the women in Alejandra's SAT group, Sonia, took the idea from their communal *chiclera* and started her own independent shop out of her home, far from the center of town on a hill that has a beautiful view of the ocean. The larger *pulperias*, convenience stores, were far from where she and her neighbors lived. Sonia decided to start a small shop to sell candies, flour, soap, rice, and other basic foodstuffs. Her motivation was to earn some extra money for the household, because, similar to Alejandra, she at times had no money whatsoever. With her husband's earnings in fishing, they bought their first stock to sell in the store.

> One time he [her husband] came from the islands [where he lived during the fishing season] and he saw when he arrived that times were very rough. Sometimes there wasn't even enough money to buy a pound of rice. I said to him, "What are we doing? When you come, you give me money and we buy, but then later there isn't any money, there isn't any work. I saw something in SAT and I want to try it out." And so he helped me.

With her husband's earnings they bought the goods they needed for the shop. Sonia explained that in SAT "we learned how to calculate an earning and a loss, and how to begin to invest." As of 2010, Sonia was still running the shop out of her home, although she complained that goods were so expensive that her profit margin had shrunk. She was afraid to

A view of the village from Sonia's home, with the primary school in the foreground

raise her prices because she might lose customers, so she decided to keep prices low and hoped that her costs would decrease in the near future.

Sonia's decision to start a small business illustrates how education opens up new choices or options. Sonia described how she gained knowledge (specifically, accounting skills) through the program. SAT also increased her confidence in interacting with people, as we have seen. Sonia now believed having friends was important. Sonia was able to start a small business because education changed the way she viewed the world, as well as provided her with the concrete skills to "extend her possibilities for being and doing" (Mosedale 2005, 252).

Juanita also started a small business, teaming up with her sister, Inita, who was in the same SAT group in her village. When they heard of plans to construct the road, Inita decided it would be an ideal time to start a roadside stall (*comedor*) to sell basic meals to travelers: "Since her [Inita's] husband never worked, and she only grew yuca, one day she said to me, "I am going to grow tired of this life. I am going to call our father to start a small business so we can survive," and she did it. She asked me to help

Juanita in the *comedor* she operates with her husband, Adan

her with a contribution and with materials." Inita's comment that she was going to "grow tired" of her life illustrates that she hoped to change it, and to take the necessary steps to improve it. The women's father, who lives in New York City, sent them some funds to start the business. The sisters worked together to build the food stall.

This food stall is now closed, for reasons described in the next chapter. However, Juanita and her husband, Adan, opened a similar stall in their village. Juanita explained that she learned basic principles of business in SAT, especially the idea of investment. She said: "Let's say I started with four cases of soda, now I am working with six or eight." Her husband worked in the fishing industry from time to time, and he also sold shellfish in the nearby city, Tocoa. She explained that they reinvest their profits from these efforts into their business. Between 2004 and 2010, they expanded the business by adding on a room for private parties and events, and they purchased two large freezers to sell frozen fish, meat products, and other goods. In the future they want to start a hotel for tourists and local travelers. Juanita's plans for the future, although ambitious, illustrate that she has a desire to continue to build on the success of her business. Like Sonia, she learned the necessary skills in SAT to take concrete actions to improve her life.

Other women in the study sample and the two men who participated in SAT show signs of increased financial autonomy and income. Saturino started a small cement block business. As he explained: "I buy five bags of cement, calculate how much cement costs and how much I pay someone to make the bricks, then I calculate the profits." A handful of women from the SAT group in one study village started a cooperative where they raise chickens and sew clothes to sell. Teodora started a bee-keeping business with a cooperative, DARADA, which in addition to raising African honeybees and selling honey has a large plot of land where they grow yuca. The collective processes the yuca into cassave and sells it, sharing the earnings. I asked Teodora if she earned more money than she had before her participation in SAT, and she replied: "Yes, yes, I don't have any problems, because I've been selling cassave. I work with my friends in DARADA. It's going pretty well. Not excellent, but enough that I can buy my daily necessities."

Finally, while in 2004 only a few women were formally employed, by 2010 a number of SAT graduates had steady jobs. Furthermore, all the women I spoke with who participated in SAT believed they were in better shape financially than they had been five years ago. Inita completed her high school studies in a nursing program and is now working in a mountain village as a nurse's aid. Ana, who working as a health promoter in her community, explained: "When I finished with SAT, I made my resume including all of the workshops and activities I had participated in." While she did not have a permanent contract, Ana had been steadily employed and earned what she considered to be a fine salary—"my economic situation has changed because now I have a salary and, well, before, I didn't." In describing her work as a community health promoter, Ana mentioned that she was "serving her community": "This was the vision of SAT, to serve communities. Well, now in my community I am a health promoter."

Soraida had worked in a handful of positions since SAT closed in her community. She was able to study for only one year in the *bachiller* program but managed to finish twelfth grade in another adult education program in her village. For one year she worked as a community outreach coordinator for *Pastoral Social* organizing women's groups. She had also worked as a teacher in two nonformal education programs. She was not sure where she would work for the 2010 academic year but seemed optimistic that she would find something. She complained that, while she earned a steady salary when working as a teacher, sometimes months would pass when she did not get paid. I asked her if her economic situation had improved or stayed the same in the past five years and she replied: "It has improved, thank God. Even though sometimes when you are working you don't get paid! They owe you two, maybe three months. So sometimes you don't have any money, but you get paid eventually!" She was also studying to be a teacher through a special program that emphasizes bilingual and intercultural education.

Napoleana worked as the administrator in a small grocery store (*bodega*) whose owners do not live in the community, and so she manages it in their absence and does the accounting. She completed SAT only through ninth grade, and I asked her if she thought the experience was worthwhile. She responded: "Yes, it was worth it. I'm grateful for it because in my job, I know how to do inventory, everything is ready when the owners come to town. . . . I feel good about my mind because of what I learned in SAT."

In the comparison group, little had changed between 2004 and 2010. Angela continued to work at the municipal offices and had a stable source of income. Susy moved to San Pedro Sula with her daughter and works in a *maquila*, a factory that makes car frames. She rented a small room and her daughter, who was fifteen, was enrolled in high school. Other than Angela and Susy, the economic condition of women in the comparison group is either the same or slightly worse than during the 2004 round of data collection.

In summary, some of women in the SAT group continued to depend on the earnings of their spouses, but over time the majority who participated in SAT demonstrated economic mobility. Their increased financial independence, although small, suggests that they may lean less on the earnings of their husbands and that their overall household wealth has increased. In the comparison group, five of the six women continue to depend almost exclusively on the earnings of their male partners. While both groups still live in poverty, and both lack access to a market and paid employment opportunities, the gap between women who participated in SAT and those in the comparison group widened over time. This suggests that education may not immediately lead to increased income but in the long run can indeed improve women's financial situation. Even moderate gains are significant in the geographically isolated and impoverished communities where these women live.

Conclusion

The idea that one of the most tangible benefits of participating in education is not necessarily financial but social confirms research conducted in other countries in Latin America. Studies in Mexico, Brazil, and El Salvador on students' experiences in adult education programs have found strikingly similar patterns to the ones described in this chapter (Bartlett 2010; Galván 2001; Kalman 2005; Prins 2006; Purcell-Gates and Waterman 2000; Stromquist 1997). In all these cases, participants emphasized that they connected with others and formed friendships and alliances through their participation in literacy classes. In Prins's (2006) study in El Salvador, participants described how even though they were neighbors, they didn't know each other well until they began studying together. Prins points out that the program met the profound human need for affiliation, to recognize and show concern for other human beings. Much like the participants in that program, SAT students became more social, and this made them feel more respect for themselves and others.

Improved social relations is particularly significant in this context because, as Hammond explains, a kind of "personal odyssey" is required to "modify the time-honored patterns of submissiveness and obedience" that characterize the attitudes and behaviors of many rural inhabitants of El Salvador and, in this case, Honduras (1998, 39). For individuals who have grown up in societies that take overtly egalitarian social relations for granted, including the United States, actions like walking over to a neighbor's house or reading from the Bible at church do not have the same significance. For the women in these Garifuna villages, becoming more vocal and participatory marked concrete actions toward personal and community betterment.

As Putnam notes in his famous study of American democracy and social capital, *Bowling Alone*, the mechanisms through which civic engagement and social connectedness operate are multiple and complex. However, he argues, hundreds of empirical studies in a dozen disciplines and subfields suggest that the growth of social capital—features of social organization such as networks, norms, and social trust that facilitate coordination and cooperation for mutual benefit—results in faster economic development, lower crime, better schools, and more effective government (Putnam 2000). These relationships have benefits for individuals but in their amalgamation also may benefit the community.

Women who participated in SAT had sustained contact with their peers, which led to social connections or friendships that they benefited from. As Sonia mentioned, after participating in SAT she "liked" being social and having friends, whereas before, she rarely left her house. The pleasure that women describe from each other's company is consistent with research that identifies the social-psychological rewards of enhanced social relationships (Bryk and Schneider 2002). In short, forming friendships is one way in which women took action toward improving their lives.

In addition to the pleasure of each other's company, interviews revealed that SAT fostered an evolving set of group norms. Participants mentioned that SAT helped them to act like a "professional." These comments overlap with Prins's (2011) discussion of how students in the Salvadoran literacy class described becoming *educado* (educated), which involved speech, respect, manners and comportment, and treatment of others. My findings suggest that there is a strong connection between women's altered self-perceptions and their actions. A new sense of self-worth or self-confidence influences the way they behave in the community. Rather than carry on "like a fool," as Isadora described, she acts like a professional. To act professional means to greet others on the street, not to participate in or react violently to gossip, and to treat others with respect.

This behavior may stem from women's recognition of their inherent nobility or "dignity." Both Rowlands (1997) and Stromquist (1995a) include dignity as part of their conceptual framework of empowerment. While the idea that women must internalize their own worth is widely recognized (Kabeer 1997; Mosedale 2005; Rowlands 1997; Stromquist 1995a), theories of empowerment have largely overlooked the way individuals view and treat others. My findings suggest that women who participated in SAT came to recognize that it is important to treat their neighbors with respect. As Teodora explained, "we are all equal." Their sense of dignity applies not only to themselves, but also to others. They attempt to demonstrate this belief by treating others with "kindness" and "respect." Again, these findings are consistent with research that conceptualizes education or *educación* as a model in which academic knowledge and cognitive development are intertwined with social competence and moral development (Bartlett 2010; Prins 2011).

The application of these shared norms may, over time, strengthen the social fabric of the community. Women were able to participate in community life and start productive enterprises at least in part because they had stronger social ties. Previous research has emphasized collective action (Rowlands 1997) as an important component of the empowerment process. Evidence of SAT's sparking "collective empowerment" is slim, as women did not describe large-scale efforts to organize and work for social improvement. However, women who participated in SAT seem to be following the Golden Rule found in all major religions and many cultures: treat others as you would like to be treated. This is an implied prerequisite of the notion of empowerment as "power with," which, Mosedale explains, refers to collective action, or the recognition that more can be achieved by individuals acting together than by individuals alone (2005, 250). Following the Golden Rule, or treating others with respect and kindness, is arguably a prerequisite of effective collective action. Likewise, the improved relationships that women described might serve as a foundation for future collective efforts to improve community life.

The findings I have described so far, including women's altered outlooks and the small but significant steps they have taken toward the improvement of their lives and their communities, are important components of the empowerment process. However, a number of structures constrain the potential of education to spark the empowerment process. The most obvious is poverty. While a handful of women earned higher incomes and thereby gained a certain degree of financial independence, the economic circumstances of study participants did not change drastically during the course of their studies. Nevertheless, my follow-up interviews in 2010 revealed that a number of SAT participants had access to a steady income, and they reported that their financial situation had improved during the previous five years. My findings suggest that over time, the income gap between those who participated in SAT and the comparison group grew. This suggests that studies attempting to investigate the role of education in empowering women financially should not expect economic gains to be immediate. In short, education does have the potential to alter women's material circumstances, which is a critical component of improving their lives and their household conditions.

At the same time, education, no matter how innovative, will not change the boundaries within which women live, work, and participate in public spaces in the short term. Nevertheless, my findings suggest that women who participated in SAT took small albeit important steps to improve their lives and improve the community.

CHAPTER 6

Behind Closed Doors

Examining the Influence of Education

on Women's Intimate Relationships

"My husband comes from a family that has the idea that a woman's place is at home and a man's the street (*la mujer es la de la casa y el hombre es de la calle*)." Wilma and I sat together in the classroom where she taught, enjoying the cool ocean breeze that wafted through the windows. Wilma calmly and openly recounted the ways in which her relationship with her husband had changed in recent years. She had been working as a SAT tutor for just over five years, and during this same time period she married and gave birth to four children. Wilma told me that her life was difficult when she first got married. She had to cook, change the babies' diapers, and do just about everything. "Even if I was washing clothes maybe, he [her husband] would call me to change the baby's diaper. He would call me to make a bottle!"

Wilma decided to speak to her husband about this situation. She found segments of the SAT textbooks that confront traditional gender roles. Her husband read them, and she would ask him what he thought about the lessons. "And then he realized that—he said that things really didn't need to be that way, the way things were before in our home. And, little by little, because of these lessons, I saw that he changed. And he changed in a surprising way!" She explained that now, if she is cooking and he is with one of their children, he will change the child's diapers. He cleans the children, changes them, bathes them, "without any problem." When Wilma had to travel to the SAT tutor trainings, he would stay and care for the children, doing all the cooking himself. Even when Wilma was at home, some nights her husband would look at her and say: "You look tired today. Sit down, watch the kids, and I will take over in the kitchen."

Wilma's fourth child was now just a few months old. She told me that in her ninth month of pregnancy, she searched desperately for someone to help her take care of the house and the kids while she recovered from the birth. She had a difficult time finding anyone. In the midst of her search, her husband turned to her and said: 'I'm here, don't worry!" After she had the baby, her husband did "everything." "He'd come into the room all the time, 'What would you like? What can I do for you? What do you want to eat? What do you want to drink? I'll make you oatmeal. I'll make you cornflakes.'" Wilma concluded this story by saying that her husband had become a very collaborative man, and that this collaborative spirit was lacking most in him during their first years of marriage. She said that he was *machista*, sexist. Now, their relationship is much more collaborative.

Wilma attributed her husband's behavioral changes to the lessons they studied together in the SAT texts. He came to realize that "things really didn't need to be that way." With relatively little prodding by Wilma, her spouse embraced a different division of labor and became much more col-laborative in the household.

Wilma's case was fairly atypical among the women in the SAT pro-gram. Nevertheless, it illustrates an important facet of women's lives largely overlooked in previous research on education and women's empowerment: relationships with their spouses.

Why Might Relationships Change?

In examining the links between education and women's empowerment in intimate relationships, I draw on a theoretical model developed by sociolo-gists Orly Benjamin and Oriel Sullivan (1999). They propose that change in marital relationships involves the interplay of gender consciousness, re-lational resources (the combination of interpersonal and emotional skills and resources one brings to a relationship), and material circumstances.[1] In their research, they find that a combination of increased gender con-sciousness and the development of particular interpersonal skills facilitate negotiation and change in the boundaries regulating communication and the domestic division of labor.

With regard to the role of material or structural resources, Benjamin and Sullivan explain that changes in structural conditions do not trans-late in simple ways into the household. While important, structural fac-tors do not play the most significant role in their conceptual model; they emphasize instead the importance of women's gender consciousness and relational resources. More specifically, they argue that women with expo-sure to therapeutic discourse have greater gender consciousness and de-velop particular interpersonal skills. This in turn facilitates negotiation and change in their communication with their partners and in the domestic division of labor.

According to Benjamin and Sullivan, therapeutic discourse encompasses a range of practices and media, including individual therapy and counseling; group or family therapy; self-enhancing workshops; and self-help books, tapes, and other programming. Therapeutic discourse often includes the goal of helping individuals develop and improve the interpersonal skills that they use within their relationships. Through therapeutic discourse, the authors find, people are able to learn how to communicate their feelings, how to change their feelings, and how to manage situations so as to maintain a sense of being in control. Other interpersonal skills that one may develop through exposure to therapeutic discourse include change-directed negotiating skills, the ability to express thoughts and feelings more clearly, and the controlled use of anger in conflictual situations, according to Benjamin and Sullivan.

Participation in SAT seems to function in a way similar to exposure to therapeutic discourse, particularly in how the program assists women to develop gender consciousness and relational resources. Through the stories that follow, I describe how SAT participants demonstrated interpersonal skills, including the ability to talk to their husbands, express their feelings, and use change-directed negotiating skills. I draw heavily on interview and observation data for five couples in the study whose experiences spotlight change through daily interactive processes.

Juanita and Adan: Working Together for Change

Juanita was seventeen years old and three months pregnant when she started her studies in SAT, the first in her family to complete secondary school. She joined the program reluctantly, under pressure from her mother and brother, who wanted her to continue her education. She explained: "I used to say that I was just passing the time in SAT . . . but then I liked the program." Finishing her studies in SAT is one of the things she is most proud of, because she now "feels like a professional."

Shortly after her daughter was born, Juanita began living with her current husband, Adan. Even though he is not the biological father of Juanita's daughter, she says he acts as such. Together Juanita and Adan operate a small *comedor*, or restaurant, that sells hot meals, snacks, and cold drinks.

Juanita told me that her relationship with Adan is not like most relationships in her community: "I don't think we are like others." She emphasized that their roles are *compartidos*, or shared, for example: "When I am going over to my mother's, I tell him where I am going, and he will cook and clean. He does whatever I would do and most men wouldn't do this." Adan also described a more equitable division of labor than is typical in the community: "The home is shared." He helped Juanita both with the business and in her agricultural work, which is, according to them, uncharacteristic of most men. "When she goes to the fields, I go with her," Adan said. "If she is going to bring back a heavy load, I take the heaviest part. She comes back with a light load (*liviana*)—that's what I do with her." Juanita used this same word, *liviana*, to describe her workload. She explained: "There are some men who don't help, but he [Adan] helps me with everything."

Adan emphasized how much they talk to each other: "Everything that happens to me when I go out, I tell her. If a woman comes here to borrow two *lempiras*, I tell her that I lent the woman two *lempiras* [ten U.S. cents]. Everything that happens to me, she knows." This everyday talk seemed to be important for their relationship and was something both of them described.

In my interview with Adan, I asked about how he and Juanita met. He explained that they grew up in the same village, but that he spent some time in San Pedro Sula (Honduras's second-largest city). When he returned to the village, Juanita had been studying in SAT for three months. Adan explained that for the first few months of their relationship he saw Juanita "just as any other person." He said that "she only had a few months of being in SAT. But two, three years afterwards, I saw a big change in her, even in the way she spoke." He said that over time, she started teaching him what she learned in SAT. "She even corrected my speaking."

Adan also said that at first, he was not thinking about a long-term commitment with Juanita, and in fact harbored thoughts of leaving her. I asked if their relationship had changed in the six years that she was in SAT. He replied: "At the beginning it wasn't so good. . . . Maybe because I was young, closed-minded, I used to say, 'What am I going to do with her? I am just going to pass the time with her.' I thought I would leave her. And, at the end of a few months, she behaved herself, she showed a lot of love. She won me over and I couldn't separate myself from her."

Adan explained that Juanita began to "talk and behave like a professional" and he liked this about her. She demonstrated care ("she showed a lot of love"). She could explain things to him and was patient. He realized that he, too, could benefit from what she was learning in SAT: "I like that she has studied because I see that over time she can help me. I am fighting for a better life. I won't get in her way of studying; . . . if I can't [do something], she can help me."

Juanita's ability to communicate with Adan and the way she interacted with him made him rethink his plan to leave her. His comments that her way of speaking changed, that "she began to talk and behave like a professional," and his description of how Juanita would explain things to him patiently if he didn't understand indicate Juanita's ability to express her ideas clearly. One way Juanita expressed her feelings and thoughts with Adan was by explaining the SAT textbooks and what she learned in the program: "Whatever I learn, I share with him; . . . I tell him, this is how we can get ahead." Her participation in the program seemed to have opened a window of opportunity for her to talk to him on a regular basis and to explain the material she was studying. Adan and Juanita stressed this sharing of the SAT lessons as an important feature of their relationship. As Adan recalled: "There were things that I didn't understand, and whatever word I didn't understand, she would *explain* it to me" (emphasis mine).

When asked how their relationship was different from most in the community, both Juanita and Adan emphasized relational resources, particularly communication skills. I asked Juanita why she was able to communicate while others don't. She replied: "Maybe because of our education—others are less educated." Her response was interesting because Adan had finished only the sixth grade and therefore was not more educated than most community members his age. Juanita explained to me that she has shared much of what she learned in SAT with Adan.

> Erin: But you are the only one who has studied? He hasn't studied?
> Juanita: No, he hasn't. . . . But whatever I learn, I share with him. I tell him this is how we can get ahead.
> Erin: And is he open to learning?
> Juanita: Yes, he is open to learning.

Education acted as a structural resource for Juanita and combined with her relational resources, it shifted her position within the relationship. Juanita had more power—in this case the power of knowledge, which she shared with Adan. She was also able to apply concrete skills, such as accounting, to improve their material circumstances.

Juanita and Adan planned to invest their money to expand the business, and they talked to each other about what the expansion priorities were. Juanita explained that they invest the money that Adan earns fishing to expand their business: "With this money we built the little building, this is the money we are working with now." However, they do not always agree on how they should spend this money and therefore have to negotiate (change-directed negotiating skills being another relational resource). Adan provided one concrete example of how these conversations go:

> If I want to buy a table [for the kiosk], I will tell her that I think it is important. She might say, "Let's not get a table. There are other more important things like getting windows. A window is more important than a table." So I will start analyzing what I think is more important, to get a table or a window. I'll tell her the table, and she thinks a window! But the most important thing is to come to some sort of agreement. I'll tell her, "Sometimes we'll do what you think is important and other times we'll do what I think is important." Then we'll decide. So because of this there are fewer problems between us.

When I asked Juanita to relate any general observations about her experience in SAT, she responded that she believed that the program changed the way she relates to others. "I was moody. Someone would walk by me on the street and I wouldn't talk to them—they didn't do anything to me but I wouldn't talk to them. Today I don't do this because I learned those things." Juanita described improved interpersonal skills, a key component of relational resources. Adan mentioned a similar change in Juanita. He said that before her SAT studies, she "didn't respect people very much." Now, he says, she is "social with people, because sometimes people come around and she chats with them and it is good for our business, the way she relates to customers, she can entertain them just with her words!"

Juanita also described improved self-confidence: "Before I felt like less when I was around professional people. But now I think we are equal." That she feels equal to professionals may also involve gender consciousness. She spoke extensively about gender issues in our interview, stating her opinion that many men in her community were "*machista* . . . they don't help with anything, but the one I am with helps with everything." During our 2010 interview, Juanita continued to express satisfaction with her relationship with Adan—she said that things hadn't changed since we spoke five years ago, and that they continue to manage the business and share responsibilities equally.

The experience of Juanita and Adan suggests that the ability to demonstrate love and care for one's partner may be another critical relational resource that can foster change in marital relationships. Previous research on renegotiating gender roles points to love and intimacy as powerful forces for change (Benjamin and Sullivan 1999; Deutsch 2007). Deutsch explains that "men sometimes need and want love, and care for women enough to be willing to trade power for it," which is consistent with Adan's experience (2007, 121–122). He was willing to give up a form of men's traditional control over women (the threat of abandonment) in exchange for a loving relationship. Feminist scholar bell hooks discusses the role of love in dismantling patriarchy and argues that we must engage in a visionary feminist discourse on love in order to end relationships based on domination and coercion (2000). In short, these findings hint at the power of love as a transformative force. The role of love and care in relationships supports feminist theories of power as capacity rather than as domination (Hartstock 1983; Karlberg 2005).

Ana and Mauro: Creating Different Gender Roles

Ana began studying in SAT when she was thirty-two. She lives with her husband, Mauro, and six children, who range in age from seven to twenty-five. She and Mauro grew up in the village where they currently live. As Mauro explained, he and Ana were *novios*, a couple, from the time they were small children. He left the village for a few years when he was a young teen to serve in the Honduran army. A few years later, when Mauro saw Ana again after living in Tegucigalpa, his strong feelings for her returned. "It was really surprising when I saw her. I felt something in my heart, and I felt the same love for her." Shortly thereafter they resumed their relationship. They have been together for twenty-five years.

Despite Mauro's professed love for Ana, in 2004 she was not happy in their relationship. I asked Ana about the division of labor in their home.

> Erin: What are his [Mauro's] responsibilities at home? What does he do? Ana: His responsibility is to help me with the children, to feed them, but in Garifuna culture men are in charge.
> Erin: And what is it like in your case?
> Ana: In my case I would say he helps me about 60 percent. He drinks. He smokes and he likes to hang out with his friends and go to parties. He spends the majority of his money on the street.
> Erin: So are you more or less happy about this situation? How do you see it?
> Ana: Look, I am not truly happy.

Ana explained that she had thought of leaving Maura to go look for work in the city. Yet this option was not appealing to her because she would have to leave her children. "So, I stay here for my children. I go up into the hills and find us something to eat."

One of the things about Mauro that bothered Ana the most was that he spent more time out with his friends than at home with his family. She was also frustrated about the money he spent on his "vices," such as cigarettes. I asked her whether they talked about these issues. She said: "Look—before, this was my problem. But now I see that everything is changing, because I recently had to talk to him because I couldn't stand it anymore." She had wanted to discuss her feelings with him for quite some time, but as she explained, she didn't have the opportunity: "The problem was that when he arrived home he would get on his bike and take off for the street. He came back late at night, and, well, all day I am working hard and I was tired. I didn't feel like talking with him so late. In the morning I would wake up and he would get up and leave again, so there wasn't an opportunity."

When Ana finally found an opportunity to talk with Mauro about her feelings, she described their conversation as follows:

> I told him that it might be better for us to separate because there was no dialogue or understanding between us. I saw that he spent his money badly on the street, and at home we have many needs. I told him this calmly, I said, "You have to decide. If you like being on the street, then it is better that you stay there because it is better for our children to think that they have a father who is on the street who doesn't help than for them to have one who is living with us who doesn't help!"

This confrontation demonstrated Ana's relational resources, including change-directed negotiating skills and the ability to express her feelings and control her anger. Ana had more to say to Mauro: "I told him that I would like him to be at home during his free time, to see how the kids are doing, so that he can help me educate the children, because education is not just in school but also at home. That is where education begins." Following this exchange, Mauro told Ana that he did not want to separate and that he would think about what she had said to him. This conversation provides an example of the slow and piecemeal change that Sullivan (2004) describes. For twenty years Ana and Mauro had been together, and so asking Mauro to change his ways was a potentially radical action.

In my interview with Mauro, I did not directly ask about this exchange, but he nevertheless indicated that he was aware of his "vices." Mauro had many good things to say about his wife. He described Ana as a "very caring person," one who "struggles to accomplish whatever goal she sets for herself." Of himself he said: "I am the one who is sort of weak in our home." I asked him what he meant, and he explained:

> I say I am sort of weak for the simple reason that I do not share her religion. She is Pentecostal and I am Catholic. I have my vices but I don't forget about my home. I smoke. I drink. But not in excess. The worst vice that I have is cigarettes, but I am begging God to help me forget them because they are harming me. Just now I came from a *velorio*, so my eyes are red, . . . so I am the one who is not on the straight path, doing things that I shouldn't.[2]

Although their conversation took place only about a month before I interviewed Ana in 2004, she had already seen an improvement in Mauro's behavior: "I see a change in him because now when he comes home, he leaves his bicycle and he sits down to think or read. He talks with his kids, and before, he never did that."

Ana believed that communication was very important in getting Mauro to change his ways: "Look—before, this [lack of communication] was my problem, but now I see that everything is changing." She thought things had improved since their conversation, although Mauro himself admitted he was "not on the straight path." However, Ana's ability to confront him and express her feelings illustrates the application of relational resources.

Like Juanita, Ana attributed changes in her interpersonal skills to participation in SAT: "I used to fight with people, but now I don't. I have changed my ways." I asked her why, and she said that after she joined SAT, "it made me ashamed." Ana also believed that she had better communication with her husband and children as a result of her studies. I asked what she thought the characteristics of a good communicator were. She replied, "Talking, knowing what to say to people."

Erin: And do you have these characteristics?
Ana: Yes.
Erin: Have you always had these characteristics?
Ana: No. Before, no. Before, well, because when I was young my father died, and my mother lived with a man who was a little violent. He used to hit me and that had a bad effect on me . . . but then I

studied, I became educated, and I started changing—that was what marked my life.

Here Ana described her belief that her communication skills changed through her exposure to education; in her words, it "marked" her life.

Ana was overall quite optimistic about the potential role of education in challenging community gender norms. I asked her to name any problems or challenges in her community, and she explained that one of the problems she sees is that men are irresponsible. She explained that sometimes women go up to work in the fields and when they come home their husbands are drunk and mistreat them. I asked her if she had any ideas about resolving these issues.

Ana: Yes, there are ways to resolve them.

Erin: How?

Ana: Through education, raising people's awareness through workshops, especially for men. I think that we need to talk with men, give them advice, and tell them that we are equal. Women have changed but men have not.

Ana seemed to have followed her own advice in talking to her husband and asking him to share responsibilities more equally. She hoped that Mauro would become a better husband and father.

While Mauro mentioned Ana's religious beliefs as a source of difference between them, Ana did not attribute any of the changes in her outlook or her abilities to her involvement in Pentecostalism, although she did mention God more broadly. The outcomes she describes, including reduced drinking and increased male involvement in family life, are also associated with conversion to Pentecostalism (Brusco 1995; Drogus 1997, 2000). While Ana did not directly mention the influence of her involvement in the church, it is possible that she gained relational resources through a combination of her involvement in SAT and in her church.

Ana's case demonstrates that education, like therapeutic discourse, can improve material resources, gender consciousness, and relational resources simultaneously. Ana had been married for more than twenty years at the time of our 2004 interview but had only now confronted her husband about her frustrations, possibly because she now had the option of moving to the city for work. She demonstrated gender consciousness through her critical examination of the community where she lived: "We need to talk to men and tell them that we are all equal."

Ana holding her SAT diploma

When I interviewed Ana again in 2010, she said things had continued to change since she had confronted Mauro five years before, and that he no longer behaved irresponsibly. She explained that "what happens here is that men see women, so humble, and they take advantage of this. It is *machismo*." She said that Mauro was proud of her because when they married she had only a primary school education. Then, with five children (and another born during her studies), she was able to finish her degree and got a steady job as a community health promoter:

> Ana: He sees that I get a salary; I am not the same as before. He has changed.
>
> Erin: When you say that he has changed, what do you mean, in what ways? What is he like now?
>
> Ana: Well, because before he left the house, he'd come home at 2:00 a.m. I used to hear a lot of gossip about him—that he was with other women. He used to waste his money. What happened at home didn't matter to him. But now he doesn't do this. Because he knows that if he were to keep doing it, well, now I know what I can depend on. I don't depend on him directly. I depend on my salary and my knowledge.

Ana coupled her altered material conditions (her salary) with her knowledge. She explained that SAT gave her "a different standard of living. . . . I am not the same as before in my ways of living and thinking." Over time, as her financial position changed, she was able to negotiate a more equitable relationship with Mauro.

Shortly after Ana made these remarks, Mauro came into the house. He greeted me warmly, and I asked him if he had been at a party the night before that everyone in the community was talking about, and several were recovering from. He replied: "Me, no. And her"—pointing at Ana—"she is too good, she is from a different world!" Ana blushed and I laughed, nodding in agreement.

Isadora and Ricardo: Resisting Change

At forty-four, Isadora was the oldest woman in the first cohort of SAT students. She had seven children, who ranged in age from thirteen to twenty-three. Isadora's kitchen was always bustling with teenagers. When we first met, in 2004, her twenty-three-year-old son was cooking *tajadas*, fried plantain chips. The oil spattered in the background as the room filled with the smell of sizzling plantains and his friends waited for their share. As Isadora told her story, her children and their friends listened quietly, sometimes giggling and speaking among themselves in Garifuna.

When I asked Isadora about her perception of challenges or problems facing women in the community, I was somewhat taken back by her candor, given that we had just met. She answered that she could not speak to other women's problems, but that if we were to speak of her own, "we would be there all night." She went on to explain that she had serious problems with the father of her children. Isadora had been living with her husband, Ricardo, for about twenty years, and she was never happy in the relationship. Her husband drank to excess and "followed the bad example of his friends." Isadora explained that he used to yell at her and insult her, but she tried not to let it bother her. "He would insult me in our house, but I would just stay quiet, I wouldn't even answer him with a single word. I just did what I was doing and I didn't say a word."

Isadora decided that she wanted to enroll in the SAT program. Ricardo did not approve. However, she explained, "I did what I wanted to do" and did not talk to him about it. Ricardo became increasingly angry with her because of her participation in the program. Isadora was not sure why he was so angry but thought it might have something to do with the fact that he had never studied (he is illiterate): "He is really jealous. He didn't ever want me to go out." She remained in the program despite his disapproval.

One day Ricardo paid her and her classmates a visit while the SAT group was in class. "He came in while the group was in session," she recalled, "and he took my by the hair, and the shirt, too." Her classmates offered their support and encouraged her to go to the municipal authorities to report his abuse. "The next day I went to report him in Iriona [the municipal capital where local authorities are located]. My classmates gave me help as well." But his harassment of Isadora continued, and one afternoon when she was out in the fields he burned all her SAT textbooks.

One night she was sleeping in bed with her daughter and "he almost killed me and my daughter. I saw that he had the machete to kill us in our sleep." Isadora decided to leave her home and go live with her parents. Her children followed her shortly thereafter, as their father continued to threaten them with the machete. Isadora had not spoken to her husband since, and her children have next to no contact with him.

Isadora explained that when her children were little, she had to stay in this abusive relationship because her husband supported her financially. "When the kids were little, I couldn't do anything." In 2004, Isadora continued to live with her elderly parents, helping out in the small *pulpería* they owned. All her children were still enrolled in school, and Isadora, too, wanted to continue her studies.

This case illustrates that the process of women's empowerment is complex, and that men can stand in the way. Unintended and negative consequences of programs that attempt to empower women are rarely discussed in studies of women's empowerment. Unlike Wilma's or Ana's husbands,

Ricardo was unwilling to relinquish his power over his wife. In fact, as she became more independent, he tried to tighten his control over her.

Isadora did not describe using communication or change-directed negotiating skills to encourage Ricardo to change his attitudes (perhaps she did not yet have these skills, since the scenario she described occurred early on in her studies). However, making the decision to leave him illustrates that Isadora took an important step toward improving her life. She was not willing to tolerate abuse and used a combination of resources (self-esteem, support from her family and friends) that enabled her to terminate the relationship. Inita's story, told later, is similar to Isadora's. Given the small number of women in the sample, it is striking that two men reacted to women's increased empowerment by violently resisting change.

Isadora died in December 2009, just two weeks after her teenaged daughter died from cancer while undergoing treatment in San Pedro Sula. Isadora had spent the last year taking care of her. According to Isadora's former classmates and tutor, the stress of her daughter's death put too much strain on her weak heart and lungs. I was told that Isadora suffered from tuberculosis, but I was unable to confirm this. She was just fifty-three years old. These losses are a reminder of how the social context, particularly precarious health conditions, can constrain women's potential.

Inita and Nelson

Inita was twenty-two when she began her studies, and she had two young children. She studied in SAT through the *bachiller* level. According to her tutor and the program coordinator, she was one of the brightest students in SAT. Her story is remarkably similar to Isadora's.

Inita lived with her partner, Nelson, for roughly ten years. Her aunt, Ana (of Ana and Mauro), told me a little bit about their courtship. Inita was living with a different aunt at the time, whom Nelson approached to ask for Inita's hand in marriage. Inita was not interested. However, the aunt was getting tired of having to support her, and so she forcefully encouraged Inita to start living with Nelson. As Ana explained: "Her aunt wanted her to go with him just because this guy had a job. She [Inita] was never in agreement about the marriage."

Inita started a small food stand (*comedor*), drawing on some of the practical business skills she had learned in her studies. As she explained: "I started the business when I learned how to do it in SAT." As mentioned earlier, she borrowed money from her father to purchase the construction materials and supplies. At first Nelson was agreeable to the idea and helped construct a small building. However, Inita explained, "he started changing because when we first started he would tell me how much money we got that day, but toward the end I didn't see any money—he was the one that managed the business, and he had me as his worker."

In addition to the tension about who was in charge, the business began to cause personal problems for Inita, because her husband, similar to Ricardo, became very jealous. Inita decided to begin the business, her sister explained, because Nelson hardly earned any money. But once she became more independent, "he didn't like her going out, going to meetings or anything. He wouldn't even let her smile or laugh in the *comedor* with other men. He said she had other husbands." He also accused her of having an affair with her SAT tutor.

One night in early September 2003, after shouting at and verbally abusing Inita, Nelson began sharpening his machete. He threatened to kill her. Luckily, her sister and brother, who live in the same lot, were awoken by Inita's sobbing and intervened. Her sister later recalled: "He said he was going to cut off her head with the machete. It's a good thing that their kids were there, because who knows what would have happened if they weren't."

The following day Inita decided to move in with her mother, taking the kids with her. When she went back to get her things, she saw that Nelson had already thrown them outside. Inita explained to me that "there was hardly any communication between us. We were fighting and I decided to leave the house. . . . I thought that the business would change him, but he got even worse. . . . I now know that he will never get himself together. For ten years I stood by his side trying to help him get himself together; . . . he won't [change]." Inita said she was torn because she didn't want to break up her family. However, she decided for her future and her children's future to move to the city. Inita moved to La Ceiba and enrolled in nursing school.

Inita did not tolerate the verbal and physical abuse of her husband. She took a dramatic step in deciding to leave for La Ceiba. Such decisions are not easy for women who are the victims of physical and emotional abuse. A social worker at a local NGO dealing with women's issues explained that for women to successfully leave an abusive situation, they must take "radical" action: "There are some women who say 'enough is enough, I am not staying with this man.' But to follow through on this they need to leave the region because if they stay here, in one way or another they always wind up back with this man. Things are calm for a while, and then the violence returns. So, they have to take a radical step." This social worker's experience working with women in the region makes Inita's story even more noteworthy.

Although I wasn't able to interview Inita in 2010, I learned from her family that she completed her nursing degree and was engaged to a pastor. They planned to marry as soon as Inita could legally divorce Ricardo, who had refused to sign the paperwork. They live together with Inita's children in an isolated mountain community a few hours from her home village.

Inita and Isadora both had resources that allowed them to leave their abusive relationships. Inita's additional years of education enabled her to move to the city and enroll in a nursing program. Her sister was able to take care of her children. Isadora could move in with her parents and help them in their *pulperia*. In short, both cases illustrate that women's empowerment may lead to the escalation of violence against women. Some men seem open to change, while others violently resist giving up their traditional control of women. That Isadora and Inita were resilient, had the necessary resources, and chose to terminate their relationships supports the hypothesis that their studies sparked a process of empowerment. Nevertheless, their empowerment involved courage, sacrifice, and suffering and was possible only because of some measure of personal or familial resources.

Sonia and Julian

Sonia was thirty-three years old and has four children with her partner, Julian. They met when she was working on the Bay Islands. He is from a Garifuna community closer to La Ceiba. They got to know each other over several years and decided to start living together. Sonia wanted to return to her village, but Julian was less keen. His village had better infrastructure. It was accessible by road, and there was electricity. In the end they decided to settle in Sonia's village because Julian spends long times away from home when he works in the fishing industry, and so it made sense for Sonia to be near her family.

After roughly six years of living in the city, Sonia and Julian returned to her village about the same time the SAT program started. She enrolled in the program, and Julian supported her decision, he said: "I thought it was important that she learned; that way we could both benefit." As a result of her studies in the program, Sonia started her small *chiclera*, as described earlier. She also encouraged her husband to put his earnings toward the construction of their own house, because they were living in her mother's house at the time. Sonia told me that as she progressed in her studies, she noticed that Julian became more cooperative and helped her more around the house. When I asked her to describe what he did around the house, she explained that he helped her take care of the children, he cooked and cleaned, and in general was very helpful.

> Before, he hardly ever helped. When I said to him, "Why don't you help me to do this," for example, to go get some water, he would say, "Ah, people will think that you have me as your *burro*, as your worker!" That is what he thought. But I would tell him that no, we had to mutually help each other. So I saw that he began to reason, and now he helps me with this.

Sonia seemed happy that Julian had become more helpful in recent years. However, she told me that she does not like his drinking too much, from time to time. She had encouraged him to go to church with her, with the hope this will make him change his ways.

Another of Julian's behaviors that Sonia was struggling with was his infidelity. She explained: "My husband, about two years ago, he stopped taking care of his three children and of me. He took another woman on the islands, and now he has two children with her." Sonia suffered during the years that her husband lived with this other woman partly because he stopped sending her money. She was forced to take in the laundry of the local pastor in order to buy food and school supplies for her children. "He didn't even send money to buy a single pencil one year!"

Sonia also wanted the father of her children to be present. She wanted her household to be intact. She said that she remained in the relationship for the sake of her children. However, just before our 2004 interview, she gave Julian an ultimatum: "I spoke with him to tell him that he needs to decide, because a person can't be waiting and waiting; . . . the truth is that I am not happy." Because Sonia was not happy, she decided to do something to make her situation better: confront her husband.

When I went to visit Sonia about a month after this initial conversation in 2004, her husband still had not returned from the islands. She said he had recently sent her money and told her to buy a new bed with the funds. She bought the bed and continued to wait for his return. When I visited Sonia another month later, her husband had returned. She said that things looked optimistic, but she still had reservations and said that she did not completely trust him. When I spoke with Julian, he did not mention that he had children with another woman. He did hint at a source of tension in his relationship with Sonia. He explained that he had never really grown accustomed to life in Sonia's village, because he is from a village that is "more advanced" (*delantado*). "The problem is that I am from another environment. There is something different about me. She [Sonia] is from here, and there [his village] it's different."

Julian mentioned in our 2004 interview that he was thinking of going to the United States to look for work. Indeed, after the birth of their fourth child in August 2005, Julian went there *mojado*, or illegally, and found work as a day laborer in New Orleans. Sonia said that she spoke with him frequently by phone. She was not sure if he still has contact with the other woman he was involved with, or if he continues to support the children from that relationship. He does send Sonia money periodically to help with their children's school fees and other household expenses. She mentioned that it is difficult to have him gone, but that she did not feel "so alone" because of her involvement in the community. She was not sure if Julian will return to Honduras.

When I last spoke to Sonia in 2010, she was uncertain what the future would bring. Nevertheless, her decision to talk with Julian about her feelings demonstrates relational resources. Similar to Juanita's case, it also illustrates that education acts as a structural resource, providing Sonia with other potential means to support herself. During the course of her studies, Sonia started a *chiclera* within her home, where she sold basic foodstuffs such as rice, beans, cooking oil, and candies. Until then, she had no access to cash income. Her material circumstances thus changed, in terms of both the number of years of schooling she completed and her income, which altered her negotiating position within the household. Furthermore, she became much more involved in community life and was elected to the village council as well as other organizations. A combination of relational resources, material resources, and gender consciousness prompted her to talk to her husband and to urge him to change his behavior. In contrast, neither of the women in the comparison group whose husbands had other wives had this trio of resources. They remained in situations they were unhappy with.

Intimate Relationships in the Comparison Group

While I did not interview the male partners of women in the comparison group, I was able to get some sense of their relationships from my in-depth interviews with the women. Of the six women in the comparison group, four were in an intimate relationship at the time of my 2004 interviews. Of these four, two had husbands who practiced polygamy (Esmeralda's husband had a wife and children in another town, and Dulcinea's husband had another family in the same community). Both women were less critical of this situation than Sonia was.

For example, in 2004, Esmeralda explained that what bothered her was that "normally what a man can save is for one woman, but I have to share it with another. Because we are two, he has to share." She said that there were positive things about her husband that she liked very much. For example, when he had his first child with her, he gave up drinking and smoking altogether. He had consistently supported Esmeralda financially, and as she pointed out, "with three children, who is going to help me more than him?" In short, while she didn't like the fact that he has another woman, she planned to remain in her relationship with him.

However, when I visited Esmeralda in 2010, she had not heard anything from her husband in three years. He simply stopped coming to the village and had not sent any money for the children. She explained that if he runs into someone from the community, he tells that person to send his regards (*saludos*) to Esmeralda. She said, quite seriously, that she told these intermediaries that the next time he tried to do that they should respond, "*Los hijos no comen saludos*"—the kids can't eat regards. Through tears, Esmeralda described her situation as "miserable" and said she had no financial help from family or friends.

Dulcinea, the other woman in the comparison group whose husband had another wife, also expressed frustration with her situation but said that, "since I am the first, he helps me a lot," and that she was "trying to be patient." In 2010 her husband continued to live primarily with his other family and from time to time would call upon Dulcinea and help financially, "but sometimes weeks pass and he doesn't visit." In 2008, Dulcinea had a stillborn premature baby. After this experience her husband suggested she have her tubes tied so this would not happen again. Her youngest and last child is five years old.

Maria Josefina was another woman in the comparison group who did not describe dialogue or change-directed negotiation in her relationship. She is the mother of seven children, from three different fathers. In 2004 she had recently begun living with a man (not a father of her children) whom she used to do washing for. She explained to me that it was a relationship in which she "helps him and he helps [her]." When I asked what a happy relationship would be, she replied that she would like to have someone who "helps" her. Often the term "help," *ayuda*, refers to financial help, although Maria Josefina did not specify exactly what she meant. She did mention several times that the appropriate role for men is to "help" women. Referring to her last husband, she said: "He hardly helped me at all, he was just bumming around on the street." I asked her what she thought of her assertion that women work more than men and she replied that it was bad because "men have to work and help women." She also said that "if a man doesn't help me, I have to look for another one." Maria Josefina did not mention communication as a strategy to improve her relationships or to encourage her partners to change their behavior. If a man does not help her, she "looks for another one." When I visited Maria Josefina in 2010, she was once again living with a father of her children. I was unable to learn how and when they got back together, as her husband was present during our interview and I decided the subject was too sensitive to bring up.

Carolina, one of the women in the comparison group who was single, lived with her former husband for several years. When Hurricane Mitch hit in October 1998, Carolina's kitchen was destroyed. She was able to acquire new construction materials from donating organizations, and she told her husband to rebuild the kitchen. Weeks went by and he still hadn't built the kitchen. She couldn't live without a kitchen, so finally she asked her brother to help. She subsequently threw her husband out, because she realized that he "wasn't any good" to her. "I came and I said to him, 'Since you don't want to do anything good, get out of here!' I packed up his things and I sent him back to his house." She did not describe trying to talk to her partner about her feelings, or to suggest that he change his ways. Carolina expressed frustration at being a single mother without any support network. She explained that from time to time NGOs or government groups would come to visit, promising that they would help the single mothers, but they never followed through. She was also frustrated by the level of male irresponsibility in the community.

Angela, who worked in the municipal offices and was the only woman in the study sample with a regular source of cash income, said that her husband was "a little *machista*." However, she did not describe trying to negotiate more equitable sharing of domestic duties. She was somewhat critical of men's behavior: "One arrives home from work tired and has to take care of the kids and the man doesn't help, doesn't cooperate." However, when I asked what she thought of this situation, she replied: "Since the beginning, man has been the head of the household. God made man; . . . he is the head of the household, and the woman follows him." She concluded one of our interviews by saying: "I have to be satisfied [*conformar*] with my situation, with what I have." Her case illustrates that material resources alone may not change a woman's negotiating position in a relationship. Even though Angela had access to regular cash income, she did not describe an equitable division of labor in the household or negotiating with her husband. Rather, she used the word "conform" (*conformo*) to explain that she must be content with the status quo.

None of the women in the comparison group described negotiation in their marital relationships or communication about the domestic division of labor. Their experiences contrast with those who participated in SAT, several of whom described frequent communication and negotiation with their partners.

Conclusion

Women's intimate relationships are one of the most important yet most challenging domains to change. Around the world, women spend more time than men on housework and child care (UNDP 2007). This phenomenon was captured by a groundbreaking sociological study in the United States, *The Second Shift* (Hochschild 1990), and continues to be discussed in the media. On Father's Day, 2008, the *New York Times Magazine* ran with a cover story that asked, "Will dad ever do his share?" and explored the challenges of couples who espoused equally shared parenting yet fell into more traditional gender patterns. The article quoted Jessica DeGroot, who runs an institute that coaches families wanting a more shared lifestyle. She captured the difficulty of making the domestic division of labor more equitable, remarking that "women entering the work force changed the work force far more dramatically than it changed things back home" (Belkin 2008). Indeed, changing the domestic division of labor so that men are more involved is a key milestone toward gender equality that no country, not even the so-called developed nations, has sufficiently overcome.

Previous qualitative studies on educational or other international development interventions that have investigated women's empowerment in the household suggest that women's public and social lives change, yet their intimate relationships remain relatively stagnant. In Prins's study of a critical literacy program in El Salvador, the female students expressed dissatisfaction with the domestic division of labor, yet they reported no improvement in their decision-making power or domestic workload (Prins 2008). In Mexico, women who participated in the conditional cash transfer program, PROGRESA, reported increased domestic responsibilities and little to no change in household gender relations (Adato and Mindek 2000). Rowlands's (1997) study of two development projects in Honduras concludes that empowerment in close relationships is the area where change is least visible.

My findings are more optimistic. In the cases of the tutor Wilma, and students Ana and Juanita, their partners seemed to slowly absorb a new understanding of gender relations. Connell describes several reasons why men may embrace the call for change, and among these are men's relational interests. Connell suggests that the quality of every man's life depends to a large extent on the quality of his relationships (2005, 1812). In addition to their relational interests, men may recognize that they may directly benefit if their wives participate in educational programs, because it could lead to higher earnings. For example, the business Juanita and Adan started increased their household income. Men may thus have both relational and material interests in supporting women's expanded roles.

Alejandro, one of the coordinators of SAT, had another theory about how and why change happened for some couples. He explained that this might be the first time SAT students (and their partners) had been encouraged to think about gender equality and that simply introducing the notion that "things don't have to be the way they are" could have a powerful effect on some students, who share these new ideas with their spouses. He was realistic that in some cases change may be more difficult. He explained that the coordinators were pleasantly surprised by several "cases where spouses supported their wives in an incredible way. There were a few cases that were very good. They were very convinced that SAT was good for their wives. They even had a joke that after their wives finished their studies they were going to be left single because their wives would move on without them!" It is unlikely that all men will embrace change so easily.

The experiences of Sonia, Ana, Juanita, and Wilma, particularly when contrasted with women in the comparison group, illustrate how some SAT students were able to change the way they communicate and negotiate in their marital relationships. The daily interactions and negotiations described here are consistent with Sullivan's (2004) observation that change in marital relations is slow and uneven. Nevertheless, some SAT students described a different way of speaking and negotiating with their partners than did women in the comparison group, and these actions may "in the end effect a radical transformation if we take the longer perspective" (Sullivan 2004, 209). Women in SAT and their husbands were beginning to break with traditional gender norms in their communities in subtle yet significant ways. They used interpersonal skills, including talking day to day, expressing feelings, and using change-directed negotiating skills to encourage their partners to share household responsibilities more equitably.

The actions that women in SAT took toward improving their relationships serve as further evidence of the notion that part of the empowerment process involves agency, where women act against established gender norms (Maslak 2008). In short, change in marital relationships stems from a combination of gender consciousness, relational resources, and material resources that enable women to take steps toward more equitable partnerships.

However, as I argued in the previous chapter, the process of women's empowerment is intimately linked to the context of their lives and the structures that support or inhibit the empowerment process. In much the same way that limited access to a market for their goods, geographic isolation, and poor infrastructure placed serious restrictions on the ability of these women to improve their material resources, their intimate relationships are another social structure that can place constraints on their empowerment. Since Isadora and Inita were of the mind that their relationships were beyond repair, they expressed agency by terminating them. Previous research suggests that when women return to the classroom, established gender role patterns can make the woman's pursuit of education destabilizing to the relationship (Garland 2009). Men's violence against women who step out of traditional gender roles is rarely discussed as part of what might happen as an unintended consequence of women's empowerment.

Isadora and Inita were able to resist their husbands' violence and abuse. This required a combination of resources, including self-confidence, family support, and sufficient financial independence. The women in the comparison group did not have these resources and therefore remained in situations they were unhappy with.

My findings suggest that SAT, by increasing gender consciousness, material resources, and relational resources, has enabled several participants to adopt a more equitable household division of labor or avoid abuse. Through everyday conversation and action they are creating relationships that redefine gender norms.

CHAPTER 7

Conclusion

Gender equality and women's empowerment are human
rights that lie at the heart of development and the
achievement of the Millennium Development Goals.
—United Nations Development Program

Gender equality and the empowerment of women
are important for basic reasons—fairness, equality
of opportunity, and economic well-being. Increasing
efficiency and achieving the full potential of men and
women alike is a precursor to prosperity. Gender equality
is also vital to advancing the other Millennium Goals—
halving poverty, achieving primary education for all, and
lowering the under-five mortality rate.
—World Bank, Global Monitoring Report 2007

WOMEN'S EMPOWERMENT IS AN appealing concept. The phrase
is sprinkled throughout contemporary international development policies
and reports, examples of which are represented in the chapter epigraphs.
Often coupled with gender equality, women's empowerment is seen as a
goal of development efforts in and of itself and as a means to accomplishing
other goals, such as poverty reduction and improved health. Part of the
reason why the international development community has rallied around
the goal of women's empowerment is that research evidence suggests that
the highest return investment available is the investment in the primary
and secondary education of young girls (Summers 2004). The logic goes
that when girls and young women go to school, they become empowered
to enter the labor force and make healthier choices for their families.

For this investment to pay off, however, education must lead to altered choices and actions. Empowerment encompasses access to resources,
agency in decision making and negotiating power, and achievement of

outcomes of value (Kabeer 1999). Access to education is not enough to empower women, and the type of education matters a great deal.

Reframing Empowerment: The Importance of Recognition, Capacity Development, and Action

Recognition

The experiences of women who participated in the SAT program suggest that an early stage in the empowerment process is a new way of thinking about oneself. This altered thinking involves improved self-confidence, which is commonly described as an outcome of adult education programs (Bartlett 2010; Prins 2008; Stromquist 1997). Several of the women I interviewed hinted at feeling ashamed before their participation in SAT. For example, Soraida explained that she didn't speak in public because "I was afraid and ashamed because I . . . because I hadn't studied." Like Soraida, several women explained that they felt better about themselves, more self-confident and proud, because they had studied.

SAT served as a catalyst for changing the way women viewed themselves for two reasons. First, the act of participating in the program and working toward their secondary education diploma had symbolic value. Since few community members had studied beyond the sixth grade, the women who participated in SAT were altering their social position within the community. They were working "*para seguir adelante*," to move ahead, and this symbolic act made them feel better about themselves.

At the same time, women were learning in the program. They were not memorizing information, as they had spent much of their time doing in elementary school. The content they were covering in SAT connected with their daily lives. They went to the fields and learned new planting techniques. Their reading comprehension improved. They learned new vocabulary words. They discussed passages from the stories in the textbooks with their tutors and classmates. Everyone I interviewed, even people who dropped out, told me that they "liked" the program and that they learned a lot. The process of learning, of accessing knowledge rather than just memorizing information, sparked a virtuous cycle. As women learned, their self-perception changed, and they began to feel better about themselves. This boost in self-confidence allowed them to try new things such as speaking in public, starting a small business, or becoming more involved in the community. They became more social, gaining respect for themselves and others. These altered perceptions and behaviors further motivated them to continue their studies in SAT.

In addition to feeling better about themselves, several women described coming to recognize the equal worth of others. For example, Juanita said that before studying she felt like "less" when she was around professional people. Now she "thinks we are equal." This may also help explain the findings of increased sociability. While this was not a dominant recurrent theme in my interviews with SAT participants, the recognition of equality seems a component of empowerment that merits future study.

The themes of self-confidence and recognizing the equal worth of individuals are closely related to the concept of affiliation. Nussbaum proposes that affiliation is one of the central human capabilities that constitute human life. She explains that it consists of two interrelated ideas:

1. Being able to live with and toward others, to recognize and show concern for other human beings, to engage in various forms of social interaction; to be able to imagine the situation of another. (Protecting this capability means protecting institutions that constitute and nourish such forms of affiliation, and also protecting the freedom of assembly and political speech.)
2. Having the social bases of self-respect and non-humiliation; being able to be treated as a dignified being whose worth is equal to that of others. This entails provisions of non-discrimination on the basis of race, sex, sexual orientation, ethnicity, caste, religion, national origin and species. (Nussbaum 2000, 79)

My findings suggest that having self-respect is a precursor to living with goodwill toward others. As women's self-confidence grew, they became more social and their friendship networks expanded. I concur with Nussbaum that these concepts hang together theoretically, that respect for oneself is intimately linked to nondiscrimination and the ability to recognize and show concern for other human beings. Building affiliation is a key mechanism by which education can empower individuals.

Religious identity may also be an important dimension of empowerment, and it is possible that SAT's emphasis on unity, justice, and gender equality as important spiritual principles influenced SAT students to create stronger social ties and adopt new beliefs. There are good theoretical reasons to believe that religion may positively interact with the empowerment process. A substantial body of literature positively links religion to physical and mental health (George, Ellison, and Larson 2002; Larson,

Swyers, and McCullough 1998; Seeman, Dubin, and Seeman 2003). Psychologists Peter Hill and Kenneth Pargament posit that "a felt connection with God" may be tied to better health status, and that people who experience a secure connection with God may experience greater comfort in stressful situations and greater strength and confidence in everyday life (2008, 7). Likewise, religion may provide individuals with a sense of purpose. "Spiritual strivings are *empowering*—people are likely to persevere in the pursuit of transcendent goals; . . . people can hold on to a sense of ultimate purpose and meaning even in the midst of disturbing life events (ibid., 8; emphasis mine).

Religion and spiritual values are piquing the interest of scholars and practitioners who work in the field of international development. An area ripe for research is the connection between women's empowerment and their religion or spiritual beliefs. This is particularly important because religion can also be used to justify women's subjugation to men (Nussbaum 2000). Angela from the comparison group is a case in point. She explained, drawing on her understanding of the Bible, that "since the beginning, man has been head of the household. God made man; . . . he is head of the household, and the woman follows him." The role of religion and spiritual beliefs in fostering or prohibiting women's empowerment merits greater attention.

In summary, recognizing one's own worth and the worth of others is similar to the "inner transformation" described by other scholars who have studied empowerment (Kabeer 1999; Rowlands 1997). These ideas resonate with the conceptual framework of SAT, which emphasizes the importance of individual and structural change to move toward the establishment of justice, unity, and equality. Empowered women come to recognize their inherent dignity and their equality with others. They believe they have the ability to contribute to personal and social betterment. They also develop the capacity to critically analyze their lives and their communities. It may take time for them to meaningfully contribute to social or structural change. To return to the words of Martín, an important first step is the recognition of their "latent" talents and capacities.

Capacity Development

The idea of power as capacity (Hartstock 1983) is at the core of how I conceptualize empowerment. A key capacity of an empowered woman is to critically examine her life and the broader society, that is, her critical consciousness (Freire 1973). Stromquist (1995b) calls the ability to develop a critical understanding of one's reality the "cognitive" dimension of empowerment. It is important to reiterate here that the purpose of criticism is not faultfinding, rejection, or backbiting. Rather, it is to foster intellectual engagement and develop language that penetrates the core of relations of domination (Leonardo 2004). Developing the capacity to critically examine oneself and community allows individuals to recognize inequality and work toward social justice.

Women who participated in SAT mentioned that the program "opened their minds" and helped them see the world differently. More concretely, they were able to identify challenges facing their communities as well as solutions to overcome these challenges, whereas women in the comparison group could not. Likewise, women who participated in SAT were more critical of gender inequality than those in the comparison group. These are two concrete examples of the critical consciousness that SAT fostered among participants.

Empowerment also entails the development of specific capacities that can be applied to improve one's livelihood. Through SAT, women learned concrete skills such as accounting and agricultural techniques that they were able to apply immediately. The SAT curriculum stresses both theoretical and practical concepts. Education that combines building critical consciousness together with practical skills is a promising approach to fostering the empowerment process.

Action

Stemming from a critical understanding of one's reality, action that leads to personal and social betterment is also a core component of empowerment. The purpose of empowerment is to challenge oppressive relationships and structures and spark social transformation. It is insufficient for women's outlooks and dispositions to change; they must take action.

Some previous research on empowerment has also mentioned action. For example, Mosedale describes empowerment as the process by which women redefine their gender roles in ways that extend their possibilities for being and *doing* (2005, 252; emphasis mine). I suggest that empowerment entails not only what is possible for women to do, but also what they are actually doing. This conception of empowerment is consistent with Kabeer's (1999), mentioned earlier, which outlines three interrelated domains of empowerment, one of which is the achievement of outcomes of value. The notion of agency, or the culturally constrained capacity to act (Ahearn 2001), is also used to clarify what women's empowerment entails.

Women who participated in SAT acted in ways that differed from both those of the comparison group and their own previous behavior (e.g., enrolling in higher education, starting small businesses, increasing social activity, speaking in public, participating in community events, etc.). However, in analyzing action as a component of empowerment, the expectation should be that change is a difficult and lengthy process. In her study of changing gender practices within the household, Sullivan argues that change is uneven, and daily practices and interactions are linked to attitudes and discourse. She explains that incremental change can be slow and piecemeal yet "still in the end effect a radical transformation if we can take the longer perspective" (2004, 209). Sullivan encourages research that focuses on the daily interactive processes of change as described by the actors themselves. Similarly, research on empowerment should focus on the daily actions in women's lives that may, over time, contribute to personal and social transformation.

Another important consideration when examining the ways in which women's actions change is how social structures may facilitate or impede the process. The geographic isolation of the communities where SAT students lived, as well as lack of access to credit, limited their earning potential. Social structures—including norms and practices within schools, families, and communities; economic provisions and opportunities; and health care—serve as key contextual variables that interact with women's potential for empowerment.

Regarding women's relationships with their husbands and the household division of labor, which previous research suggests are among the most stubborn social structures to change (Adato and Mindek 2000; Hochschild 1990, 1996; Lorber 2000; Prins 2008; Sullivan 2004), my findings suggest that some participants in SAT, specifically the tutor Wilma and students Juanita, Ana, and Sonia, were able to successfully alter the domestic division of labor with their husbands. This action, negotiation with their partners, demonstrates the interconnection between the various components of empowerment: gender consciousness (implying the recognition of self-dignity and the equality of all individuals), improved communication skills (capacity), and altered material resources (again, concrete capacities such as accounting). These women engaged in what Sullivan (2004) would call a "daily interactive process," actions that seemed to open up the possibility for change.

Sonia's case serves as an example of the interconnection of recognition, capacity building, and action as components of empowerment. During the course of her studies she asked her husband, Julian, to play a more active role in the household, even though he worried that people would think he was her *burro*, or beast of burden. Her action implies increased gender consciousness, as she came to think that in her relationship they should "mutually help each other." She also started a *chiclera* in their home from which she earned a small income. While her husband began to help her with household tasks, he also started a relationship with a woman in the Bay Islands. Rather than tolerate his infidelity, Sonia decided to confront him, and she used her relational resources to talk with him about her feelings. She explained to him that he needed to decide between her and the other woman, because "a person can't be happy waiting and waiting." In contrast with the two women in the comparison group whose husbands had other wives, Sonia did not tolerate Julian's behavior. The combination of resources she gained through participation in SAT, namely, her increased gender consciousness, her access to material resources, and her ability to negotiate and communicate with Julian, allowed her to take action and attempt to change a situation she was "not happy" with.

Sonia's intolerance for Julian's behavior represents an important contestation of traditional gender norms in these communities. Because the majority of women are dependent on the earnings of their male partners, they are left with few options and may stay in relationships that they are unhappy with. Esmeralda, one of the women in the comparison group whose husband lived with a woman in another community, said: "With three children, who is going to help me more than him?" This remark illustrates that she is dependent on her husband financially and thus is "trying to be patient" with a situation she viewed as less than ideal.

In contrast with the comparison group, women in the SAT program seemed to be taking small yet significant steps to challenge inequitable gender norms. Over time, a shift in the household division of labor in a few households may serve as an impetus for change in others. Slowly, gradually, unevenly, men in these communities may become more involved in family life, benefiting themselves, their wives, and their children. If, like Sullivan (2004), we view these small changes from the potential of the long-term change they might represent, they could be seeds for a more substantive and radical transformation.

As the international community agreed in the Beijing Declaration, "a harmonious partnership between men and women is a critical aspect of ensuring the well-being of families" (Beijing Declaration, paragraph 15). This implies that men, too, must act differently for women to become empowered. In the cases of Isodora and Inita, however, we see that change is not always easy and that men may fervently resist women taking on new roles in the household and the community. Drawing on her experience with women's empowerment programs in Southeast Asia, scholar/activist Srilatha Batliwala argues that women's empowerment must change the nature of women's relationships with their male partners:

> Women's empowerment, if it is a real success, does mean the loss of men's traditional power and control over the women in their households: control of her body and her physical mobility; the right to abdicate from all responsibility for housework and the care of children; the right to physically abuse or violate her; the right to abandon her or take other wives; the right to take unilateral decisions which affect the whole family; and the countless other ways in which poor men—and indeed men of every class—have unjustly confined women. (quoted in Rowlands 1997, 23–24)

Batliwala goes on to say, however, that the process of women's empowerment will also liberate men, as they will be able to move beyond gender stereotypes. While some men may fervently resist giving up their control over women, others may be more willing. There are several reasons why men may embrace the call for gender equality. Among these are men's "relational interests" in gender equality, because the quality of every man's life depends to a large extent on the quality of his relationships (Connell 2005, 1812). The International Men and Gender Equality Survey found that women are more satisfied in their relationships when the man plays an equal or greater role in one or more domestic duties (Barker et al. 2011). Sharing responsibilities involves negotiation and is not easy, but it can lead to very rewarding outcomes.

In her study of couples in the United States who equally share household and parenting responsibilities, Deutsch holds that men have "a world to gain" from more equal participation in the household. "Equality means some sacrifices from men, but the men I interviewed told me, each in his own way, that the rewards reaped were well worth it. The bond they forged with their wives, the special relationships with their children, and the development they saw in themselves were priceless" (1999, 228, 230). A nuanced discussion of the sacrifices and benefits for men of sharing more equally with women has been missing from previous research and policy documents in the field of gender, education, and international development. Gaining a better understanding of what serves to constrain or foster changed male behavior should be the goal of future research on education and empowerment.

Finally, while my findings suggest that SAT participants took on new roles outside and inside the household, I did not uncover evidence that they undertook collective action. The agricultural projects that students engage in might provide a site for collective empowerment, but more research is necessary to explore this possibility. Previous research on empowerment emphasizes women's ability to act collectively (Rowlands 1997). While I agree that long-term social change demands collective action, this outcome is overly ambitious in the short term. Again, social structures can facilitate or impede the empowerment process. If strong civil networks already exist, it may be more feasible for women to engage in collective action. However, in the absence of social institutions, sustained collective empowerment will take time to develop. Nevertheless, actions including stronger social ties, improved friendship, and increased involvement in the community are precursors to collective action, and these intermediary steps should not be overlooked.

When Is Education Empowering?

Not all educational experiences are empowering. The tendency in international development discourse has been to equate years of schooling or literacy with empowerment, as if the two are unquestionably linked. For example, the ratio of literate women to men fifteen- to twenty-four years old and the ratio of girls to boys in primary, secondary, and tertiary education are two indicators of the Millennium Development Goal to "promote gender equality and empower women." Missing from the discourse on education and women's empowerment is a discussion of the process by which education can transform dominant values and gender inequality (Robinson-Pant 2004).

Of course, achievement of formal credentials matters. Earning a diploma in the SAT program served as an important social marker for women. Completing secondary schooling allowed individuals to enroll in higher education and seek paid employment. A secondary education degree acted as an important resource for women that increased their choice set, aside from the knowledge gains or behavioral changes they may have attributed to their participation.

However, the content and the purpose of SAT are the key characteristics of the program that make it empowering. As critical education scholars describe, these characteristics include linking education with social change, the roles of students and teachers, and relevancy (see, e.g., Kincheloe 2005; Shor 1992). Again, the purpose of SAT is to help students develop capabilities that enable them to take charge of their own intellectual and spiritual growth and at the same time contribute to the building of better communities and the transformation of society (Arbab and Arbab

2003). The program explicitly links education with social transformation through student action. Important components of this process are critical reflection and dialogue. The textbooks that students study together with their tutors are rich in content. Through discussion questions, the texts spark conversation and debate.

A number of elements of the curriculum and pedagogy in SAT are potentially empowering:

- *Emphasis on understanding*: Rather than using rote memorization and dictation, the textbooks and tutor attempt to cultivate a deep understanding of the subject areas students are studying. The interdisciplinary nature of the curriculum facilitates this, since the textbooks do not divide knowledge into traditional subject areas but rather integrate knowledge around specific capability areas. That students have their own textbooks is helpful, as they are able to read the exercises, write out the answers, return to previous lessons, and study the materials at home.

- *Relevance to local context*: The curriculum is relevant to rural life, and it asks students to describe their environments as part of the lessons. Students also visit households in their communities to learn about and from community members in an attempt to generate local knowledge. The textbooks were written with a rural context in mind, wherever possible use language and examples that students find accessible, and ask students to think about actions that could improve community life.

- *Teaching style*: The tutors in SAT play an important role in the learning process. The tutor is expected to learn alongside students and are not thought of as the ultimate authorities. They are expected to be honest when they do not know something, and together with students attempt to find out the answer. Tutors get to know the students well, and staying with an SAT group for six years may increase their incentive to encourage student progress (they cannot pass a struggling student off to another teacher at the end of the school year). The pedagogy that tutors use and the special training they receive are key features of SAT. Even if tutors are deficient in some area or absent, the textbooks provide academic content for the students so that they can continue to learn and work through the lessons.

- *Agricultural component*: In the vast majority of SAT communities in Honduras, the main livelihood strategy is agriculture. In addition to the contextual relevancy that this feature of the curriculum adds, growing crops as a group may have other beneficial outcomes.

Research from the United States suggests that incorporating gardening into school curricula is associated with improved self-esteem, better attitudes toward school, improved social skills, increased group cohesion, and improved interpersonal relationships (Bunn 1986; Campbell et al. 1997; Klemmer, Waliczek, and Zajicek 2005; Robinson and Zajicek 2005). All these are important components of empowerment. Additional research should investigate how the agricultural component of SAT plays a role in empowerment, particularly in collective empowerment. In the meantime, the women in this study mentioned the agricultural content as one of the most satisfying aspects of the program.

Mainstreaming Gender in SAT

A distinguishing feature of SAT is that the principle of gender equality is mainstreamed into the curriculum, emphasizing that both individual and structural changes are required to achieve gender equality. Furthermore, the struggle for gender equality is linked with the broader goal of justice. This approach is consistent with current research and theory on undoing gender, which highlights the need for analysis of the links between social interaction and structural change and an emphasis on justice (Deutsch 2007; Lorber 2000; Sullivan 2004). The following excerpt from a textbook used to train tutors and program coordinators elaborates FUNDAEC's approach:

> Many feminist thinkers recognize, for example, that oppression will remain in society even if action is taken against discriminatory practices. They take "feminist praxis," then, beyond questions of law, norms, and regulations for the elimination of discrimination to a profound examination of the fundamental elements of social theory and methodology in the context of the status of women. . . . Some of this discourse clearly indicates that the challenge is not to simply open room for women in the present social order but to create a new one which embodies among other things the equality of women and men. . . . One of the reasons we insist on relating the status of women with the principles of justice is that we are not satisfied to see some women liberated from that form of oppression that is based on sex only to join the institutions of oppression operating in the context of class, race, nationality and political and economic power. The challenge for us is to bring about the kind of changes, both in people and in social structures, that turn relationships of domi-

nation into relationships of collaboration, cooperation, and reciprocity. We hope that, in the process of achieving the equality of women and men, humanity will be able to eliminate oppression and create a society that embodies the principles of justice. (Arbab and Arbab 2003)

This strategy, to link the equality of men and women with a broader vision of society that is governed by the principle of justice, echoes an observation made by Stromquist, who argues that the task in front of educators is to construct a new vision of society, one that requires changes in the processes, structures, and content of education (1995a, 446–447). FUNDAEC's approach to gender recognizes the need for such deep and radical changes.

The SAT curriculum does this by encouraging participants to engage in a discourse that emphasizes equality. According to two of the program's developers, "the main instrument of our pedagogy is an ongoing dialogue pursued by the student—with us [staff at FUNDAEC], with the tutor, with other students, and increasingly with the community and the institutions of society. . . . Our textbooks are records of this dialogue" (Arbab and Lample 2005, 186). The explicit gender content thus attempts to promote discussion about gender and at the same time to convey the principle of gender equality. This strategy is consistent with Sullivan's observation that new or altered discourses on gender are an important step toward gender consciousness (2004).

A lesson on the digestive system illustrates this approach, as we have seen. Recall that it asks students to "think of one of your convictions, for example, your belief in the equality of men and women. . . . Can you describe what you thought and did until it became part of your systems of beliefs?" Students are to respond individually to this prompt in writing, and then share what they have written with their classmates. This approach opens space for the dialogue about gender that, as many feminist scholars have argued, is most likely to happen in schools (Connell 1989; Haywood and Mac an Ghaill 2003; Stromquist 1995a). Discussing gender allows SAT students to think through their assumptions and recognize instances of inequality in their own lives and communities. Because these lessons appear in the texts, they could even share these with their families, as the tutor Wilma did with her husband.

Another feature of SAT that challenges oppressive gender relations is that tutors are given the opportunity (in training sessions) to reflect on their own beliefs and daily interactions and analyze social structures that perpetuate inequality. The role of the tutor is critical because teachers are the change agents of educational reform. In training sessions, tutors discuss questions that are intended to allow them to identify their assumptions about gender as well as to engage a process of critical reflection, for example:

> We have mentioned that one type of knowledge, mainly, one's understanding of one's own human nature, is of special importance in the struggle against oppression. Consider then the question of human identity in general. In this respect, both men and women are offered entirely false definitions and are bombarded by harmful images of what a human being actually is. How are these false definitions and images propagated? How are they transmitted from generation to generation?
>
> The structure most affected by the relationship between men and women is the family. . . . Discuss in your group the profound changes that the unit of the family as a basic structure of society must undergo in order to reflect the principle of the equality of women and men. (FUNDAEC 2007)

Finally, SAT emphasizes the family as a "basic structure of society," as illustrated in the foregoing excerpt from the tutor training materials. Through narratives in the text that portray family life and pose discussion questions, tutors and students engage a process of critical reflection on the domestic division of labor and daily interactive processes in the family. SAT introduces the family as a social structure that requires "profound" transformation in order to reflect gender equality. This emphasis is crucial, particularly in light of overwhelming evidence that gender relations in the domestic sphere remain unchanged (Benjamin and Sullivan 1999; Hochschild 1990, 1996; Lorber 2000; Sullivan 2004).

These features of the SAT program make it a transformative innovation in secondary education, one that sparks the empowerment process among participants.

Conclusions

SAT: A Viable Model of Secondary Education

While this research has focused on SAT and women's empowerment, the program is also of interest to policy makers because it appears to be a viable means to expand secondary education coverage and improve its quality in rural areas of Latin America. In the region, many countries are close to reaching the goal of universal primary education; estimates from the World Bank place net enrollment rates in primary school at 94 percent, on average (diGropella 2006). However, significant deficits in secondary education enrollment remain throughout the region, particularly in the low-income countries of Honduras, Nicaragua, and Guatemala, where net enrollment rates hover around 35 percent (ibid.).

Providing access to secondary education is one challenge. Ensuring that all students have access to high-quality secondary education is another. High rates of grade repetition and early dropout are serious problems in many Latin American countries (diGropella 2006; Urquiola and Calderón 2006). One possible explanation is poor education quality: policy documents of the World Bank and the Inter-American Development Bank argue that there are urgent and acute problems with education quality in Latin America (diGropella 2006; IDB 2004).

Research on how to improve the quality of education in developing countries often focuses on the role of specific inputs, such as teacher training, textbooks, class size, pedagogical materials such as flip charts, or curricular innovations such as radio instruction. In a recent review of research from developing countries on the factors that affect student outcomes, Glewwe and Kremer (2006) summarize the results of randomized experiments, natural experiments, and retrospective studies and come up with a mixed picture. However, they suggest that one interpretation of their findings is that the most effective way to improve the quality of education in developing countries is to address the problem of weak teaching.

Closely related to the issue of teacher quality is the curriculum that teachers are expected to implement. In Latin America, the secondary education curriculum is another possible culprit for the poor quality. One common concern is that the curriculum is divided into too many subjects, presented to students as independent and unrelated (Alvarez 2000). Twelve to fourteen fragmented, compartmentalized subjects are too many for students to study and schools to adequately cover per academic year (IDB 2000). These curricula also pose cognitive demands that are beyond the abilities of most of those available to teach. The curriculum encourages rote memorization, little creativity, and has little relevance to students' daily lives (Braslavsky 1999).

Another concern is that the secondary school curriculum in Latin America does little to meet the public purposes of schools, particularly the goal of preparing future participants in a democratic society. Reimers argues that citizenship education and the development of global values should be an explicit objective of efforts to improve educational quality throughout the world. He does not advocate that schools should focus exclusively on these goals, but rather believes that helping students develop a sense of public purpose is a means to facilitate higher levels of engagement with other subject areas (Reimers 2006). In short, citizenship education is seen as an important component of educational quality because it addresses the goal of preparing future citizens *and* it is a way to make school more relevant and engaging (Cox, Jaramillo, and Reimers 2005).

SAT responds to these common critiques of secondary education through its emphasis on tutor training and pedagogy, the interdisciplinary nature of the curriculum, and the incorporation of values. My current research project (together with Patrick McEwan of Wellesley College and Renan Rapalo Castellanos of the Honduran National Pedagogical University) investigates a number of features of SAT that will speak to its ability to offer high-quality education to rural students. Among other outcomes, we are measuring students' achievement on standardized tests of Spanish and mathematics and their participation in community life, and a number of measures related to citizenship education.

However, even if the results of our research suggest that SAT is of high academic quality and fosters participation in community life, the experience in Honduras to date suggests that widespread implementation of the program will face continuing resistance from those with a vested interest in preserving the status quo, including teachers in traditional primary and secondary schools and other educational authorities. Research from the United States suggests that educational reform is a tediously slow process (Tyack and Cuban 2003). Reforming secondary education in Latin America will require financial resources and political will on the part of governments and donor agencies. Finally, it requires readiness to experiment coupled with a posture of learning among policy makers, teachers, parents, and students.

Need to Widen the Gender Lens

Another emerging issue in the study of secondary education in Latin America is a gender gap that favors girls and women (Duryea et al. 2007). A 2006 UNICEF report on the state of the world's children finds that in Latin America and the Caribbean, boys generally have higher repetition rates and lower academic achievement levels than girls and, in some countries, a higher rate of absenteeism (UNICEF 2006). Research by economists at the IDB confirms this and estimates that the gender gap in attainment has moved in favor of females at a pace of 0.27 years of schooling per decade for the birth cohort born between 1940 and 1980 (Duryea et al. 2007). Gender disparity starts to appear around age ten, when boys begin to leave school at a higher rate than girls (UNICEF 2006). By ages fifteen to seventeen, 19.2 percent of boys have dropped out altogether, compared with only 8.5 percent of girls (UNICEF 2006). These trends are also found in the United States, Australia, and the United Kingdom. A growing body of research explores boys' experiences in school and the underlying social norms that push them out of the school system (Connell 1989, 1995; Ferguson 2000; Haywood and Mac an Ghaill 2003; Kimmel 2004; Pascoe 2007).

One of the possible reasons why boys drop out of school at higher rates in Honduras is because they enter the labor market at a younger age than do women (INE 2007). Extreme poverty coupled with traditional gender norms that dictate that it is a man's responsibility to earn money for the family are likely responsible for this trend. This is a clear example of how the current gender system can keep men as well as women from reaching their full potential. The chapter on boys from the *2006 State of the World's Children* report, which discusses the statistics on boys' disadvantage just noted, concludes: "Gender sensitivity means what it says: being clear about the needs of both girls and boys, and creating school systems, classrooms and societies in which all children flourish" (UNICEF 2006, 67). The emphasis of the international development community on women and girls, rather than on gender, has often overlooked how gender norms can push boys out of the education system. It is time to widen the gender lens to include men and boys.

While progress has been made in recent decades with regard to expanding educational access to girls and women, the root causes of their educational disadvantage remain, including social norms and gender bias. Unfortunately, most social programs targeting gender deemphasize the importance of challenging oppressive gender norms. Connell (2005) provides a comprehensive overview of gender-equality reform, detailing recent research and policy on men and masculinity, and argues that, in almost all policy discussions, to adopt a gender perspective means to address women's concerns. The field of international development education needs to broaden the discussion of gender to examine boys, men, and masculinity.[1] In particular, research should investigate the individual attributes and circumstances that contribute to men's willingness change (Benjamin 1998; Connell 2005). A major challenge to women's moving ahead is that men may not want them to. Education can play a role in changing the way men and women think about gender, but only if educational programs are spaces where students both thrive intellectually and find their attitudes about gender challenged.

Education can promote more equitable gender relations; it can mine gems of inestimable value inherent in both males and females. However, change will take time. Nevertheless, I agree with Deutsch (2007), who urges scholarship on the social processes that underlie resistance against changing conventional gender relations. My hope is that by exploring the experience of SAT students in Honduras, this study has highlighted how education can empower individuals to improve their lives and the communities in which they live.

"It Opened the Door and Showed Us the Way"

In this book I have demonstrated how education can spark positive change in women's and men's lives. However, not every kind of education will do this. Several features of the SAT program, including its emphasis on critical thinking, relevancy to the local context, the teaching style, and the incorporation of specific values including gender equality make it a particularly innovative educational program.

Other SAT participants echoed the reflections of Juana, one of the first SAT *bachiller* graduates, on how SAT had altered her life trajectory: "SAT opened the door and showed us the way." After finishing SAT, Juana won a scholarship to Earth University in Costa Rica, where she completed her degree in agronomy in February 2009. When she graduated, she was offered a job in Honduras at Standard Fruit Company (Dole). She turned it down, despite its higher pay, to work for Bayan, the NGO that sponsors SAT. Juana explained: "I feel like a child of Bayan . . . because they have helped me so much. Also, I consider that working in education I can help foster certain changes." She is now working as a SAT program coordinator in Puerto Lempira, a small regional city in the eastern part of Honduras near the Nicaraguan border. She hopes to strengthen the agricultural component of SAT, bringing her technical expertise as an agronomist. She also hopes to turn the agricultural projects of SAT groups into something that can evolve into small businesses for the students. As a program coordinator she earns a stable salary and is the main breadwinner in her family. She and her partner recently had a baby boy, Denzel. Her husband takes care of the baby while Juana is at work.

I asked Juana what she thought it would take to empower women and improve gender relations in the community. Her remarks were strikingly

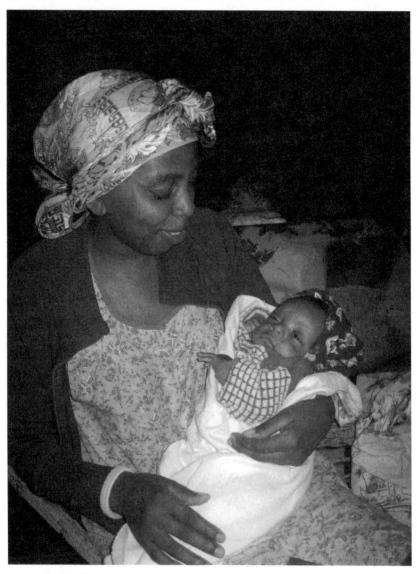

Juana and her baby, Denzel

similar to the findings of my research (which I had not shared with her). It is with her words, and expression of hope, that I conclude.

> I think that instead of working with women, we have to work with men. Because women already know what they need to do, but men haven't taken into account what their responsibilities are. Programs have arrived—programs for women. But I think the problem is that we have left the men behind. Here in the community there are more women that have studied than men. Here there are more women working than men. Women know that their rights are this, this, and this. Women know. Now it is men that have to know.

Looking down at the newborn boy in her arms, I asked: "Will Denzel be different?" She replied: "I hope so."

Betty, holding her baby, studying a PSA text with the help of her tutor

EPILOGUE

SAT in Africa

With Joseph Lample

To RESPOND TO THE interest being shown in a number of countries worldwide to adopt SAT, FUNDAEC modified the curriculum for use in Asia and Africa (and translated the textbooks into English). The resulting program is called Preparation for Social Action, or PSA. There is a great deal of overlap between PSA and SAT, as students study very similar texts. However, SAT is recognized by governments as equivalent to secondary school, whereas PSA has not received this recognition. PSA's target population includes youths and adults like Betty Mugimba, a twenty-year-old woman who lives in rural Uganda. She dropped out of school because she couldn't afford the fees.

"PSA Has Given Us a Chance to Show We Are Worthy"

Her hands moist with the dough of samosas she would sell later that day, Betty noticed her friend Jesca walking by with books under her arm. After a few days of this, Betty wondered where Jesca was going. She asked her: "What is it all about?" Jesca told her she had joined a new program, PSA. Betty was immediately intrigued, because "Jesca told me that it was all about preparation for social action, and because I love education, I love knowledge, I love going to school, and I also love working in the community. And because of what Jesca explained to me, I became interested in joining PSA."

Betty, like many adolescents in the Ugandan countryside where she lives, had dropped out of school because she couldn't afford it. She was also pregnant. Since most schools don't permit pregnant students, she didn't think she'd be able to enroll. But Jesca encouraged her to come along: "She [Jesca] was like, it's okay, so I was like, okay, tomorrow if you're going you will pick me up and we will go together. So the next day she picked me up and I came to school and I joined just like that, something that was not common."

Roughly a year after joining the program, with her baby placed in the center of a small classroom on an empty sack of maize, Betty described how her participation in the program had allowed her to make a useful contribution in her community: "After you drop out of school, most people in the community see you as useless. But PSA has given us a chance to show that we are worthy." In addition to her studies in PSA, Betty holds weekly classes for children, and she has worked with her classmates on a number of service projects and educational campaigns in the community. Betty enjoys the service projects and the opportunity to develop her spiritual qualities.

> Honestly, . . . while I was still in the Ugandan curriculum and before I joined PSA, there is something called spiritual qualities. . . . I knew all about them, [but] I didn't know that someone could be good and I would just act and behave the way I wanted to. But now, before I do, before I act, I have to first think of the action that I'm going to take. First think about its repercussions, then I can do it. Honestly speaking, before, I was bad. But now I'm fighting it and I'm trying to be good just because of the PSA program. And I'm also fighting to see that I build my spiritual qualities to 100 percent, though I'm not yet really 100 percent but at least I'm trying.

In addition to fighting to be "good" and thinking about the consequences of her actions, Betty felt her experience in PSA was different from that in traditional Ugandan secondary schools. She stressed that in PSA the students cooperate, consult, and make decisions together, whereas students compete for first place in traditional schools: "In the Ugandan curriculum there is competition and selfishness. Because in class you will not be able to share your knowledge with other people, because if you share they will learn and they will try to compete with you for the first position. So you have to keep everything you know to yourself so that you will be the first." She also believed that in Ugandan schools, the teacher tells students everything, whereas in PSA students can generate their own ideas: "It's difficult to bring up people's different talents, for example, the capabilities of us to keep our minds running and thinking of new ideas. In PSA we are able to do that, but in the Ugandan curriculum, it's the teacher who thinks for the students."

The PSA program gave Betty an opportunity to return to school, and she said it taught her and her classmates skills that will improve their parenting: "In Uganda it's believed that once you've produced a child, you've produced for the nation. And as you groom that child well, due to the skills you've learned in PSA, you're grooming the nation's child. So that's also another advantage we have."

PSA in Africa

Betty is one of approximately 750 students who study in the PSA program in Africa. Currently, the PSA program consists of twenty-six textbooks, each organized around the development of one or more capabilities. As in the SAT program, the textbooks are interdisciplinary and do not mimic traditional subjects normally found in secondary schools. The texts are grouped into the same five capability areas as SAT texts: language, mathematics, science, technology, and service to the community. Students study these textbooks under the guidance of a trained tutor. Again, while students in PSA do not currently receive any formal recognition for their participation in the program, the curricular content is intended to cover what would normally be the last two years of primary school or the first two years of secondary school, depending on the educational system of the country.

FUNDAEC, whose offices are still located in Colombia, collaborates closely with local institutions to implement the PSA program. In 2007, FUNDAEC received a grant from the Hewlett Foundation to support the implementation of PSA in Kenya, Zambia, and Uganda. FUNDAEC provided training to local institutions in each country to ensure that they could successfully oversee and expand the PSA program in their region. Several times each year, representatives from FUNDAEC went to Africa and ran training sessions, usually of two or three weeks in duration, to give the tutors and coordinators an opportunity to learn more about the pedagogy and conceptual framework of FUNDAEC through firsthand collaboration with members of its staff. In addition, FUNDAEC attempts to collect data based on the experiences of its many partner organizations in implementing the PSA materials, often synthesizing this information into documents for future training.

A Closer Look at PSA in Uganda

Uganda is a landlocked East African country that was coined the "pearl of Africa" by Winston Churchill because of its magnificent scenery and friendly culture. The vast majority of Ugandans live in extreme poverty; many are illiterate. Compared with other countries in East Africa, Uganda experienced comparatively slow educational expansion in the first two decades following its independence from Great Britain in 1962 (Oketch and Rolleston 2007; Penny et al. 2008). Despite its somewhat delayed start, Uganda eventually adopted universal primary education (UPE) policies, as well as a fairly ambitious set of universal secondary education (USE) policies (Oketch and Rolleston 2007; Stasavage 2005). While UPE in Uganda has largely been considered a success because enrollment increased from 2.8 million to 7.6 million between 1997 and 2004, gains at the secondary level have been much more modest (Chapman, Burton, and Werner 2009).

The universal secondary education policy seems to be more of a symbolic government decision to increase opportunities for attendance than a far-reaching policy change (Chapman, Burton, and Werner 2010). As of 2009, attendance rates at the secondary level had increased just 15 percent since the establishment of USE. Uganda has one of the lowest secondary school gross and net enrollment rates (both around 25 percent) in East Africa (EACS 2010; UNESCO 2010a). The PSA program hopes to respond to the pressing need to expand secondary education coverage for adolescents and adults who have not had the opportunity to study beyond primary school.

In Uganda, PSA is run by the Kimanya-Ngeyo Foundation for Science and Education (Kimanya), a small, nongovernmental organization based in Jinja, in the southeastern part of Uganda. (Kimanya-Ng'eyo means "the large enterprise of knowing.") Kimanya was created through the efforts of a few expatriates in collaboration with local educators to implement PSA in Uganda. Selam Ahderom—a native Eritrean, the executive director, and one of the seven founders—explained that, for a number of years, he and his cofounders had been very interested in FUNDAEC's work with the SAT program. Through his contacts in the Bahá'í International Community, Ahderom was aware of ongoing efforts at FUNDAEC to prepare a modified, nonaccredited version of their rural educational materials in the form of PSA. Ahderom along with his wife, Debbie Singh-Ahderom—an Australian physician, member of the Council of Founders, and now the national director of Kimanya—set out in late 2006 to identify potential sites for the program's implementation. The program has been running in Uganda since 2007.

In June 2010, Joseph Lample, a doctoral student who works as my research assistant, visited Uganda to conduct a case study on PSA. During his trip, he observed PSA groups and conducted mainly one-on-one interviews with tutors and students in the program. Students, who were often shy and reserved during one-on-one interviews, also were interviewed in focus groups, where they were more talkative.

In all, participatory observation (involving visits of varying frequency and duration) was conducted for seventeen PSA groups, one PSA group field trip, and part of a tutor training. Nine interviews were conducted, including three group interviews. The interviewees were three coordinators (two of whom were also board members), three tutors, fourteen students, and Kimanya's executive director. The interviews were recorded and transcribed, and Joseph took extensive field notes during his observations of PSA classrooms. We see this research as a first step in what will be a longer and more comprehensive study on the PSA program and empowerment in Uganda.

We found striking similarities between the early challenges of implementing SAT in Honduras and the Ugandan experience to date. We also found similarities in the ways PSA participants in Uganda and SAT students in Honduras spoke about their experiences. These preliminary findings suggest that the impact of SAT/PSA may be similar across contexts, and that the notion of empowerment as a process of recognition, capacity development, and action is a relevant framework for exploring the relationship between education and empowerment in other regions of the world.

Early Challenges and Institutional Learning

As was the case in Honduras, the initial implementation of PSA in Uganda was not an easy process. Kimanya has attempted to document its experiences and considers itself, as an organization, in a "learning mode." It has experimented with a number of methods of delivering the PSA program (e.g., linking with private schools, targeting adults that have dropped out of the formal system, etc.). PSA in Uganda is likely still several years away from bringing PSA to scale (as of this writing there are approximately thirty tutors working with 350 students). Nevertheless, the early years of PSA implementation in Uganda informed Kimanya's current operations and strategy. As with SAT in Honduras, the early history of PSA in Uganda demonstrates that implementing innovative educational programs takes patience and the institutional capacity to respond to the opportunities and challenges each context presents.

Tutor Recruitment, Training, and Retention

In January 2007, Kimanya began a focused effort to initiate the PSA program in southeastern Uganda. Two representatives from FUNDAEC went to Uganda to provide the first training for aspiring PSA tutors. The weeks before the training were occupied with attempts to introduce the aims of PSA to as many individuals and communities as possible. "Of course we had to visit the communities, talk to the local leaders, recruiting tutors," explains Kalenga Masaidio, an early collaborator and current program coordinator for Kimanya Ngeyo. "After all [that], then those selected tutors were invited for the training."

Spreading information about the program, attracting support and attention in new localities, would not have been successful without the involvement of a few key individuals. As time went on, those individuals—Kalenga Masaidio, Mary Kayongo, and Joseph Kisame—would eventually prove an invaluable part of Kimanya's organization, later becoming three of its earliest coordinators (similar to Alejandro and Ricardo in Honduras). By the time the training began, around twenty-five individuals from the Kamuli, Mukono, Kampala, and Jinja districts had been recruited. The two-week training focused on the first three textbooks of the PSA curriculum. This experience with tutor training clarified that, similar to the case in Honduras, recruiting and successfully training tutors was going to be a major challenge. In the early months of the program, Kimanya experienced particular difficulty in sustaining the involvement of its newly trained tutors.

After the training finished and tutors were asked to recruit study groups of fifteen members or more in their communities, it became clear quite quickly that many of the tutors were not able to follow through—only five or six would eventually go on to establish a group. "Most of them [tutors] did not continue," Kalenga points out.

> And one of the reasons is that we selected very old people. You could find a tutor that is seventy years old, sixty years old. [*Laughs*] The selection was not really done properly, because . . . that was the initial stage

and also we did not understand the whole program. So we thought that anyone could be recruited as a tutor. . . . They came knowing that maybe they will have, you know, [a] big reward at the end of the day, which we did not tell them. . . . But after the training, when they realized that it was something small, then they left. And of course we can't blame them, they have huge responsibilities, so they had to leave.

Among the primary factors contributing to the low retention rate of these volunteer tutors was that Kimanya had underestimated the time commitment required, often twenty to thirty hours per week. Kimanya quickly realized they would have to pay tutors to keep the program viable. According to Selam Ahderom:

> The reality that we found was that people actually have to be very careful about how they use their time. . . . The way that the rural economy is set up means that a person actually has to use his labor outside of his garden to do a number of other things to be able to supplement his income. And so, to be able to devote fifteen or twenty hours in a week is actually a very large commitment, no matter what the timing is.

Challenges also arose at this stage when it came time for newly trained tutors to recruit interested participants. Because there were no trained coordinators at this stage, many tutors presented their own understanding of the aims and goals of PSA, with the result that many prospective PSA students held unrealistic expectations about the program. Among the common claims, for example, was that participants in PSA could expect their efforts to lead to jobs after only a short period of study. A realistic sense of the time commitment required to complete the entire sequence of PSA texts was also unclear. Just as in Honduras, a number of early participants dropped out of the program, and the number of groups dwindled. Through these experiences, Kimanya developed a better estimate of the time commitment expected of their tutors and participants. These insights influenced their recruitment and training of new tutors in the remaining half of 2007.

Student Recruitment and Retention

Kimanya has struggled with student recruitment and retention. By 2009, based on two years of experience in implementing PSA, a basic set of guidelines had materialized for selecting where to start a group, and whom to invite. Through an assessment of participation in the program up to that point, Kimanya identified participants in PSA as primarily from three groups, each with its own set of challenges and advantages:

1. *Youths attending the small private school of a PSA tutor.* Unlike the strategy in Honduras, in Uganda, Kimanya trained teachers at private schools to become tutors, who would deliver the PSA curriculum to their private school students. Among the challenges faced by these participants was the need to balance time dedicated to completing PSA with time necessary to complete their schoolwork. These students, along with their tutors, have struggled to create a learning environment distinct from that of the traditional classroom. Tutors, for example, have had little time to work with pedagogies introduced by PSA, and often there is only a superficial transition from the private school to the PSA study environment.

2. *Youths who had dropped out of school.* These students struggled to balance their time commitments between PSA activities and work at home in support of their families. Many in this group drop out of the program to support their family full time. Fluency in reading, writing, and speaking English has also varied greatly among these participants.

3. *Adults who had dropped out of school before enrolling in or completing secondary school.* These participants often join PSA to develop their language and agricultural skills, yet due to their age and family responsibilities they face many challenges in acclimating into an intensive study environment, particularly in English. Exceptions exist however, including those who have spent more time in urban areas and therefore have had more exposure to English, giving them a slight advantage over their peers.

At the beginning of 2009, looking closely at the challenges and advantages of working with each of these populations, Kimanya made a series of calculated decisions about the types of PSA groups they would aim to support. As a direct result of conversations with representatives from the Ministry of Education that year, Kimanya began working with two new target groups: five PSA groups (with a hundred Senior 1 students) at a large, privately run day- and boarding school, and one group at a polytechnic/vocational school. Kimanya decided to provide its own trained tutors in these schools, rather than train existing teachers at each institution. These tutors dedicate their entire attention to the needs of their PSA students, rather than splitting their attention between the requirements of PSA and of other classes at the school.

In addition, Kimanya started groups that had no direct affiliation with a school. Because PSA was initially created by FUNDAEC as an alternative, nonaccredited approach to promoting locally driven community development, Kimanya wanted to support groups of young people (and often some adults) in using the PSA materials regardless of school affiliation or formal accreditation. The next series of tutor trainings in 2009 focused on selecting tutors who would work within specific communities rather than through the support of a given school. In 2009, twenty new tutors were trained and sixteen new groups started.

In 2010, Kimanya's focus shifted from expanding the PSA program to improving the coordination and the overall quality of groups. Through consultation with FUNDAEC and other organizations implementing PSA, Kimanya decided that to more effectively expand the program in the future, they needed to monitor and coordinate a manageable number and distribution of groups rather than attempt a large-scale expansion of the program.

As part of this new strategy, Kimanya is working to improve the quality of its existing coordinators, who are high school graduates. It is also training a cohort of university-educated coordinators. As part of their intensive study, this new cohort of coordinators will simultaneously study the specialization course FUNDAEC offers and work with PSA groups. It is too early to determine if this new strategy will be effective. In the meantime, Kimanya remains confident that a continued effort to make decisions in light of ongoing experience with their groups, tutors, and coordinators provides the most promising strategy to avoid regression or stagnation as an organization.

Impact of PSA in Uganda: Initial Findings

Kimanya is currently working with approximately 350 students. In focus group interviews, the students described a number of areas where PSA has improved their lives, particularly in their ability to communicate in English, their involvement in community life, and their acquisition of agricultural skills. Our interviews offered a first glance at how PSA might work to empower students in other contexts, more specifically in East Africa.

Recognition and Capacity Development

As was the case with Honduran SAT students, several PSA students in Uganda believed they had increased their ability to communicate and think critically. Several participants who spoke about differences between the traditional Ugandan curriculum and PSA said that PSA helped them think, rather than be "spoon-fed" information. Joshua, a young male student, explained:

> In our traditional education, they prefer spoon-feeding, and they like spoon-feeding. But here, before getting any explanation from the tutor, you have to . . . first know something, even if it is wrong or right, but you have to first get something. In our traditional education, the teacher just come in class and just tell you what is inside the book. But here, the tutor can give you a book, you go with a book every day, and you get a chance to know something about what is inside in the book. So, it also develop your reasoning capacity, reading capacity.

Joshua said that in traditional Ugandan secondary schools, students might be able to read well, but they don't necessarily understand what they have read. Speaking of a hypothetical student, he said: "He can't explain what insight [is] in the book. He just know[s] reading, but reasoning, it's a problem."

Joshua's classmate, Charles, agreed with this depiction of the traditional Ugandan schools. In his experience, teachers would ask questions, and if nobody answered they would just write the answer on the board. He explained that this was "hindering our thinking capacity." He said that in PSA, "now we have a chance of thinking. We can read a paragraph and then start to bring out our minds, how we understood this paragraph." In traditional secondary schools, "they were giving us answers, no room for thinking." He said that in PSA he has a chance to express himself.

Richard, a student in a different PSA group, said: "In PSA program, we share different ideas because we sit in a circle. So while in the Ugandan curriculum the teacher just writes notes on the board and we just copy. So by the time you go back home you won't even be having an idea of what you learned." He explained that another difference between PSA and traditional Ugandan schools was the absence of corporeal punishment. "In PSA there is no punishment like in Ugandan curriculum. When you do something, they'll beat you. But in PSA they'll just maybe counsel you, advise you to change."

In their classes, students study the PSA textbooks in English and have the opportunity to speak English with their classmates and tutor. This practice allows them to develop greater English language fluency, which in turn boosts their self-confidence. They recognize that they are not "useless," as two PSA participants said. A forty-year-old participant, Julius, explained how he no longer feels afraid when he communicates his ideas to others.

> Sincerely speaking, me, I left studies, it was roughly in 1984. When you count from '84 up to now, it's a long journey. In fact, some sort of English words have flown away from my knowledge, my head. And expression towards people has become a problem to me. But as we have gone on, I have gone on recovering lost words. The way how to use English has been improved. And I can now stand on myself and express towards the public or the community or any collection of people while having no fear.

In addition to gaining a sense of confidence through the program, Moses admitted to antisocial behavior before his PSA participation, as had Ana and Juanita in Honduras. "Before I joined PSA, I couldn't even say something in public because I was shy. And sometimes I was cruel because I used not to talk to people. I would like just to be alone all the time. But right now, at least I can converse with anyone." Looking at Joseph, he said with a smile: "And I couldn't know that one day I would talk with a *mzungo* [foreigner]."

Julius, like many of the students I interviewed in Honduras, said that practical agricultural skills and capacities were an important benefit of program participation:

> I have found it very interesting because most of my work was to grow crops. I am a farmer. We do things on the garden, but at times we find that we failed to get good crops because of lack of knowledge. But things we do and we study I found them here when studying, that they are the usual things we do at our gardens. But because of lack of reminders, we can fail to get yields from our crops. So, as we have been dealing with this program I have found that I have improved myself on my farms; whatever I do, I use the knowledge in growing crops, finding the good species to apply, and so many good things.

Our initial interviews with PSA students suggest that the experience can be transformative. In addition to concrete agricultural skills, students described a new appreciation of their worth. They improved their communication skills and this improved their self-confidence. Their studies in PSA have allowed them to be more sociable with others, an important first step in becoming more involved in the community. As another PSA participant, Mathieu, explained, his time in PSA has allowed him to grow up: "The change I can see, it is not even *a* change, but changes. Like something grew up in me, about confidence."

Strikingly similar to how Juanita said that SAT "opened her mind," Joshua spoke about the program "expanding his mind." He used the analogy of breastfeeding to describe the differences between PSA and traditional Ugandan education. He explained that PSA doesn't "feed" anyone. This is similar to the "banking" analogy of education that is often used to describe the differences between traditional schools and critical pedagogy. He believed traditional schools "breastfeed," or offer easy, free-flowing facts and require little effort, which students become accustomed to in the way that babies grow fond of (and dependent on) suckling at their mothers' breasts. Other students said that traditional schools use "spoon-feeding." According to Mathieu, unlike traditional schools, in PSA you "develop your capacity":

> Basically I can say everything was fine in this traditional education. But now I can see a difference with it if I tried to compare it with the PSA program, there is a difference there. The first thing is about [*Laughs*], um . . . can I call it breastfeeding? This program of PSA, really it doesn't feed anyone. The other one, we used to just copy notes from the blackboard, you write everything, they give you the answer. Anyway, it is easy but it's blocking your brain. Like, it doesn't expand your mind. I mean, it doesn't build your attitude. But this program, but the way it approaches its education is different. And I like it because you just, you know, you discuss everything. You develop your capacity, your thinking capacity, your reasoning capacity.

In our interview, Betty provided a concrete example of this critical thinking capacity. She explained that, as part of the community service projects her PSA group carried out, she had spoken with her friends and neighbors to find out what they knew about the transmission of malaria. They told her that when you eat a lot of mangos or maize, you get malaria. Also, when you are pregnant, you get malaria. "Scientifically it isn't correct, but if you look deep into what they've said, it's correct. Because during the season of mangoes and maize there is a lot of rubbish, and in this rubbish it increases the breeding places for mosquitoes and so malaria increases."

Betty continued: "Also, when you are pregnant, you are more vulnerable to malaria," demonstrating her understanding that pregnancy reduces a woman's immunity to the disease. Betty does not dismiss local knowledge (that mangos and maize are correlated with malaria), but at the same time she demonstrates the ability to use scientific knowledge to make sense of her local context.

"A Heart of Service": Action toward Self- and Community Improvement in PSA

As is the case in the SAT curriculum, in PSA a capability area of the texts is "service to the community." The texts in this area—*Environmental Issues, Ecosystems*, and *Nurturing Young Minds*—introduce a number of practical service projects that include improving community sanitation, the education of young children, and agricultural practices. Consistent with FUNDAEC's theoretical framework, practical activities are an essential and complementary component of PSA. The texts provide numerous opportunities in the form of assignments for participants and tutors alike to carry out acts of service in the community.

As a result, over the course of completing each textbook, participants in Uganda engage in an assortment of service projects Short-term projects are often the result of consultation with local community leaders and members about immediate needs, for example, cleaning up trash in local neighborhoods, filling potholes in the road and clearing water passages, and even constructing a temporary home for an elderly woman. Service projects of longer duration have more often taken the form of public health campaigns (usually of fixed duration), as well as educational programs for the spiritual and intellectual training of children and youth. From January to June 2010 alone, Kimanya recorded having collaborated with 650 individuals (from communities in each of the four districts where PSA groups are located) on activities ranging from malaria visits to classes for children and gatherings for youths.

A number of students said that these social action projects changed the way they viewed themselves and their potential contribution to the community. For example, Moses explained that before his participation in PSA, he was like a man without any "use." Through his experiences with service projects he has become a recognized community member and now sees himself as a "responsible man": "When serving the community we've become really known by the people. Because for me, I was like a man which doesn't have any use. But right now in my community everyone looks at me as a responsible man. Which, eh, I've got it from PSA."

Charles said that in his community people are motivated by earning money, and rarely out of a desire to improve the community. He believed that his own attitude toward service changed as a result of his experience in PSA.

> Another thing is about service, before I used to think that now if like, if Sara come and tell me that "come and help me somewhere," she has to pay me, she has to pay for that work. But now there's this thing that has grown in me of service. I know that if I do this, I know I'm helping people, I'm helping my community to develop. Because in our communities people like money, pretty much. But if you come and say now, "I'm going to do this," like cleaning the road without paying, then a person, or an understanding person, can say now, "This thing is good." In life, we don't always have to always work for money. But we have to, I can say, sacrifice.

The idea of selfishness came up in several interviews, with students explaining that they were self-centered before their participation in PSA. Charles, for example, described his plan to study in a high school and then get a job so that he could help only his family. He said that "now there is this opportunity whereby I have to help myself, I have to help my family, and also my community." Charles elaborated further that the traditional Ugandan curriculum reinforces a self-centered attitude:

> I can say that maybe in the Ugandan curriculum there is a lot of self-satisfaction. Because a person grows when he knows that I have to do this, and help this, I have to have money. But now at least, a person can grow. Though it's not bad to have money, but you have to help your community. I mean, I have money, I have to go like, there is these orphans, I have to help them. But many people here, if he has money, he doesn't care about other people. He cares about himself or he cares about his family. And that's not good, and here in Kimanya there is no that.

Tutors also have worked with students to identify potential income-generating projects. One tutor, Mohamed, recounted that part of the difficulty of implementing PSA is that it is very different from what people in his village are used to in terms of development initiatives. Rather than giving out material goods, Kimanya is attempting, metaphorically, to teach people how to fish.

We have this problem of poverty being really rampant among most of us in the communities where we come from. Most of these agencies, when they come, like I've said, they always come and just dish out things. No education, no nothing—[just] cash and maybe some things to start with like cows or goats. And this is not something that [Kimanya] does. Why? Because it has its own way. It already, I don't know, assessed and saw that maybe one of the reasons the other organizations haven't been effective, mostly, with helping the problems most people are facing in our communities, is [that they] just [give] out anything they have. So it decided to offer education, maybe. But it could not stop at just giving education. Because really, like I said, teaching someone how to fish is really important.

Kimanya has learned through experience that, for many participants, involvement in PSA is not simply a means to intellectual and practical training to be shared within the community; it is also a means by which individuals intend to support and improve the lives of their families. As a result, efforts in this area have aimed to encourage a balance between preparation for individual and community benefit. Chief among its concerns in designing such projects, however, is that proposed activities be carried out in a fashion still conforming to the overall pedagogy and philosophy of PSA.

For example, one opportunity for income generation, in light of the themes covered in the PSA curriculum, is agricultural production. As an extension of the practical components involved in such texts as *Planting Crops* and *High-Efficiency Diversified Plots*, Kimanya has made an effort to provide additional training opportunities to PSA groups by hiring experienced farmers to meet with participants and share local methods and experiences. Additionally, Kimanya has supported various PSA groups in efforts to acquire a diversity of seeds needed to sustain locally designed projects. In doing so, Kimanya has seen PSA groups use practical activities as opportunities not only to benefit their learning, but also to generate income if they sell their crops. Many of these exercises also serve as opportunities to engage outside community members in collective learning.

Beyond agricultural projects, Kimanya has funded other local entrepreneurs to offer training to PSA groups in their areas of expertise. One individual provided training to PSA groups in the Mukono district on how to raise chickens and how to prepare fresh jam. Kimanya makes a conscious effort to maintain the delicate balance between supporting these income-generating projects and making sure they reinforce learning from the textbooks, and equally important, that their aims neither distract from nor contradict the underlying goals of PSA.

"PSA Is the Type of Education That Uganda Really Needs to Go Ahead and Develop"

Betty, the PSA student whose story we shared earlier, believed that PSA is "the type of education that Uganda really needs to go ahead and develop." While PSA has been operating in Uganda for close to five years, there are already signs that it can open the minds and improve the lives of participants. Although we did not engage in extensive data collection, nor did we focus specifically on gender relations, the initial interviews and focus groups we conducted make us optimistic that PSA is a viable model for the East African context. Students' testimonies about their experiences in the program are consistent with the notion of empowerment as a process of recognition, capacity development, and action. Time and research are needed to more fully determine the ways in which PSA is a viable model for the East African region.

We expect that it will take time, as it did for SAT in Honduras, for PSA to grow from a small, grassroots initiative working in one region of the country to a large, nationally accredited program. We expect that Kimanya too will face resistance from traditional secondary school teachers and other educational authorities who have a vested interest in maintaining the status quo. The strategy that Kimanya is using to identify the challenges of recruiting and training students and tutors, as well as to determine which model will be most effective in Uganda, rather than expanding too quickly seems like an informed and careful approach. In Honduras it took roughly ten years for the program to expand. With each change in government (at the departmental and municipal levels), the program confronts resistance. It also struggles to find funding from donors to maintain operations. While PSA and SAT show great potential as tools to empower youths and adults to improve their lives and their communities, change is never easy. It will require the sustained efforts of individuals and institutions.

APPENDIX

Examples from SAT/PSA Textbooks

The lessons in this Appendix come from two SAT textbooks that have been translated into English for use in the PSA program in Africa (in Honduras and other Latin American countries, the students study these texts in Spanish).

The first two lessons, "The Gastrointestinal System" and "The Nervous System," are extracted from a language textbook entitled *Primary Elements of Descriptions: Systems and Processes*. This book follows in sequence a book called *Elements of Descriptions*. Each SAT text begins with a "To the tutor" section that explains the main goals of the lessons. In the note to the tutor at the beginning of the *Systems and Processes* text, the authors explain the main goals:

> In order for individuals to act in the world with efficacy and promote constructive change, they must be capable of perceiving the reality around them and describing it at higher and higher levels of sophistication. The two units that make up the text *Primary Elements of Descriptions* were designed with this in mind. Together they seek to develop in the students the capabilities required to describe the world they see and experience with increasing clarity. . . . The present unit builds on this understanding to introduce words and concepts needed to speak about the many processes that continually unfold in the world and the systems in which they occur.

The next two lessons, "Addition and Subtraction" and "Values and Ethics in Business," are extracted from the third book of a sequence titled *Basic Arithmetic*. In the note to the tutor, the goals are described as:

> This ["Addition and Subtraction"] and the next unit, "Multiplication and Division," are dedicated to the twofold capability of performing the four

arithmetical operations quickly and accurately and applying them to real-life situations. . . . Emphasis is placed on clarifying concepts, on developing skills and, above all, on the application of knowledge. . . . The latter lessons offer an overview of the principles of accounting. . . . Apart from the opportunity this affords to show participants one immediate application of what they have studied, the discussion and exercises in these lessons make it possible to seamlessly weave elements of knowledge about social and spiritual reality into the course content. Individual initiative, honesty and truthfulness, transparency and accountability—these are examples of issues raised throughout the lessons and addressed explicitly in the last one.

The lessons included here illustrate some of the main features of the SAT curriculum, including:

- an interdisciplinary approach
- the explicit discussion of spiritual principles and values, with an emphasis on justice
- an attempt to link academic content with the practical application of knowledge to improve individual and community well-being
- use of informal language ("imagine you are eating an apple") to draw out what students already know, or generate local-level knowledge
- gender equality as an explicit component of the curriculum
- emphasis on critical thinking, discussion, and debate

13 The Gastrointestinal System

Imagine you are eating an apple. What would have to happen to the apple so that, ultimately, the cells of the body can use its nutrients to carry out their functions? It has to be broken down into its very small building blocks, does it not?

When you first pick up the apple, it is whole and hard, and you cannot fit it all in your mouth, let alone swallow it. So the first thing you do is to take a bite and chew it. The mouth is the first component of the gastrointestinal tract, in which begins the process of breaking down food into smaller and smaller pieces.

Once the pieces of apple are small enough, you swallow them, sending them through the esophagus into the stomach. There the apple stays for a while to be broken down further and further. The stomach produces a substance called *hydrochloric acid* that works on the apple and dissolves it. There are also other substances called *enzymes* that are produced in other parts of the body and sent to the stomach to help break down food. By the end of this process, the apple you ate is part of a liquid that can now pass to the small intestine.

In between the stomach and the small intestine there is the *pyloric sphincter*. The sphincter is like a valve. There are muscles all along the gastrointestinal tract constantly pushing the food downward. This downward push causes the valve to open. Each time the sphincter opens, it allows a very small amount of the liquid in the stomach to pass into the small intestine. The process of breaking down the apple into its small building blocks continues as the liquid goes down the small intestine. The resulting small particles are picked up by the capillaries in the walls of the intestine, and constitute the nutrients that the blood takes to the cells of the body.

What we have seen up to now seems to indicate that the gastrointestinal tract has at least two major parts. The main function of the first, beginning with the mouth and ending in the stomach, is to break down food into small building blocks. The main function of the second, consisting of the *small intestine*, is to allow for the absorption of nutrients by the blood stream. But there is also a third major portion, called the *large intestine*. Not all the apple you ate can be absorbed through the capillaries. There are certain building blocks, mostly those called *fibers*, that must go through the tract and finally be eliminated. Elimination is the primary function performed by this third part of the gastrointestinal tract.

With this brief description of the process of digestion in mind, you should now look carefully at the following sketch of the gastrointestinal system, and think about the structure and functions of each of its components.

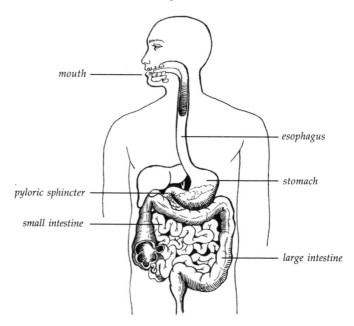

mouth

esophagus

stomach

pyloric sphincter

small intestine

large intestine

■ **Extension**

1. We have said that food is broken down into its building blocks in order to enter into the blood. You have probably heard often of three essential components of food we eat, namely, protein, fat, and carbohydrates. Do you know what the smallest building blocks of each of these are? The building blocks of protein are amino acids, and of fat, fatty acids. Carbohydrates come in two forms: simple carbohydrates or sugars, and complex carbohydrates or starches. The basic building blocks of both simple and complex carbohydrates are the same: units of the sugar glucose. These units combine in many ways to produce different kinds of simple and complex carbohydrates. Other substances that are absorbed into the blood are vitamins and minerals, and, of course, water.

2. Where do digestive enzymes come from? Look at the diagram below which shows the pancreas and a tube that connects it to the small intestine. Enzymes needed for breaking down carbohydrates and proteins are produced in the pancreas and from there are delivered to the small intestine. The substance needed for the digestion and absorption of fat is called *bile*, and is stored in the gall bladder near the liver.

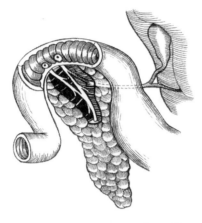

3. Look carefully at the sketch below that shows finger like projections in the wall of the small intestine. These are called *villi*, and are full of capillaries through which absorption of nutrients takes place. What would happen if these projections did not exist, and the wall of the intestine was smooth? How many capillaries would then come in contact with food?

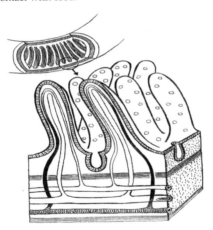

The Gastrointestinal System   77

4. We have said that the main function of the first part of the gastrointestinal tract is to break down food, and that the second part is in charge of absorption. But do you think any nutrients get absorbed in the stomach or even in the mouth? Can you think of any evidence to support your answer?

_____

_____

_____

_____

5. You have surely noticed that after eating some foods you soon get hungry, while other foods satisfy hunger for a longer time. Order the following foods according to how long they keep you from getting hungry.

   vegetables, meat, pasta, fruit, lentils, rice, cheese, yogurt, butter, bread

_____

_____

_____

Generally, carbohydrates are digested more or less quickly, usually within about two hours; protein takes about three to four hours to be digested; and fat takes the longest of all. Can you see a relationship between this information about digestion and the way in which you have ordered the foods listed above?

6. Here are some words you may have heard that indicate problems of the gastrointestinal system. Match each one with one of the short descriptions that follow the list.

   a. Dental caries   d. Peptic ulcers   g. Constipation

   b. Mouth ulcers   e. Gallstones   h. Diarrhea

   c. Esophageal reflux   f. Pancreatic cancer   i. Hemorrhoids

   _____ Cancerous growth in the long gland that lies behind the stomach and manufactures insulin and digestive enzymes

   _____ Erosions of the lining of the stomach or the first part of the small intestine

   _____ The inability to pass bowel movements easily

   _____ Sores or open lesions in the mouth

   _____ Enlarged, swollen, often painful veins in the anal area

   _____ Holes that damage the structure of the teeth caused by plaque that dissolves tooth enamel

_____ Frequent, watery bowel movements, often accompanied by stomach pain

_____ Sudden return of stomach contents into the esophagus

_____ Hard lumps produced by the hardening of mineral salts, formed in the gall bladder or biliary passages

■ Reflections on Internalizing Ideas

Our digestive system is in charge of taking in food and converting it to a form that can be absorbed by the cells of our body. This is an entirely physical process over which we have little control once we have swallowed the food. In the world of thought, our mind does something similar to digestion. It receives ideas and works with them. Some it keeps and makes its own. Others it rejects and tries to forget. Think of one of your convictions, for example, your belief in the equality of men and women. Do you remember when you first encountered this idea? Were you convinced of its truth immediately? Can you describe what you thought and did until it became part of your system of beliefs?

14 The Nervous System

All of you have, at one point or another, hit a nerve in your elbow. Can you describe the sensation? What you felt was caused by the transmission of a nervous impulse, much like an electrical current. This impulse traveled through peripheral nerves to the spinal cord, and then to the brain. Peripheral nerves run throughout the body and are in charge of transmitting the stimuli they receive as the body interacts with things outside.

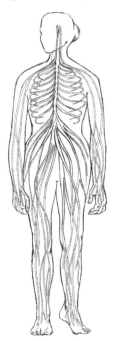
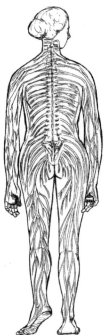

81

This process can be illustrated by the following diagram:

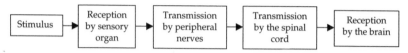

The "sensory organ" in the second box of the above diagram refers to the sense of touch. The sense of touch is spread all over the body and allows every part of the body to act as a sensory organ, receiving messages to be transmitted to the brain.

The other senses—sight, hearing, taste, and smell—function through relatively small organs of the head: the eyes, the ears, the tongue, and the nose. These organs send the messages they receive from the outside world to the brain through another set of nerves called cranial nerves. Messages received by the sense of touch on the face also go through the cranial nerves. The following diagram illustrates such a process:

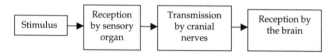

The process we have described up to this point is the reception of information from the world around us and its transmission to the brain. The information we receive through the eyes, for example, can be the shape, the size, or the color of something. This information is carried by the light that comes from the object causing the eyes to form an image of it. How is information received by the senses of hearing, smell, and taste?

Once information is received by the brain it must be processed. How does the brain process information? For one thing, it compares it to the information it already holds. Think of yourself, for example, walking around a room in the dark. Your hands touch various objects and the peripheral nerves send the corresponding information to the brain. Your brain already has information about the position of the objects in the room from previous occasions when the light was on. Also, over the years, your brain has accumulated information about how different things feel to the touch. By comparing all this information, it can figure out where you are with respect to the objects, even in the absence of visual stimuli. But how does this processing of information allow you to walk? Messages are formulated in the brain, transmitted through the spinal cord to peripheral nerves, and finally to the muscles of your legs, ordering them to move in certain ways. Here is a diagram illustrating this process:

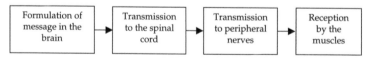

The diagram below illustrates the entire process of receiving a message and responding to it. What do you think the word *effectors* in the box before the last means?

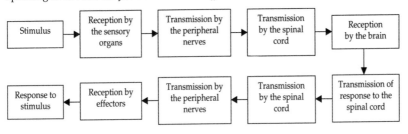

▮ Extension

1. Look carefully at the following sketches of nerve cells. Can you think of how their shape is related to their function?

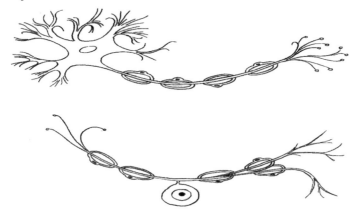

2. Take two sharp pins or needles, and simultaneously prick the back of a friend with both pins without hurting him. Keep bringing the points closer to each other until they join. Each time that the needles come closer to one another, ask your friend how many pricks he feels. Describe what happens.

3. We have said that when the brain receives a message, it processes it. What do you understand by the word *processing*? Is there more to it than comparing it with the information held in memory? What goes into the formulation of a new message? Do you always decide to do something once your brain has received a message? What is the meaning of the word *will*? How is it mustered?

4. The formulation of a message in the brain that leads to some kind of action is not automatic. Different people will act differently in response to the same message. One example of a life-long process that trains people to act in specific ways is education. Do you think education actually has a physical effect on the nervous system? Does it do something to the cells of the nervous system of the person being educated?

5. Draw similar diagrams using boxes and arrows as we have done in the body of the lesson but now for a specific stimulus and the response that follows:

   a. Your hand touches something hot and you quickly pull it back.

   b. You hear a strange sound.

   c. You hear a beautiful poem that touches your heart.

   d. You hear a very funny statement.

   e. You hear a melody and follow the rhythm with your feet.

   f. You enter the kitchen, smell food cooking, and decide to eat.

   g. You are engaged in carrying out this exercise.

   h. You reflect on some of the problems of your community and decide to work harder to build unity.

6. The first example in the previous exercise belongs to a category of acts so rapid that it has been given its own name: *reflex*. The goal-keeper of a soccer team cannot give himself the luxury of thinking about which side the ball will go to; he has developed certain reflexes which enable him to act quickly in such situations. A very important function of reflexes is to help protect us by enabling us to act quickly when faced with danger. Are we born with reflexes or do we develop them through experience?

Reflections on the Flow of Information in a Community

In this lesson, a number of very basic but highly important ideas have been presented to you, all related to the way a person receives, processes and responds to information. There are, of course, thousands of questions that we have not considered about this complex subject. We should remember, however, that information is a subject that needs to be studied not only from the point of view of the individual human being, but also in the context of the community and of society as a whole. The way information is produced and propagated is one of the strongest factors determining how the world will develop in the crucial years ahead. As a promoter of community well-being, therefore, you will have to be well aware of the flow of information in the communities you serve. This is a matter that we will have to address in future courses, but we take the opportunity now to ask you to carry out a simple exercise.

First, identify in your group as many channels as you can through which information flows into your community. Give examples of the kinds of information that each channel carries. Next, choose two or three instances in which important information reached your community recently through one or more of these means and try to describe in some detail what happened to it. The type of questions you will wish to address include: How was the information received? How was it propagated? To approximately how many? Did some people in your community make decisions based on the information they received? How? Did receiving this information and the subsequent decisions lead to some community action?

 Inequalities

The knowledge we have acquired of addition, subtraction, and simple equations allows us to work with mathematical expressions that involve inequalities. Consider the expression 16 < 20. What makes us say that 16 is less than 20? How much must be added to the number 16 to make it equal 20? Similarly, what can we say about the expression 30 > 25? Why is 30 greater than 25? How much should we take away from 30 to be left with 25?

Analyze the following inequalities, explaining in each case why one of the numbers is greater than or less than the other:

$$7 < 10$$
$$21 > 15$$
$$11 < 38$$

Single numbers are not the only mathematical entities we can compare with each other. Sometimes we have to compare more complicated numerical expressions. In order to do so, we need to explore a few of the properties of inequalities. You are going to discover the first of these properties by doing a short exercise. Decide whether or not the following expressions are valid:

$3 < 50$	T ☐	F ☐
$3 + 10 < 50 + 10$	T ☐	F ☐
$12 < 22$	T ☐	F ☐
$12 + 4 < 22 + 4$	T ☐	F ☐
$18 > 9$	T ☐	F ☐
$18 + 5 > 9 + 5$	T ☐	F ☐
$19 > 25$	T ☐	F ☐
$19 + 8 > 25 + 8$	T ☐	F ☐

43

How did you decide on your answer to each case above? Did you perform the calculations? Look again at the exercise and then consider this question: What happens when both sides of an inequality increase by the same amount? Does the inequality sign change, or remain the same? Is it correct, then, to say that an inequality is conserved, when we add the same number to both sides? Complete the sentence below.

If the same amount is _____ to both sides of an inequality, the inequality is _____.

Without performing the addition, complete the inequalities below with the sign > or <, as appropriate.

$$14 + 12 \qquad 15 + 12$$

$$14 + 12 + 8 \qquad 15 + 12 + 8$$

$$30 + 5 \qquad 20 + 5$$

$$30 + 5 + 9 \qquad 20 + 5 + 9$$

$$35 + 12 + 4 \qquad 35 + 12 + 8$$

$$70 + 5 + 120 \qquad 70 + 1 + 120$$

$$18 + 7 + 20 \qquad 7 + 18 + 10$$

The second property we ask you to consider is very similar to the previous one. What happens if we subtract the same amount from both sides of an inequality? Will the inequality be conserved? Think of some examples to help you answer this question, and then fill in the blanks in the following sentence:

If the same amount is _____ from both sides of an inequality, the inequality is _____.

Now, without subtracting, complete the inequalities below with the sign > or <, as appropriate.

$$7 - 5 \qquad 8 - 5$$

$$742 - 20 \qquad 520 - 20$$

$$948 - 80 \qquad 500 - 80$$

$$745 - 20 - 5 \qquad 400 - 20 - 5$$

$$1240 - 58 - 75 \qquad 1000 - 58 - 75$$

The properties of inequalities we have just studied enable us to answer an important question. Suppose you are given the expression

$$b + 8 < 8 + 15,$$

in which the letter b represents any number. What are the values of b that make the expression valid? We can answer this question immediately by remembering one of the above properties. We know that an inequality is maintained if we add the same number to or remove it from both sides. So we can subtract 8 from both sides of this expression to obtain

$$b < 15.$$

The original expression is valid, therefore, if b takes on any value less than 15. In the following exercise, find the range of values of the number represented by a letter that makes each inequality valid:

a. If $a + 5 < 20 + 5$ then $a < 20$

b. If $70 + 15 < 70 + b$ then $b > 15$

c. If $1.45 + x > 20 + 1.45$ then _____

d. If $25 + m > 13 + 25$ then _____

e. If $0.88 + m < 0.88 + 2.93$ then _____

f. If $y - 45 < 78 - 45$ then _____

g. If $z + 30 > 80 + 30$ then _____

h. If $5.5 + 80 < 5.5 + x$ then _____

i. If $18 + 35 > 18 + b$ then _____

j. If $80 - 75 < c - 75$ then _____

Now examine the inequality

$$a + 8 < b + 8.$$

What can you say about a and b? Could you say that $a < b$? Write down the relation that exists between the two numbers represented by letters in the following inequalities, as shown in the first example:

a. $7 + c < d + 7$ $c < d$

b. $15 + d > 15 + x$ _____

c. $x + 25 < y + 25$ _____

d. $z + 18 < 18 + t$ _____

e. $z - 2.7 > y - 2.7$ _____

Inequalities   45

■ Extension

Equations and inequalities allow us to make detailed numerical statements about the world. Many of these statements contain letters that represent numbers. You have already been working with equations of this type, but you are now asked to think further about what these letters represent.

The letters that appear in equations or inequalities are sometimes called *variables*. An equation or inequality may contain one variable, two variables, or more. Variables may stand for any number, but sometimes they can only take on certain values. For example, in the expression $y < 20$, the variable y is restricted to all the numbers that are less than 20.

Suppose we define the letter a as follows:

$$a = \text{the age of a child in school.}$$

What are the different numerical values that a can take on? If you live in a place where children attend school from the age of 5 until they are 18, for example, the letter a would be any number between 5 and 18. This can be expressed mathematically as

$$5 \leq a \leq 18,$$

where the symbol $\leq$ means "is less than or equal to". The entire expression, therefore, is read "a is greater than or equal to 5 and less than or equal to 18."

Now consider a slightly different case. We will define

$$a + b = 10,$$

where a and b are whole numbers. What are the possible different values that a and b can take on? If a has a value of 1, what must be the value of b? What if a has a value of 2? Or 3? Write out all the possible values of a and b in the space below, restricting a and b to positive integers.

In each of the following cases, write out all the possible values that the variables can take on, again confining the variables to positive integers:

a. $a + b = 6$ _____

b. $c + b = 9$ _____

c. $8 - a = b$ _____

d. $a + b + c = 4$ _____

Reflections on the Concepts of Equality and Inequality

The words *equality* and *inequality* are not used in mathematics only. We often use them to speak of human beings and society as well. We say, for example, that there should be equal employment opportunities for people, independent of their race or ethnic origins, or that today's vast inequalities between the rich and the poor should be eliminated. We do not imagine, of course, that human beings should be equal to one another in every way. We find physical differences to be quite natural and easily accept that people have diverse talents and capacities. But when inequalities are the result of injustice, we feel something is wrong. We do not mind when one family in a village owns ten hectares of land and another seven, but we are enraged when we see a few landowners possessing hundreds of hectares each, while the majority of the villagers do not have a piece of land large enough to earn a decent living. Try to think of some inequalities that are acceptable and others that you consider unjust.

Inequalities   47

14 Values and Ethics in Business

In this unit we explored concepts and developed skills related to the operations of addition and subtraction. We then studied simple accounting practices as a means of applying these concepts and skills. Some knowledge of accounting will help us succeed if we want to run a small enterprise. It also enables us to be better employees if we work for someone else. And, of course, it is an important tool in our efforts to assist others in their productive endeavors.

Obviously, a business needs to be profitable, otherwise it would not be worth maintaining. But is profit the only measure of success? How would you feel if, after running your business for 30 years and making a considerable profit, you realized that what you produced did not contribute in any significant way to your community's well-being? On the other hand, how would you feel if you were part of a small business that enabled you to lead a reasonably prosperous life and at the same time benefit your friends, neighbors, and the community at large? Think about a few businesses in your microregion that, while a source of work and economic security to those who run them, are of service the community. What qualities or conditions contribute to making a business of this kind?

_____

_____

_____

_____

How are we to determine whether or not a certain type of work contributes to the well-being of humanity? Some kinds of work are obviously beneficial to the individual and society, and others are clearly detrimental. But it is not always easy to ensure that one's work brings benefit to others. In order to clarify some of the issues, discuss with your group whether or not each of the following activities contributes to the well-being of society, and, if so, how:

- Making and selling soymilk and bread made of soy flour

- Growing and selling organic produce to one's neighbors

- Selling one's body

- Selling slices of fruit to passengers on buses and to schoolchildren during recess

- Working for an advertising company that specializes in selling products using scantily clad women as models

- Working as a street vendor selling cheap household gadgets such as clothespins, hangers, barrettes, earrings, and so on. Although these items may break easily, they are inexpensive enough for everyone to afford

- Reading horoscopes and tarot cards in order to help people know and plan for their futures

- Selling lottery tickets

- Opening a family restaurant that prepares healthy, inexpensive meals for the day laborers in town

- Working as a live-in maid for a family and taking care of their children

- Getting paid well to help a politician distribute flyers with campaign promises of greater health and educational benefits that you are sure the politician will not keep

- Selling cans of beer, water, and soda at the stadium, where the prices can be raised because of the high demand

- Using your truck to transport a box of goods for your friend. The contents of the box, he says, are "better left unknown". The pay is good and your friend says it can be a regular job if you play by the rules.

- Digging wells using appropriate technology so as to provide neighbors with drinkable water

- Opening a bike repair shop

- Raising chickens, pigs, and cattle to sell at the local market

- Opening a village store with all sorts of food and household products that are bought in bulk in the city and sold at an affordable price. The frozen chicken and produce you sell is cheaper than those sold fresh by the farmers in the village itself

- Opening a video rental store, with a room that has video games for children to play

- Selling guns

- Making and selling kites

- Making and selling fireworks

- Opening a small daycare center that, although not very lucrative, offers parents an opportunity to work outside of their homes

- Opening a beauty salon

- Opening a discotheque and bar to give the local youth a place to go in the evenings

- Giving music lessons

- Offering workshops on how to make a lot of money in a very short time

It is not enough, of course, to simply choose a type of work that improves the community's well-being. The way we behave and the qualities we possess give meaning to our work, enabling it to truly benefit humanity. One very important attribute we must have is a spirit of service. When we have a spirit of service, our work does not feel like a chore. It is easier to overcome the difficulties that arise from time to time. Maintaining a spirit of service also fuels our enthusiasm and brings joy to whatever task needs to be done. Let us explore this idea a bit further by doing an exercise.

For each of the following cases, think about the extent to which the actions of the person demonstrate a spirit of service. If applicable, indicate how a greater spirit of service would have made each person act differently.

a. Martha owns the town's pharmacy. One morning at two o'clock, a neighbor comes over to buy medicine that he needs urgently, and Martha arises reluctantly to respond to him. The neighbor thanks her most graciously but feels very embarrassed, because she is grumpy.

b. Cesar sells shoes in the marketplace. For each pair of shoes he sells, he earns a commission of ten percent. One Saturday afternoon, a woman comes over with her two children and stops in front of his stand. The children are beaming, and Cesar knows that they are buying shoes to wear to school, which begins the following week. He notices that this family does not have too much money to spend but he treats them very kindly. Just then, a rich-looking customer comes in, who is bound to buy more expensive shoes. Cesar tells the woman to wait and begins helping the new customer.

c. Susana has assisted her father in his carpentry shop for years and is now able to take on a few jobs of her own. As she is still learning, she only charges for the cost of materials and a little extra for her time. However, when she realizes that the Sanchez family cannot pay her normal price for building a chicken coop, she decides to give them a special discount and allows them to pay her in installments, as she knows they are honest and are going through hard times.

d. Claudia works in a fabrics store and earns a fixed salary. When a customer comes in, she tries to show her whatever cloth is closest to the register, and does not volunteer much information about any fabric that is out of reach. Unless asked for a specific cloth, she resists going to the second floor, as she dislikes walking up and down the stairs.

e. Edmundo is a witty orange seller at the Saturday market. He makes everyone laugh with his advertising cries, "It's not my fault that I have the best!" and "They look like basketballs but they really are oranges!" He always carries a smile and is often seen giving away an orange or two to a few needy people. Nevertheless, when some of the wealthier townspeople visit the market, he raises his prices and tries to pass off a couple of over-ripe oranges to them as well.

f. Mr. Spencer has taught mathematics for twenty years at the local secondary school. He still teaches the same lessons from an old textbook he owned when he first started teaching. He has his students copy the lessons down in their notebooks and do the exercises at the end of each chapter. A number of students enjoy the fact that he never assigns homework, for he says, "Everything they need to know, they learn in class." At the end of one school day, a student asks Mr. Spencer if he can explain a concept in the textbook to her. He replies that her question has to wait until the next day because school is now over.

g. Cecilia teaches science at the same school as Mr. Spencer. She has not been teaching there for very long, but she is well known and well liked by the staff and students. She assigns meaningful homework frequently, even though this requires her to spend extra time reviewing and grading the assignments. She is often seen after school preparing for the next day's science experiment.

h. Sam owns a small store in town that sells knick-knacks. He seems to lead a double life. When he is in his shop, he is always smiling and he greets everyone with a warm and hearty, "How can I help you?" as they enter his store. But outside his store he is short-tempered and almost unpleasant. His neighbors like going to his shop, but sometimes they wonder why he behaves so differently outside of its walls.

i. Angela and her husband John have a child who is very ill, and they travel with him to the city each week so that he can receive treatment. A few months ago they opened a bar to supplement their income and pay for the costs of their child's treatment. They did not expect the success that came. Every night the bar is packed with people who are drinking, dancing, and playing pool and cards. The townsfolk say they like their bar because Angela and John treat them like family, listening to their troubles, giving advice, and always serving the drinks with respect and great care.

Through your analysis of the above situations, you have certainly discovered that a spirit of service is an internal condition of the individual and that it is developed by acquiring certain virtues and spiritual qualities. Honesty, for example, brings genuineness and sincerity to one's spirit of service. Having love towards others means that one serves out of a sense of love and respect, not just because service is socially acceptable. Justice and equity ensure that one is considerate towards others. Detachment from praise and criticism helps one labor with constant joy. What other qualities are essential to the development of a spirit of service?

_____

_____

_____

What we are emphasizing in this lesson is the importance of choosing an occupation that is beneficial to society and of showing forth a spirit of service in one's daily work. A word we use in relation to these two concepts is *ethics*. To be ethical means to live according to a certain set of standards. In the context of one's work, we believe, this means answering at least two questions. One is whether the type of enterprise we want to join or initiate is ethical, and the other is whether our behavior within an enterprise is ethical. Making such a judgment requires that we adhere to certain standards. A question that often arises is, Whose standards do we follow? Is it enough to say that our actions are in agreement with what others around us do? Should our standards come from society or should they come from a higher source or spiritual authority? Clearly, only when we look to spiritual principles do we find true guidance on how to act in an ethical way. At times, certain practices are accepted in society that go against a person's principles. For example, it is possible that the selling of alcohol to adults is socially acceptable, but if you believe liquor to be detrimental to the individual and society, this practice would go against your principles. Or it is possible that among shopkeepers it is acceptable to slightly manipulate the scale that is used to weigh the goods, because this goes unnoticed by most and does not really hurt anyone. But for a person who strives for absolute honesty this would not be an acceptable practice.

Decide whether the following practices are generally accepted in society. If so, think about whether or not they would be acceptable for someone who lives according to high spiritual principles. In each case, explain which is the relevant principle.

- A person working at an ice cream shop sells the shop's secret recipe to the competitors across town. By doing this he will make a little money, and his friends working at the other store will also benefit.

- A storekeeper gives back less change than he should to children and people who cannot calculate well, because they will never notice the slight difference.

- Even though the flowers and farm vegetables are a few days old, the woman at the produce stand insists on calling them "just picked", because she knows that nobody will buy them if she tells the truth. All the other sellers claim that theirs, too, are "fresh", so she feels justified in her actions.

- In its advertisements, a company shows its sandwiches overflowing with vegetables, cheese, and meats, even though this picture does not resemble the product for sale at all.

- A painter in town offers price estimates for painting people's houses by always starting with a high bid. This way, if a client does not like his price, he can bargain down to an amount that is reasonable for both of them.

- Another painter runs a quality painting business and is well known in town for his honesty. When he is asked for an estimate, he gives his customers a fair price, and they know that he does not play the negotiating game.

- A person is filing his taxes for his small construction business, and he slightly manipulates the figures under the "income" column so as to reduce his tax burden, especially since this year has been difficult for him.

- When the corner store fills up with lots of customers, the storeowner always helps the clients with the largest orders first, because he does not want to lose his highest paying customers by making them wait. Children who want to buy sweets do not have anything else to do anyway.

- The man who runs the village bakery ensures that his customers are always treated well. He requires his employees to wait on people in the order they come in, even if it looks like some of them are not planning on buying anything.

- A person who has many regular customers for her yogurt business decides to water down the product in order to reduce her production costs. This will help her pay off her start-up loan more quickly.

- A teacher at the local primary school likes all of his students but he cannot help preferring two students who are his "favorites". When they do poorly on an exam, he still gives them good grades but provides them with extra help in class so they do not make the same mistake next time.

- A worker is paid a fixed wage per day to sew shirts. He and his friends sew slowly on purpose because, after all, he will still receive the same pay, and his boss is mean to him anyway.

- A weaver sells her rugs and tapestries each weekend at the open-air market. She always takes great care with each piece and makes it to the best of her ability, even though her extra care does not bring her more profits.

Let us now summarize what we have said. Whether we run our own business or work for someone else, we should strive to contribute to the well-being of humanity. But this alone is not enough. Our work must be governed by the spirit of service. To contribute to the well-being of humanity and work with a spirit of service, we need a set of ethical standards. In choosing these standards we should avoid simply doing what society says is acceptable. Our ethical standards should be based on spiritual principles, and we should have the courage to uphold them, no matter how strong the pressures of the society around us to do otherwise.

Notes

Introduction

1. *mykodak.blogspot.com/2008/04/i-am-powerful.html*. Retrieved 17 July 2011.
2. *www.un.org/millenniumgoals/gender.shtml*. Retrieved 17 July 2011.
3. Child care in this context includes dishwashing, cleaning dwelling, laundry, ironing, other household upkeep, physical care of children, teaching, playing, and other child care (UNDP 2007).
4. These include the Bill and Melinda Gates Foundation, William and Flora Hewlett Foundation, Rockefeller Foundation, Ford Foundation, Inter-American Development Bank, Department for International Development (UK), Canadian International Development Association, and Irish Aid Agency.
5. The Bahá'í faith is an independent world religion founded in the mid-nineteenth century by a young Persian, Mirza-Husayn-'Ali, known by the name Bahá'u'lláh. The Bahá'í teachings include the full equality of men and women, the elimination of the extremes of wealth and poverty, the harmony of science and religion, and the need for universal education. The religion's most central teachings revolve around the promotion of unity and justice in the context of increasing global interdependence (Karlberg 2005). For overviews of the Bahá'í teachings, see Peter Smith, *The Bábí and Bahá'í Religions: From Messianic Shi'ism to a World Religion* (Cambridge: Cambridge University Press, 1987). The official website of the International Bahá'í community is *www.bahai.org*.

Chapter 1

1. Here my use of the term "recognition" differs from its usage in recent debates over the "politics of recognition" and the role of identity in political mobilization. For an overview of this debate see Alcoff 2007.
2. I conducted one interview by phone and the rest in person. I digitally recorded thirteen of these interviews and transcribed relevant portions for analysis.

Chapter 2

1. Much of the information about FUNDAEC's conceptual framework in this chapter comes from one of the participants in this initiative, Dr. Farzam Arbab, in a publication by IDRC in conjunction with this effort (Harper 2000).
2. The original group included Alberto Alzate, Gustavo Correa, Edmundo

Gutierrez, Martin Prager, and Francia de Valcárcel. Over the years, other key individuals working with FUNDAEC have included Haleh Arbab and Carmen Inez de Gamboa.

3. The specialization program is post-baccalaureate. In terms of educational degrees, it would lie somewhere between a BA and an MA.

4. *www.fundaec.org/en/programs/cubr/index.htm.*

5. In July 2004, I participated in a seminar sponsored by FUNDAEC (hosted in Toronto) to study this module of the specialization program.

6. See Henry Giroux and Anthony Penna, "Social Education in the Classroom: The Dynamics of the Hidden Curriculum," in *The Hidden Curriculum and Moral Education*, ed. Henry Giroux and Julius Purpel (Berkeley, CA: McCutchan, 1983), 100–121.

7. Most participants in Colombia and Honduras are Catholic or Protestant. While SAT's spiritual perspective was not the explicit subject of my research, my conversations with students and tutors suggest that participants appreciate it and find that it does not conflict with their religious beliefs.

8. Several examples of lessons from these textbooks are included in the Appendix. These lessons are in English because the program now operates in several countries in Africa, including Kenya, Zambia, and Uganda, where English is the official language of instruction. In Honduras and other Latin American countries student textbooks are in Spanish.

9. Claudia Uribe, personal communication, 2 March 2011.

10. As of this writing, Patrick McEwan, an economist at Wellesley College, and I are leading a comprehensive evaluation of SAT in Honduras. Our study measures student performance on assessments in language and mathematics as well as a number of other outcomes of interest, including their civic engagement, their trust in the community, the classroom climate, and altruism.

Chapter 3

1. Estimates vary widely and Honduran census data for this region is often criticized for being unreliable.

2. In much of the literature, the terms "black Carib" and "Garifuna" are used interchangeably. "Garifuna" is the term the Garifuna use to refer to themselves, and therefore the term I use here.

3. Several participants explained that because legal marriage involves a monetary fee, couples often cohabitate without legally marrying. I use the terms "husband," "wife," and "partner" interchangeably.

4. The Mexican welfare program Oportunidades (formerly PROGRESA) gave welfare subsidies directly to women, arguing that "women are generally the ones who make fair, responsible, and appropriate use of household resources, particularly to the benefit of their children"; *www.sedesol.gob.mex/html2/ PROGRESA/texto.htm.* Last accessed 16 March, 2002.

Chapter 6

1. Benjamin and Sullivan consider "gender consciousness" a continuum along

which generalized gender awareness is succeeded by consciousness of the rights associated with specific gender locations within a given system (Gerson and Peiss 1985). I use the term to signify ideological awareness of how gender shapes the lives and fortunes of men and women (Gurin 1985).

2. The literal translation of *velorio* is "wake." However, Mauro is referring to the Garifuna custom of *dugu*, an ancestral rite to honor the dead which lasts three days and three nights (Cayetano and Cayetano 1997).

Chapter 7

1. More than ten years ago, Rowlands made a similar argument: "If empowerment of women is a gender issue, there is a need to tackle the corresponding task with men that will contribute to reducing the obstacle of machismo. . . . This work has not had much recognition to date, and is very rare in the design and development of programs" (1997, 132). NGOs, particularly Instituto Promundo of Brazil, have made progress in this regard. Another promising initiative is the MenEngage Global Alliance, a network of NGOs that seek to engage men and boys in effective ways to reduce gender inequalities (see *www.promundo.org.br* and *www.menengage.org*).

Works Cited

Adato, M., de la Brière, B., Mindek, D., and Quisumbing, A. (2000). *Final Report: The impact of PROGRESA on women's status and intrahousehold relations.* Washington, DC: International Food Policy Research Institute.

Adato, M., and Mindek, D. (2000). *PROGRESA and women's empowerment: Evidence from six Mexican states.* Washington, DC: International Food Policy Research Institute.

Ahearn, L. M. (2002). *Invitations to love: Literacy, love letters, and social change in Nepal.* Ann Arbor: University of Michigan Press.

Alcoff, L. M. (2007). Fraser on redistribution, recognition, and identity. *European Journal of Political Theory 6*(3), 255–265.

Allen, A. (1999). *The power of feminist theory.* Boulder, CO: Westview Press.

Alvarez, B. (2000). *Educación secundária: Temas críticos para la formulación de políticas.* Report written for the Regional Policy Dialogue: Education and Training of Human Resources Network. Washington, DC: Inter-American Development Bank. Retrieved 12 May 2011 from *idbdocs.iadb.org/wsdocs/getdocument.aspx?docnum=627143.*

Arbab, F. (2000). Promoting a discourse on science, religion, and development. In S. Harper (Ed.), *The lab, the temple, and the market: Reflections at the intersection of science, religion, and development* (149–237). Bloomfield, CT: Kumarian Press.

Arbab, F. (2005). *Primary elements of descriptions: Systems and processes.* With S. Ahderom, A. Alzate, S. Farid, E. Gutiérrez, J. Marín, J. Roldán, C. Rosenthal, and D. Singh. Cali, Colombia: Fundación para la Aplicación y Enseñanza de las Ciencias.

Arbab, F., and Arbab, H. (2003). *Constructing a conceptual framework for social action.* Cali, Colombia: Fundación para la Aplicación y Enseñanza de las Ciencias.

Arbab, F., Correa, G., and de Valcálcel, F. (1988). *FUNDAEC: Its principles and activities.* Retrieved 12 March 2010 from *www.fundaec.org/en/institution/celater_doc.htm.*

Arbab, F., and Lample, P. (2005). *Educational concepts.* Cali, Colombia: Fundación para la Aplicación y Enseñanza de las Ciencias.

Arbab, H. (2007). Generation of knowledge and the advancement of civilization. Presentation delivered at the Annual Conference of the Association for Bahá'í Studies North America. Ontario, Canada.

Bahá'í International Community (1995). The prosperity of humankind. Statement prepared for the United Nations Summit on Social Development, Copenhagen, Denmark. Retrieved 12 May 2011 from *statements.bahai.org/95-0303.htm*.

Baily, S. (2011). Speaking up: Contextualizing women's voices and gatekeepers' reactions in promoting women's empowerment in rural India. *Research in Comparative and International Education 6*(1), 107–118.

Bajaj, M. (2009). "I have big things planned for my future": The limits and possibilities of transformative agency in Zambian schools. *Compare, 39*(4), 379–398.

Banks, J. (1991). A curriculum for empowerment, action, and change. In C. Sleeter (Ed.), *Empowerment through multicultural education* (125–142). Albany: State University of New York Press.

Barker, G., J. M. Contreras, B. Heilman, A. Singh, and R. Verma (2011). Evolving men: Initial results from the International Men and Gender Equality Survey (IMAGES). Retrieved 21 July 2011 from *www.promundo.org.br/en/wp-content/uploads/2011/01/Evolving-Men-IMAGES-1.pdf*.

Bartlett, L. (2008). Literacy's verb: Exploring what literacy is and what literacy does. *International Journal of Educational Development, 28*(6), 737–753.

Bartlett, L. (2010). *The word and the world: The cultural politics of literacy in Brazil*. Creskill, NJ: Hampton Press.

Bateman, R. B. (1998). Africans and Indians: A comparative study of the Black Carib and the Black Seminole. In N. E. Whitten and A. Torres (Eds.), *Blackness in the Caribbean: Central America and Northern and Western South America* (200–222). Bloomington: Indiana University Press.

Belkin, L. (2008). When Mom and Dad share it all. *New York Times*, June 15.

Benjamin, O. (1998). Therapeutic discourse, power, and change: Emotion and negotiation in marital conversations. *Sociology, 32*(4), 771–793.

Benjamin, O., and Sullivan, O. (1999). Relational resources, gender consciousness, and possibilities of change in marital relationships. *Sociological Review, 44*(2), 225–251.

Bernbaum, M., E. Murphy-Graham, and I. Pooshti (1999). Mid-term evaluation of the DFID-sponsored SAT program in La Mosquitia, Honduras. Unpublished mimeo.

Bourdieu, P. (1977). Cultural reproduction and social reproduction. In J. Karabel and A. H. Halsey (Eds.), *Power and ideology in education* (487–511). New York: Oxford University Press.

Bourdieu, P. (1993). *The field of cultural production: Essays on art and literature*. New York: Columbia University Press.

Bowles, S., and Gintis, H. (1976). *Schooling in capitalist America*. New York: Basic Books.

Braslavsky, C. (1999). *The secondary education curriculum in Latin America: New tendencies and changes*. Buenos Aires: International Bureau of Education. Retrieved 12 May 2011 from *collections.infocollections.org/ukedu/uk/d/Js1861e/*.

Bruce, J. (1989). Homes divided. *World Development, 17*(7), 979–991.

Brusco, E. (1995). *The reformation of machismo: Evangelical conversion and gender in Colombia*. Austin: University of Texas Press.

Bryk, A., and Schneider, B. (2002). *Trust in schools: A core resource for improvement*. New York: Russell Sage Foundation.

Bunn, D. E. (1986). Group cohesiveness is enhanced as children engage in plant-stimulated discovery activities. *Journal of Therapeutic Horticulture, 1*, 37–43.

Campbell, A. N., Waliczek, T. M., Bradley, J. C., Zajicek, J. M., and Townsend, C. D. (1997). The influence of activity-based environmental instruction on high school students' environmental attitudes. *HortTechnology, 7*(3), 309.

Carter, D. S. G., and O'Neill, M. H. (1995). International perspectives on educational reform and policy implementation. Brighton, UK: Falmer.

Cayetano, S., and Cayetano, F. (1997). Garifuna history, language, and culture of Belize, Central America, and the Caribbean. Belize City: BRC Publishing.

Chapman, C., Burton, L., and Werner, J. (2010). Universal Secondary Education in Uganda: The head teachers' dilemma. *International Journal of Educational Development, 30*, 77–82.

Connell, R. W. (1989). Cool guys, swots, and wimps: The inter-play of masculinity and education. *Oxford Review of Education, 15*(3), 291–303.

Connell, R. W. (1995). *Masculinities.* Cambridge: Polity Press.

Connell, R. W. (2005). Change among the gatekeepers: Men, masculinities, and gender equality in the global arena. *Signs, 30*(3), 1801–1825.

Cox, C., Jaramillo, R. and Reimers, F. (2005). Education for democratic citizenship in the Americas: An agenda for action. Washington, DC: Inter-American Development Bank. Retrieved 12 May 2011 from *isites.harvard.edu/fs/docs/icb.topic648757.files/Reimers_Education_for_Democratic_Citizenship_In_The_Americas.pdf.*

DaCosta, D. (2008). "Spoiled sons" and "sincere daughters": Schooling, security, and empowerment in rural West Bengal, India. *Signs, 33*(2), 283–307.

de los Reyes, E., and Gozemba, P. A. (2002). *Pockets of hope.* Westport, CT: Bergin and Garvey.

Dejaeghere, J., and S. K. Lee (2011). What matters for marginalized girls and boys in Bangladesh: A capabilities approach for understanding educational well-being for empowerment. *Research in Comparative and International Education, 6*(1), 27–42.

Deutsch, F. (1999). *Halving it all: How equally shared parenting works.* Cambridge, MA: Harvard University Press.

Deutsch, F. (2007). Undoing gender. *Gender and Society, 21*(1), 106–127.

diGropella, E. (2006). Meeting the challenges of secondary education in Latin America and East Asia: Improving efficiency and resource mobilization. Washington, DC: World Bank.

Dodds, D. (2001). The Miskito of Honduras and Nicaragua. In S. Stonich (Ed.), *Endangered peoples of Latin America: Struggles to survive and thrive* (87–100). Westport, CT: Greenwood Press.

Drogus, C. A. (1997). Private power or public power: Pentecostalism, base communities, and gender. In E. L. Cleary and H. W. Stewart-Gambino (Eds.), *Power, politics, and Pentecostals in Latin America* (55–76). Boulder, CO: Westview Press.

Drogus, C. A. (2000). Liberation theology and the liberation of women in Santo Antonio, Brazil. In J. Burdick and W. E. Hewitt (Eds.), *The church at the grassroots in Latin America: Perspectives on thirty years of activism* (85–106). Westport, CT: Praeger.

Duryea, S., Galiani, S., Nopo, H., and Piras, C. (2007). The educational gender gap in Latin America and the Caribbean. IDB Working Paper #600. Washington, DC: Inter-American Development Bank. Retrieved 12 May 2011 from *www.nip-lac.org/uploads/Hugo_Nopo.pdf*.

EACS (East African Community Secretariat). (2010). East African community facts and figures. Retrieved 13 April 2011 from *eabc.info/files/EAC_Facts_and_Figures_2009%5B1%5D.pdf*.

EPHPM (Encuesta Permanente de Hogares de Propositos Multiples). 2007. Instituto Nacional de Estadística de Honduras.

Fals-Borda, O., and Rahman, M. (Eds.). (1991). Action and knowledge: Breaking the monopoly with participatory action research. New York: Intermediate Technology/Apex.

Ferguson, A. A. (2000). *Bad boys: Public schools in the making of black masculinity.* Ann Arbor: University of Michigan Press.

Fiedrich, M. (2004). Functional participation? Questioning participatory attempts at reshaping African gender identities: The case of REFLECT in Uganda. In A. Robinson-Pant (Ed.), *Women, literacy, and development: Alternative perspectives* (219–232). London: Routledge.

Fiedrich, M., and Jellema, A. (2003). *Literacy, gender, and social agency: Adventures in empowerment.* London: Department for International Development. Retrieved 12 May 2011 from *ageconsearch.umn.edu/bitstream/12854/1/er030053.pdf*.

Freire, P. (1973). *Pedagogy of the oppressed.* New York: Seabury Press.

FUNDAEC (2001). Evaluation summary and institutional history. Unpublished grant proposal. Cali, Colombia: FUNDAEC.

FUNDAEC (2007). Empowering promoters of local prosperity. Unpublished grant proposal. Cali, Colombia: FUNDAEC.

FUNDAEC (2008). *Education: A discourse on social action.* Cali, Colombia: FUNDAEC.

Galván, R. T. (2001). Portraits of *mujeres desjuiciadas*: Womanist pedagogies of the everyday, the mundane, and the ordinary. *Qualitative Studies in Education, 14*(5), 603–621.

Garland, R. (2009). Love and literacy: What happens in couples when the woman learns to read. EdD diss., Harvard University.

George, L. K., Ellison, C. G., and Larson, D. B. (2002). Exploring the relationships between religious involvement and health. *Psychology Inquiry, 13,* 109–200.

Gerson, J. M., and K. Peiss (1985). Boundaries, negotiation, consciousness: Reconceptualizing gender relations. *Social Problems, 3*(24), 317–331.

Gilligan, C. (2006). Mommy, I know you: A feminist scholar explains how the study of girls can teach us about boys. *Newsweek,* January 30.

Ginsberg, M. (1998). NGOs: What's in an acronym? *Current Issues in Comparative Education, 1*(1), 29–34.

Givhan, R. (2009). Baring arms. *New Yorker,* 16 May. Retrieved 12 May 2011 from *www.newyorker.com/reporting/2009/03/16/090316fa_fact_givhan*.

Glewwe, P., and Kremer, M. (2006). Schools, teachers, and education outcomes in developing countries. In E. Hanushek and F. Welch (Eds.), *Handbook of the economics of education, volume 2* (945–1017). London: Elsevier.

Gonzalez, N. L. (1988). *Sojourners of the Caribbean: Ethnogenesis and ethnohistory of the Garifuna.* Urbana: University of Illinois Press.

Greenwood, D., and Levin, M. (1998). *An introduction to action research: Social research for social change*. Thousand Oaks, CA: Sage.

Gurin, P. (1985). Women's gender consciousness. *Public Opinion Quarterly, 49*(2), 143–163.

Gutmann, M. (2007). *The meanings of macho: Being a man in Mexico City*. Berkeley: University of California Press.

Hammond, J. L. (1998). *Fighting to learn: Popular education and guerrilla war in El Salvador*. New Brunswick, NJ: Rutgers University Press.

Harper, S. (Ed.). (2000). *The lab, the temple, and the market: Reflections at the intersection of science, religion, and development*. Ottawa: International Development Research Centre.

Hartstock, N. (1974). Political change: Two perspectives on power. *Quest: A Feminist Quarterly, 1*(1), 10–25.

Hartstock, N. (1983). *Money, sex, and power: Towards a feminist historical materialism*. New York: Longman.

Haywood, C., and Mac an Ghaill, M. (2003). *Men and masculinities*. Buckingham, UK: Open University Press.

Helms, M. W. (1981). Black Carib domestic organization in historical perspective: Traditional origins of contemporary patterns. *Ethnology, 20*(1), 77–86.

Herlihy, P. H. (1997). Indigenous peoples and biosphere reserve conservation in the Mosquitia rain forest corridor, Honduras. In S. Stevens (Ed.), *Conservation through cultural survival: Indigenous peoples and protected areas* (99–129). Washington, DC: Island Press.

Herz, B., and Sperling, G. (2004). What works in girls' education: Evidence and policies from the developing world. Washington, DC: Council on Foreign Relations. Retrieved 20 July 2011 from *www.cfr.org/education/works-girls-education-evidence-policies-developing-world-report-barbara-herz-gene-sperling/ p6974*.

Hicks, A., Cronin, L., Meyer, B., Scott, L., and Lim, S. (2008). Roundtable on the CARE "I am powerful" campaign. *Advertising and Society Review, 9*(1). Retrieved 15 July 2011 from *muse.jhu.edu/journals/advertising_and_society_review/v009/9.1roundtable.html*.

Hill, P., and Pargament, K. (2008). Advances in the conceptualization and measurement of religion and spirituality: Implications for physical and mental health research. *Psychology of Religion and Spirituality, 5*(1), 3–17.

Hobbes, T. [1651] (1968). *Leviathan*. London: Penguin.

Hochschild, A. R. (1990). *The second shift*. New York: Avon Books.

Hochschild, A. R. (1996). *The time bind*. New York: Henry Holt.

hooks, b. (2000). *Feminism is for everybody*. Cambridge, MA: South End Press.

Hoyos, R., Bussolo, M., and Núñez, O. (2008). Can *maquila* booms reduce poverty? Evidence from Honduras. Development Prospect Group Working Paper. World Bank. Retrieved 12 May 2011 from *www.iadb.org/intal/intalcdi/PE/2008/02381 .pdf*.

IDB (Inter-American Development Bank). (2000). *Reforming primary and secondary education in Latin America and the Caribbean: An IDB strategy* (Sustainable Development Department Sector Strategy and Policy Papers Series). Washington, DC. Retrieved 12 May 2011 from *www.iadb.org/document .cfm?id=1481874*.

IDB (Inter-American Development Bank). (2004). Honduras: Secondary education and job training program (HO-0202). Unpublished loan proposal. Washington, DC: Inter-American Development Bank.

INE (Instituto Nacional de Estadistica Honduras). (2001). *Censo 2001* [Database]. Retrieved 12 May 2011 from *www.ine.es/censo2001/index.html*.

INE (Instituto Nacional de Estadistica Honduras). (2007). Encuesta de hogares. Retrieved 12 May 2011 from *www.ine.gob.hn/drupal/*.

IRAW (International Women's Rights Action Watch). (2003). *Status of women in Honduras under specific ICESCR articles*. Hubert Humphrey Institute of Public Affairs, University of Minnesota. Retrieved 12 May 2011 from *www1.umn.edu/humanrts/iwraw/publications/countries/cescrhonduras.htm*.

ISGP (Institute for Studies in Global Prosperity). (2005). *Science, religion, and development: Some initial considerations*. New York: Bahá'í International Community. Retrieved 12 May 2011 from *www.globalprosperity.org/initial_considerations.html?SID=4*.

Jackson, C. (1999). Men's work, masculinities, and gender divisions of labour. *Journal of Development Studies, 36*(1), 89–108.

Kabeer, N. (1994). *Reversed realities: Gender hierarchies in development thought*. London: Verso.

Kabeer, N. (1997). Women, wages, and intra-household power relations in urban Bangladesh. *Development and Change, 28*(2), 261–302.

Kabeer, N. (1999). Resources, agency, achievements: Reflections on the measurement of women's empowerment. *Development and Change, 30*(3), 435–464.

Kalman, J. (2005). *Discovering literacy: Access routes to written culture for a group of women in Mexico*. Hamburg: UNESCO Institute for Education.

Karlberg, M. (2005). The power of discourse and the discourse of power: Pursuing peace through discourse intervention. *International Journal of Peace Studies, 10*(1), 1–25.

Kerns, V. (1983). *Women and the ancestors: Black Carib kinship and ritual*. Urbana: University of Illinois Press.

Kimmel, M. (2004). What about the boys? What the current debates tell us—and don't tell us—about boys in school. In M. Kimmel (Ed.), *The gendered society reader* (243–261). New York: Oxford University Press.

Kincheloe, J. (2005). *Critical pedagogy*. New York: Peter Lang.

King, E., and Hill, A. (Eds.). (1993). *Women's education in developing countries: Barriers, benefits, and policies*. Baltimore: World Bank/Johns Hopkins University Press.

Kishor, S. (2000). Empowerment of women in Egypt and links to the survival and health of their infants. In G. Sen and H. Presser (Eds.), *Women's empowerment and demographic processes: Moving beyond Cairo* (119–158). New York: Oxford University Press.

Klees, S. (1998). NGOs: Progressive tool or neoliberal force? *Current Issues in Comparative Education, 1*(1), 49–54.

Klemmer, C. D., Waliczek, T. M., and Zajicek, J. M. (2005). Growing minds: The effect of a school gardening program on the science achievement of elementary students. *HortTechnology, 15*(3), 448–452.

Kristof, N., and WuDunn, S. (2010). *Half the sky: Turning oppression into opportunity for women worldwide*. New York: Knopf Doubleday.

Lample, P. (2009). *Revelation and social reality: Learning to translate what is written into reality.* West Palm Beach, FL: Palabra Publications.

Landsdale, J. (2002). Education to combat abusive child labor activity: Child labor and fishing for crustaceans in Honduras. Unpublished report prepared for Creative Associates International, Washington, DC.

Larson, D. B., Swyers, J. P., and McCullough, M. E. (1998). Scientific research on spirituality and health: A report based on the Scientific Progress in Spirituality Conferences. Bethesda, MD: National Institute for Healthcare Research.

Leonardo, Z. (2004). Critical social theory and transformative knowledge: The functions of criticism in quality education. *Educational Researcher, 33*(6), 11–18.

Lewis, M., and Lockheed, M. (2006). Inexcusable absence: Why 60 million girls still aren't in school and what to do about it. Washington, DC: Center for Global Development. Retrieved 12 May 2001 from *www.cgdev.org/content/publications/ detail/11898/.*

Lorber, J. (2000). Using gender to undo gender: A feminist degendering movement. *Feminist Theory, 1*(1), 79–95.

Lukes, S. (2005). *Power: A radical view.* Basingstoke, UK: Palgrave Macmillan.

Lunn, J. (2009). The role of religion, spirituality, and faith in development: A critical theory approach. *Third World Quarterly, 30*(5), 937–951.

Mac an Ghaill, M. (2003). *The making of men: Masculinities, sexualities, and schooling.* Buckingham, UK: Open University Press.

Machiavelli, N. [1513] (1961). *The prince.* London: Penguin.

Malhotra, A., and Mather, M. (1997). Do schooling and work empower women in developing countries? Gender and domestic decisions in Sri Lanka. *Sociological Forum, 12*(4), 599–630.

Malhotra, A., Schuler, S., and Boender, C. (2002). *Measuring women's empowerment as a variable in international development.* Paper commissioned by the Gender and Development Group of the World Bank. Retrieved 14 April 2009 from *hdr.undp.org/docs/network/hdr_net/GDI_GEM_Measuring_Womens_ Empowerment.pdf.*

Marx, K., and Engels, F. [1846] (1967). *The German ideology.* London: Lawrence and Wishart.

Maslak, M. A. (Ed.). (2008). *The structure and agency of women's empowerment.* Albany: State University of New York Press.

Maslak, M. A. (2011). Education, employment, and empowerment: The case of a young woman in northwestern China. *Research in Comparative and International Education, 6*(1), 119–129.

Mason, K. O. (2003). Measuring empowerment: A social demographer's view. Paper presented to the workshop Measuring Empowerment: Cross-Disciplinary Perspectives. Retrieved 12 May 2011 from *siteresources.worldbank.org/INTEMPOWERMENT/ Resources/486312-1095970750368/529763-1095970803335/mason.pdf.*

McCauley, E. (1981). No me hables de la muerte, sino de parranda. Tegucigalpa: ASEPADE.

McLaren, P. (1999). A pedagogy of possibility: Reflecting upon Paulo Freire's politics of education. *Educational Researcher, 28*(2), 49–56.

Miller, J. B. (1982). Women and power. *Work in Progress, 82*(1), 1–5.

Monchinski, T. (2008). *Critical pedagogy and the everyday classroom.* New York: Springer.

Monkman, K., Miles, R., and Easton, A. M. (2008). The dance of agency and structure in an empowerment educational program in Mali and the Sudan. In M. A. Maslak (Ed.), *The structure and agency of women's education* (107–126) Albany: State University of New York Press.

Mosedale, S. (2005). Assessing women's empowerment: Towards a conceptual framework. *Journal of International Development, 7*(2), 243–257.

Murphy-Graham, E. (2005). *Para seguir adelante*: Women's empowerment and the *Sistema de Aprendizaje Tutorial* (SAT) program in Honduras. EdD diss., Harvard University.

Murphy-Graham, E. (2007). How secondary education can be used to promote participation in public life: Evidence from the *Sistema de Aprendizaje tutorial program* in Honduras. *Prospects, 37*(1), 95–112.

Murphy-Graham, E. (2008). Opening the black box: Women's empowerment and innovative secondary education in Honduras. *Gender and Education, 20*(1), 31–50.

Murphy-Graham, E. (2009). Constructing a new vision: Undoing gender through secondary education in Honduras. *International Review of Education, 55*(5), 503–521.

Murphy-Graham, E., Vega de Rovelo, A., Del Gatto, F., Gijsbers, I., and Richards, S. (2002). Final evaluation of DFID tutorial learning system (SAT) rural education project on the north coast of Honduras 1997–2002. Unpublished report.

Nussbaum, M. (2000). *Women and human development.* Cambridge: Cambridge University Press.

Nussbaum, M. (2003). Women's education: A global challenge. *Signs, 29*(2), 325–355.

Nussbaum, M. (2011). *Creating capabilities: The human development approach.* Cambridge, MA: Belknap Press of Harvard University Press.

Oketch, M., and Rolleston, C. (2007). Policies on free primary and secondary education in East Africa: Retrospect and prospect. *Review of Research in Education, 31*(1), 131–158.

Pascoe, C. J. (2007). *Dude, you're a fag: Masculinity and sexuality in high school.* Berkeley: University of California Press.

Penny, A., Ward, M., Read, T., and Bines, H. (2008). Education sector reform: The Ugandan experience. *International Journal of Educational Development, 28*(3), 268–285.

Perfetti, M., Leal, S., and Arango, P. (2001). Experiencias alternativas para la expansión del acceso a la educación secundaria para los jóvenes en las zonas rurales: El Sistema de Aprendizaje Tutorial (SAT) y el modelo de posprimaria rural de Escuela Nueva. Paper commissioned by the Inter-American Development Bank, Centro de Estudios Regionales Cafeteros y Empresariales (CRECE), Colombia. Retrieved 12 May 2011 from *idbdocs.iadb.org/wsdocs/getdocument.aspx?docnum=776338.*

Pigem, J. (Ed.). (2007). Faith-based organizations and education for sustainability: Report of the International Experts' Workshop, Barcelona. Retrieved 12 May 2011 from *www.arcworld.org/downloads/Barcelona%20Report.pdf.*

Porta Pallais, E., and Laguna, J. R. (2007). Educational equity in Central America: A pending issue for the public agenda. USAID EQUIP 2 Working Paper. Retrieved 14 July 2011 from *www.equip123.net/docs/ e2-EducationalEquityCentralAmerica-English_WP.pdf.*

Prins, E. (2006). Relieving isolation, avoiding vices: The social purposes of participation in a Salvadoran literacy program. *Adult Education Quarterly, 57*(5), 5–25.

Prins, E. (2008). Adult literacy education, gender equity, and empowerment: Insights from a Freirean-inspired literacy programme. *Studies in the Education of Adults, 40*(1), 24–39.

Prins, E. (2011). On becoming an educated person: Salvadoran adult learners' cultural model of *educación*/education. *Teachers College Record, 113*(7). Retrieved 12 July 2011 from *www.tcrecord.org/library ID Number: 16075.*

Prins, E., and Drayton, B. (2010). Adult education for the empowerment of individuals and communities. In C. E. Kasworm, A. D. Rose, and J. M. Ross-Gordon (Eds.), *Handbook of adult and continuing education* (209–219). San Francisco: Jossey-Bass.

Proscio, T. (2000). *In other words: A plea for plain speaking in foundations.* New York: Edna McConnell Clark Foundation.

Psacharopolous, G. (1988). Education and development: A review. *Research Observer, 3*(1), 99–116.

Purcell-Gates, V., and Waterman, R. (2000). *Now we read, we see, we speak: Portrait of literacy development in an adult Freirean-based class.* Mahwah, NJ: Lawrence Erlbaum.

Putnam, R. (2000). *Bowling alone: The collapse and revival of American community.* New York: Simon and Schuster.

Ramírez, R. L. (2003). Sistema de Aprendizaje Tutorial: Experiencia innovadora de educación rural en Colombia. Unpublished report prepared for presentation to the Ministry of Education of Colombia for SECAB.

Raynor, J. (2007). Education and capabilities in Bangladesh. In M. Walker and E. Unterhalter (Eds.), *Amartya Sen's capability approach and social justice in education* (157–176). New York: Palgrave Macmillan.

Reimers, F. (2006). Citizenship, identity, and education: Examining the public purposes of schools in an age of globalization. *Prospects, 36*(3), 275–294.

Richards, M. (2005). Integrating moral values in rural education and sustainable development in Latin America: The System of Tutorial Learning (SAT). *Bahá'í Studies Review, 13*, 105–117.

Rihani, M. (2006). Keeping the promise: Five benefits of girls' secondary education. Washington, DC: Academy for Educational Development. Retrieved 12 May 2011 from *www.aed.org/Publications/upload/Girls-Ed-Final.pdf.*

Robinson, C. W., and Zajicek, J. M. (2005). Growing minds: The effects of a one-year school garden program on six constructs of life skills of elementary school children. *HortTechnology, 15*(3), 453–457.

Robinson-Pant, A. (2004). Education for women: Whose values count? *Gender and Education, 16*(4), 473–489.

Roldan, L. A. V. (2000). El Sistema de Aprendizaje Tutorial (SAT): Una propuesta educativa para el desarrollo rural humano, armónico y sostenible. Retrieved 12 May 2011 from *www.yorku.ca/hdrnet/images/uploaded/Roldan_SAT.pdf.*

Rowlands, J. (1997). *Questioning empowerment: Working with women in Honduras.* Oxford: Oxfam.

Sachs, J. (2005). *The end of poverty: Economic possibilities for our time.* New York: Penguin Books.

Schensul, S., Schensul, J., and LeCompte, M. (1999). *Essential ethnographic methods.* Walnut Creek, CA: AltaMira Press.

Schultz, T. P. (1987). *Education investments and returns in economic development.* New Haven, CT: Yale University Press.

Schultz, T. W. (1971). *Investment in human capital: The role of education and research.* New York: Free Press.

Seeman, T. E., Dubin, L. F., and Seeman, M. (2003). Religiosity/spirituality and health: A critical review of evidence for biological pathways. *American Psychologist, 58*(1), 53–63.

Selener, D. (1997). *Participatory action research and social change.* Ithaca, NY: Cornell Participatory Action Research Network.

Sen, A. (1993). Capability and well being. In M. Nussbaum and A. Sen, *The quality of life: Studies in development economics* (30–53). Oxford: Oxford University Press.

Sen, A. (1999). *Development as freedom.* Oxford: Oxford University Press.

Shor, I. (1992). *Empowering education: Critical teaching for social change.* Portsmouth, NH: Heinemann.

Stasavage, D. (2005). Democracy and primary school attendance: Aggregate and individual level evidence from Africa. AfroBarometer Working Paper #54. Retrieved 20 July 2011 from *www.nyu.edu/gsas/dept/politics/faculty/stasavage/APSA2005%20education3.pdf.*

Stiglitz, J. (2006). *Making globalization work.* New York: Norton.

Stromquist, N. P. (1995a). Romancing the state: Gender and power in education. *Comparative Education Review, 39*(4), 423–454.

Stromquist, N. P. (1995b). The theoretical and practical bases for empowerment. In C. Medel-Añonuevo (Ed.), *Women, education, and empowerment* (13–22). Hamburg: UNESCO Institute of Education.

Stromquist, N. P. (1997). *Literacy for citizenship: Gender and grassroots dynamics in Brazil.* Albany: State University of New York Press.

Stromquist, N. P. (1998). NGOs in a new paradigm of civil society. *Current Issues in Comparative Education, 1*(1), 62–67.

Stromquist, N. P. (2002). Education as a means for empowering women. In J. Papart, S. Rai, and K. Staudt (Eds.), *Rethinking empowerment: Gender and development in a global/local world* (22–38). London: Routledge.

Sullivan, O. (2004). Changing gender practices within the household: A theoretical perspective. *Gender and Society, 18*(2), 207–222.

Summers, L. (1993). Foreword. In E. King and A. Hill (Eds.), *Women's education in developing countries: Barriers, benefits, and policies.* Baltimore: World Bank/Johns Hopkins University Press.

Summers, L. (2004). Education for all. Harvard Graduate School of Education, Askwith Forum. Cambridge, MA, 26 October.

Sunshine, C. A. (1996). *The Caribbean: Survival, struggle, and sovereignty.* Washington, DC: EPICA.

Tercero, G. (2002). Cosmovisión, comportamiento y SIDA: Un estudio de antropología médica entre los Garífunas. Unpublished report commissioned by the Inter-American Development Bank, Tegucigalpa, Honduras.

Thomas, S. M. (2004). Building communities of character: Foreign aid policy and faith-based organizations. *SAIS Review*, *24*(2), 133–147.

Thorne, B. (1993). *Gender play: Girls and boys in school*. New Brunswick, NJ: Rutgers University Press.

Tyack, D., and Cuban, L. (2003). *Tinkering toward utopia: A decade of public school reform*. Cambridge, MA: Harvard University Press.

Tyndale, W. (2003). Idealism and practicality: The role of religion in development. *Development*, *46*(4), 22–28.

Umansky, I., Hernandez, R. Alas, M., and Moncada, G. (2008). Alternative upper secondary education in Honduras: Assessment and Recommendations. Unpublished report commissioned by the United States Agency for International Development.

UMCE (2003). Informe nacional de rendimiento académico 2002, Tegucigalpa: Honduras.

UNDP (United Nations Development Program). (2007). Human development report 2007/2008. New York: Palgrave Macmillan.

UNDP (United Nations Development Program). (2009). Human development report 2009. New York: Palgrave Macmillan.

UNESCO (United Nations Educational, Scientific, and Cultural Organization). (2003). The leap to equality: Education for All global monitoring report 2002–2003. Paris: UNESCO.

UNESCO (United Nations Educational, Scientific, and Cultural Organization). (2005). The quality imperative: Education for All global monitoring report 2004–2005. Paris: UNESCO.

UNESCO (United Nations Educational, Scientific, and Cultural Organization). (2010a). Reaching the marginalized: Education for all global monitoring report 2009–2010. Paris: UNESCO.

UNESCO (United Nations Educational, Scientific, and Cultural Organization). (2010b). Global education digest 2010: Comparing education statistics from across the world. Montreal: UNESCO Institute for Statistics.

UNICEF. (2006). *State of the world's children*. New York: UNICEF.

Unterhalter, E. (2007). *Gender, schooling, and global social justice*. London: Routledge.

Unterhalter, E. (2011). How far does this go? Reflections on using the capability approach to evaluate gender, poverty, education, and empowerment. Presented at the Comparative and International Education Society Conference, Montreal, May.

Unterhalter, E., and Aikman, S. (2005). *Beyond access: Transforming policy and practice for gender equality in education*. Oxford: Oxfam.

Urquiola, M., and Calderón, V. (2006). Apples and oranges: Educational enrollment and attainment across countries in Latin America and the Caribbean. *International Journal of Educational Development*, *26*(6), 572–590.

Vavrus, F. (2003). *Desire and decline: Schooling amid crisis in Tanzania*. New York: Peter Lang.

Walker, M., and Unterhalter, E. (Eds.). (2007). *Amartya Sen's capability approach and social justice in education*. New York: Palgrave Macmillan.

Weber, M. [1910–1914] (1978). *Economy and society: An outline of interpretive sociology*, Guenther Roth and Claus Wittich (Eds.). Berkeley: University of California Press.

Weiler, K. (1988). *Women teaching for change: Gender, class, and power*. Westport, CT: Bergin and Garvey.

Weiler, K., and Middleton, K. (1992). *Telling women's lives: Narrative inquiries in the history of women's education*. Buckingham, UK: Open University Press.

World Bank (2001). *Engendering development through gender equality in rights, resources, and voice*. Washington, DC: World Bank

Yuscaran, G. (1991). *The Garifuna story*. Tegucigalpa: Nuevo Sol Publicaciones.

Index

Page numbers in boldface refer to illustrations.
The letter "t" refers to a table.